STAR PASS RECEIVERS OF THE NFL

Exciting profiles of nine great NFL pass catchers. Included are Otis Taylor, Raymond Berry, Fred Biletnikoff, Paul Warfield, Lance Alworth, Charlie Sanders, Bob Hayes, Don Maynard and Danny Abramowicz.

STAR PASS RECEIVERS of the NFL

by JOHN DEVANEY

illustrated with photographs

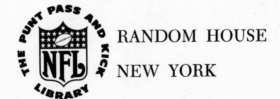

RANDOM HOUSE
NEW YORK

THE PUNT PASS AND KICK
NFL
LIBRARY

For Bumbi

Library of Congress Cataloging in Publication Data
Devaney, John.
Star pass receivers of the NFL.

(The Punt, pass, and kick library, no. 17)
SUMMARY: Brief career biographies of nine pass receivers in pro football. Included are Otis Taylor, Fred Biletnikoff, Paul Warfield, Lance Alworth, Charlie Sanders, Bob Hayes, Raymond Berry, Don Maynard, and Danny Abramowicz.
1. Football—Biography—Juvenile literature.
2. National Football League. [1. Football—Biography.
2. National Football League] I. Title.
GV939.A1D42   796.33'2'0922   [B][920]72–1591
ISBN 0–394–82439–3
ISBN 0–394–92439–8 (Gibraltar lib. ed.)

CONTENTS

INTRODUCTION

The tall quarterback ran back a few paces. He turned and threw the ball at me. The ball whizzed loudly through the air. It seemed to jump into my hands, smacking my reddened and swelling palms. *Now I know what it's like to be a pro football pass catcher,* I thought.

I was catching the passes of Detroit quarterback Greg Landry. One afternoon when he was warming up during practice I had asked him if I could catch a few of his passes. For ten minutes he whizzed the ball at me from 20 yards away. Soon my hands ached. I dropped only two or three passes, but each time Landry threw, I leaned backward to soften the sting of the ball.

"Are you throwing at game speed?" I shouted to him.

"Oh, no," he said. "I'm throwing at half-speed."

Right then I began to appreciate how difficult it is to be a pro football pass receiver. Unlike a receiver in a game, I wasn't being pushed and shoved and elbowed by defenders. I didn't have to run a complex pass route. And I wasn't hearing the footsteps of a 240-pound linebacker pounding toward me as I waited to make a catch.

Later I talked to Detroit pass receiver Charlie Sanders, one of the nine receivers included in this book. "The easiest part of our business is catching the ball," Charlie said. "The hard parts are getting open, being where you are supposed to be—and then holding on to the ball after you have caught it."

For each of the nine receivers in this book, there was toil and trouble learning the skills of being a pass catcher in the pros. But each of them mastered those skills. The stories of other great receivers, people like Don Hutson of the 1930s and Dave Parks of today, have been told in *Great Pass Receivers of the NFL* (Punt, Pass & Kick Library #6). Some of the outstanding pass receivers of today, notably San Francisco's Ted Kwalick and Gene Washington, still must prove they can be great year after year. But any NFL pass receiver has some amazing talents. Greg Landry's passes taught me that the ball comes very hard and very fast to them all.

John Devaney

STAR PASS RECEIVERS OF THE NFL

1. OTIS TAYLOR

"I
AM
AN
ATHLETE
FOR
MY
OWN
HEART"

Otis Taylor walked slowly up to the line of scrimmage. He always seemed to walk slowly, as if he were walking to the gallows. His teammates even called him "Slug," short for "sluggish." Now, at the line of scrimmage, Otis casually watched quarterback Len Dawson as the Kansas City quarterback called the signals.

This was no ordinary game. This was Super Bowl IV, in January 1970. The AFL champion Chiefs were facing the NFL champion Minnesota Vikings for pro football's world championship. The Chiefs were ahead, 16-7, but the Vikings had scored a few

In Super Bowl IV, Otis Taylor runs past the last Viking defender on his way to a touchdown.

minutes earlier and seemed to be rolling. Now the Chiefs had the ball on the Viking 46 and they needed some points for insurance. In the huddle Dawson called for a pass.

Dawson hut-hutted the signals. He took the snap and stepped back, then looked to his right. He saw Otis Taylor veer toward the sideline near the Viking 35. Dawson fired the ball to Taylor, who caught it just as a Viking defensive back, Earsell Mackbee, rushed up to tackle him. The lanky Otis did a little Indian dance, and squirmed away from Mackbee. He raced down the sideline.

Another white Viking uniform angled toward him. Suddenly, Otis changed direction, cutting toward the middle of the field. The Viking back tried to brake to a stop. He reached out a hand and grasped Otis's jersey. Otis pushed him away with a stiff-arm, then galloped the rest of the way for a 46-yard touchdown. Now the Chiefs led 23-7.

That touchdown seemed to take the sting out of the Viking attack. They failed to score again and the Chiefs were football champions of the world. In the clubhouse, Chief coach Hank Stram told everybody that Taylor's touchdown catch had clinched the game.

It was a typical catch for Otis. All during his career with the Chiefs he often caught a big pass in a big ball game, broke a tackle or two and went on to score a clutch touchdown. In the AFL championship game against Buffalo in 1966, Otis caught a pass on the 10-yard-line. Tough Tom Janik, a cornerback, hit Otis with a flying tackle. Otis spun, flinging off Janik. Another back, Butch Byrd, ploughed into Otis head-on. Otis smashed right over Byrd and ran into the end zone for a touchdown. The Chiefs went on to win the championship 31-7.

Writer Bill Richardson once asked Otis about all those important catches. "I think I can catch the ball and come up with the big play in desperate situations," Otis said in his solemn manner. "I've been fortunate at times to make the big play. To be honest, that is what I play for—to catch the ball for a touchdown. Every receiver wants to make that big play, to catch the ball for a touchdown."

And later he said, "I think I make a lot of big plays because I can run with the ball after I catch it. I catch it, I run hard with it, and running is just as important as catching."

In the mid-1960s coaches in the old American Football League argued who was the better pass receiver, Lance Alworth or Otis Taylor. Most agreed with a Boston Patriot coach who said, "Toss a coin." But by the 1970s many spectators claimed that Otis was probably the NFL's all-around best pass catcher. Otis could catch the ball, he could run with it, and he could do what most pass receivers don't do well: he could block. "If you can make a block and open up a path for a touchdown for someone else," Otis said, "that can be as rewarding as catching a ball and running 80 yards for a touchdown."

At 6-foot-3 and 215 pounds, Otis had the rangy size to be a good blocker. He had speed to run with jack rabbits, something he did as a boy back in Texas. And most important of all, he could leap high. Once, in college, the 6-foot-3 Otis played center in a basketball game against a 6-foot-9 fellow named

Willis Reed, who later led the New York Knicks to
the world championship of pro basketball. Although
Taylor was six inches shorter, he held Reed to 13
points while scoring 13 himself.

Pro quarterbacks love to throw to leapers like
Taylor, for he can turn a bad throw into a reception.
And he can leap to bat away a bad throw before it is
intercepted. In one game against the Jets in 1967,
Lenny Dawson threw long to Otis. The pass was un-
derthrown and two Jets closed in on the ball as it
came down. Otis sped between them, leaped and
caught the ball—with one hand.

That one-handed catch was no accident. "In practice I work at catching the ball with one hand," Otis
said. "I'll try catching the ball only with my left
hand for a while and then I'll try catching it only
with my right hand for a while. I'll even work at
catching it with my hands folded behind my back. A
ball can come to you in a lot of different ways and
you can be tied up so you can't use both hands."

In a game against Washington in 1971 Otis cut
across the end zone and saw a pass from Dawson
spiraling toward him. A Washington defensive back,
Pat Fischer, saw that the taller Otis was going to
catch the ball. In desperation Fischer grabbed Otis,
pinning his left arm to his side. Otis reached up with
his free right hand and caught the ball one-handed.

A few years earlier, against Boston, he was speeding down the sideline after a long pass. This time he
reached out with his *left* hand and made a one-
handed over-the-shoulder catch. "I was sure the pass
was way beyond his reach," Boston coach Mike
Holovak said later. "It was about the most amazing

Taylor leaps high to catch a pass against the Chiefs' arch-rivals, the Oakland Raiders.

catch I've ever seen in a football game."

Kansas City quarterback Len Dawson appreciated those miracle catches. When someone asked him why the Chiefs won the AFC's Western Division title in 1971, the laconic Len said, "Otis Taylor was healthy. Our approach has been to go out and throw. And to throw, you've got to have someone like Otis who can catch the ball."

In that 1971 season only Fred Biletnikoff caught more passes than Otis among AFC receivers. But Otis, with 1,110 yards, led all the AFC receivers in total yardage. After playing only seven seasons he already ranked among the top ten in the AFC in career catches. He had 295 to his credit, an average of more than 40 per season.

"That's pretty good for a man who moves as slowly as Slug," one Chief said early in 1972. Slug answers that he sees no need to rush. He agrees with former great golfer Walter Hagen, who believed that one should go through this world taking time to sniff the flowers along the way.

Some fans and even some coaches were fooled into thinking that Otis was lazy because of his slow-moving ways. But his quarterback, Len Dawson, knew better.

"Otis has got a deceptive way about him," said Dawson. "He'll seem to be only gliding along and then suddenly he'll take off. But what I like about him is that not only has he got fast feet and good hands, he has a good head. He sees things out there. He'll come off the field and often he'll diagram a pass pattern in the dirt. We've scored touchdowns on some of those patterns he's drawn in the dirt."

In one game against the Chargers, Otis loped through what the Chiefs call backside patterns, the patterns a receiver runs when the pass is going to the other side of the field. Otis seemed to run each pattern a little slower. He noticed that defensive back Speedy Duncan was covering him a little differently. During a time-out Otis sketched a pattern he thought would set him free. Dawson looked at the pattern and said, "All right, let's try it."

On the snap of the ball Otis started to lope through a pattern. Then suddenly—*vaaaa-rooom!* He dashed right by Duncan on a straight line, caught the pass and raced some 48 yards before the speedy Duncan caught him from behind.

Otis was born August 11, 1942, in Houston, the son of a school custodian. "I never needed anything," Otis said. "My mother never refused me anything—the best pants, suits, shoes. But I always wanted something new. She'd get it for me. But my mother really ran the house and she didn't tolerate any foolishness. She used to tan me when I'd come home from playing football with a bloody nose or with my new clothes ripped."

First Otis wanted to grow up to be a baseball player. Then he played forward for his high school basketball team and he wanted to become a basketball player like Elgin Baylor. "I saw this man while I was in high school and I just fell in love with him," Otis said. "I tried to do the things Elgin Baylor did. I wasn't a great shooter, though. But playing helped me as a football receiver by making me quicker and more agile."

Otis was the quarterback on his high school football team, whipping passes as far as 70 yards. He went to Prairie View A & M as a quarterback. One day in his sophomore season he was catching passes on the sideline. A coach noticed Otis grabbing the ball one-handed. From that moment on, Otis was a receiver. Jim Kearney (later a safety man with the Chiefs) became the team's quarterback.

"Jim and I, we did some fantastic things together at Prairie View," Otis said. "Jim would just tell me to go out there and run and then he'd whip that ball 50, 60, 70 yards. I would run with the drive of a trackman, and then at the last second I'd put my hands out. If you run with your hands out, you'll never get it."

The only trouble was, Otis sometimes stuck out his hands and dropped the ball. He was trying to run with the ball before he caught it. "I just don't settle for a catch," Otis told his exasperated coaches at Prairie View. "I love to run. I'll jump, I'll skip, I'll dance sideways, anything to get the ball farther downfield."

The Prairie View coaches impressed on him that to get downfield he had to hold onto the ball. Otis began to do what all the good receivers do: "look" the ball into his hands before he took off on one of his dashes. He stopped dropping passes.

In 1964, Otis's senior year, the American Football League and the National Football League were competing with each other for good football players. Scouts offered huge salaries and bonuses and used all sorts of tricks to lure players into signing with teams in their league. Although Otis came from a small school, the Dallas Cowboys of the NFL and the Kansas City Chiefs of the AFL were interested in him. One day an insurance man who worked for the Cowboys phoned Otis. "We're going to have a Thanksgiving party in Dallas just for football players," he told Otis. "Come on down from Prairie View for a few days."

Otis drove to Dallas and found about a dozen other football players at a party in a Dallas hotel. There were trays of hot and cold food, tall cold drinks, and a lot of music and laughter.

Otis joined in the fun. The insurance man was a good host, telling the players to eat and drink as much as they wanted. His job was to keep these players hidden from AFL scouts while scouts from the Cowboys and other NFL teams tried to sign them to contracts.

The Kansas City Chiefs were trying to find Otis to sign him for the AFL. A Chief scout, Lloyd Wells, was looking for him in Dallas. He called the Chiefs' offices in Kansas City. "I've been trying to find Otis Taylor for three days," he told the Chiefs. "I got a tip that he's hidden somewhere in Dallas, but I've looked in dozens of places and can't find him. I might as well come back home."

"Stay," the Chiefs told Wells. "We want to sign Otis."

Sighing, Wells hung up. He found a girl who knew Otis. "Where is Otis Taylor?" he asked her. She knew, but she wouldn't say. Wells called Otis's mother and told her that the girl wouldn't tell him where her son was. Mrs. Taylor phoned the girl and briskly told her to tell Mr. Wells where he could find

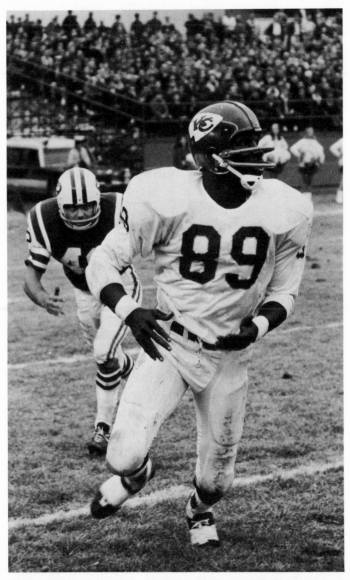

Taylor looks for the pass as a New York Jet defender comes up behind him.

Otis. Finally the girl told Wells that Otis was at a party for football players in a motel in a Dallas suburb. Wells drove to the motel.

Meanwhile, Otis was enjoying the party with Seth Cartwright, another player at Prairie View. Then a Cowboy scout told Taylor why Cartwright was there. "We only invited him along to be company for you," he said. "You're the one we're interested in."

Otis was insulted. Although Cartwright was a good player, the Cowboys were only using him to help sign Otis Taylor. Taylor was also tired of hearing about the greatness of receiver Bob Hayes. He began to wonder if the Cowboys would have room for another wide receiver.

A Cowboy official walked over to tell Otis that a newspaperman had come to see him. Otis went to the door and saw that the "newspaperman" was Lloyd Wells of the Kansas City Chiefs. "Hey," he said, "you're not a newspaperman."

"Shhh," Wells whispered. "The Dallas people wouldn't let me in here if they knew who I was."

Wells then made an offer to Otis. If he signed to play for Kansas City he would receive a car, a bonus of $10,000, and a $14,000 salary. The Cowboys had made a similar offer, but after talking to the Cowboy officials at this party, Otis had decided he'd rather play for Kansas City.

"I'll sign with you," he told Wells.

The time was now near midnight. The party was ending. The Cowboys had rented rooms at the motel for the players, so they couldn't be contacted by

AFL teams. Wells left the motel, drove his car to a
road near the motel, and waited.

At three in the morning he saw a tall, shadowy
figure scurry out of a motel door, whisk around the
pool, and come running toward him. Wells threw
open the door. Otis jumped in and Wells gunned the
car, streaking back to Dallas. A few days later Otis
signed with the Chiefs. The Cowboys had been out-
smarted.

When Otis reported to the Kansas City camp, he
was worried. He was not one of the highly publi-
cized rookies. "Some rookies think they got it
made," he told a friend. "But I'm going to be worried right up to the last cut."

Otis made the team and two years later the Chiefs
won the AFL championship. "The biggest factor in
winning the championship," said tight end Fred Ar-
banas, "was Taylor. He not only gave us the long
ball threat but he blocked. Most flankers don't care
much for hitting but Otis doesn't mind sticking his
head in there."

Those long Dawson-to-Taylor passes put a new
zip in the Kansas City offense. "We used to travel by
bus," Hank Stram said, speaking of his offense.
"With Otis we go by jet."

After Otis joined the team, the Chiefs were usually winners in post-season playoffs, too. They twice
went all the way to the Super Bowl, losing to Green
Bay in Super Bowl I, then winning Super Bowl IV
against the Vikings. The Chiefs paid Otis well for his
pass catching, as much as $50,000 a year.

A lot of that money went into Otis's closet. He

During a muddy game, Taylor takes a rest.

liked clothes. He wore $200 suits, $100 shoes, and $50 sweaters.

"I paid $240 for a double-breasted suit in New York," he once told writer Arnold Hano. "It's so beautiful I could go to bed with it on."

In 1971 he told a friend, "I just got some more clothes the other day. I didn't need them, considering all the stuff that's lying around that needs pressing. But I can't help buying clothes. I don't like to talk about the number of suits I have, but if you came to Kansas City and interviewed the Chief secretaries, they would tell you how many days I've gone in a row without wearing the same thing twice."

At times he didn't seem to enjoy football. On the day before a game Otis became testy and moody. "I'm very nervous," he said. "I eat a light breakfast that Sunday morning and I won't be able to eat again until Monday. In the dressing room I get into uniform and I won't say very much."

But the thing that kept Taylor going—proving over and over that he was the greatest receiver in football—wasn't the clothes or the money.

"I'll tell you something about Otis Taylor," he said. "He wants to be the best—always. There hasn't been a year he played when he didn't want to score more touchdowns than anybody else. At the start of every season he starts out aiming for the top ten. And he doesn't quit aiming. It's a day-to-day thing, every week, every game."

Then he said, "I am not an athlete for the money or the fame or the Super Bowl. I am an athlete for my own heart."

2. RAYMOND BERRY

*"YOU'VE
GOT
TO
PRACTICE"*

Johnny Unitas ducked into the Colt huddle. "Slant," he said in his gravelly voice. The Colts clapped hands and wheeled out of the huddle.

The scene was Yankee Stadium on a raw and gloomy December afternoon in 1958. Some 62,000 Giant fans were roaring, "Hold, Giants, Hold, Giants," as the Colts lined up on their own 25-yard-line, a long 75 yards from the Giant goal. The Colts were losing 17-14 with only 90 seconds remaining. If they failed to score they would lose not only the game but the NFL championship.

Raymond Berry trotted toward his end position.

Even in his white Colt helmet and padded jersey, he seemed too fragile to be a pass catcher. The official figures said Raymond Berry was 6-foot-2 and 187 pounds, but he looked skinny. Those who knew him knew he also had a weak back and needed contact lenses to see normally. But now he would be the target of Johnny Unitas's passes as the Colts made one last try at victory.

Unitas called the signals and took the snap. He stepped back, looking for Raymond Berry. On the snap Berry had charged straight at a Giant defensive back. The defender stepped back, afraid that Berry would get ahead of him. Raymond jabbed his right foot into the ground and changed direction, slanting toward the sideline and opening a gap between himself and the defender. When Berry turned, the ball was already halfway toward him.

The defender was cutting now toward the ball. But it arrived before he got there. Berry brought it down just as he was flattened by the defender.

Raymond got up and looked at the sideline. He was on the 50-yard-line, for a gain of 25. The Colts still had a chance.

Again Raymond went out for a pass, this time running a Z-like pattern toward the sideline. Again Unitas arched a pass, again Raymond caught it, this time for a 16-yard gain.

The Colts were at the Giant 35, still too far away for a good chance at a field goal. And the clock kept running—20 seconds, 15 seconds. . . .

Unitas was back in the pocket, looking desperately for an open man. Berry took two steps toward the center of the field, then veered toward the sideline

In the 1958 championship game, Berry plows into Giant tackler
Jim Patton.

on the Z-pattern. Unitas lofted the ball toward him and Berry raced under it, knowing he had to make this catch or time would run out on the Colts.

Raymond reached up and the ball settled into his hands. He hugged it to his chest like a baby. Just then a Giant defender hit him from behind. Raymond slammed into the hard ground, but he held onto the ball. Then the whistle blew and the play ended.

Raymond jumped up. He was on the 13-yard-line. He saw a clump of players rushing onto the field from the Colt bench. They were the Colt field-goal-kicking team, led by kicker Steve Myhra. The clock was stopped with only seven seconds remaining. Myhra's kick was good, tying the game 17-17. The clock ran out and the players returned to their benches to rest a minute before pro football's first sudden-death overtime began.

Early in the overtime the Colts had the ball, third down, 15 yards to go for a first down. The Giants knew Unitas would be passing and they knew his number one target would be Raymond. Two Giant defenders closed in on Raymond as he blasted off the line. But Raymond made a move that lost one man. He made another move and the second man, Carl Karilivacz, slipped and fell down. Unitas flipped the ball to Raymond, who caught it on the Giant 42 for a Colt first down.

Unitas scanned the Giant defense. He figured the Giants would be spreading their outside linebackers wide, trying to cut off Berry's pass routes toward the sidelines. Unitas sent his big back, Alan Ameche,

plunging up the thinned-out middle, and Alan the
Horse thundered to the Giant 20.

The confused Giants grouped toward the middle.
On the next play Berry faked running toward the
sideline, then veered over the middle. Unitas lined
the ball right at him, Raymond caught it and then
disappeared under a cloud of blue New York jerseys
at the Giant eight-yard-line.

Two plays later the Colts were on the one. Unitas
handed off to Ameche, and the Horse burst into the
end zone for the touchdown that won the game, 23-
17, and the championship.

In the Colt clubhouse reporters surrounded Berry.
Some were surprised, seeing him close-up for the
first time. With his thin, almost ascetic face, he
looked more like a high school English teacher than
a pro football player.

"It was simple stuff really," Raymond told the reporters. "In a slant pattern I'd veer toward the sideline. On the Z-out pattern I'd go downfield about
ten yards, take about two steps toward the center of
the field, then turn and break diagonally toward the
sideline. But you've got to practice that fake toward
the center of the field or you'll fall flat on your face."

Practice. Practice. Practice. That could have been
Raymond Berry's middle name. One day the following summer he was on a practice field at West-
minster, Maryland. Most of the other Colts had left
the field; only Unitas and Berry remained. They had
been working out for two hours, but Unitas and
Berry went on working. Berry ran straight down the
field for ten yards, then cut to the sideline on a

square-out pattern. Unitas threw him the ball, and
Raymond snared it moments before he stepped out
of bounds. For 20 minutes they practiced that pass,
first to the left, then to the right. Then Unitas finally
headed for the dressing room. For another ten minutes, under the hot afternoon sun, Raymond kept it
up, running through that square-out pattern again
and again.

A few years later Raymond married a pretty Baylor University co-ed and she became a practice partner. Beginning in July, before the opening of the
Colt camp, Raymond and Sally would drive to a
practice field near their home every afternoon.
Then, for two hours, Sally would toss short passes to
Raymond as he weaved through his patterns.

All that practice helped to make Raymond Berry
the top pass-catcher of pro football. He caught 631
passes during his 13 seasons with the Colts, more
than anyone in the 50-year history of the National
Football League. He ran 9,275 yards with those
catches, more than five miles. Only the Jets' Don
Maynard has surpassed Berry's yardage record.

Maynard had an advantage—he was fast. Raymond Berry wasn't. Once Berry raced 235-pound
defensive end Gino Marchetti. They finished in a tie.
Most pass receivers would have left Marchetti floun-
dering behind them. Maynard's speed allowed him
to go deep, sometimes gaining 50 yards or more on
one reception. But Raymond Berry, weaving his
short patterns, usually had to catch three or four
passes to gain 50 yards.

The amazing part of the Berry–Unitas combina-

Berry makes an off-balance catch as a Detroit defender approaches.

tion was its consistency. When Unitas threw those short passes to Berry, it sometimes seemed they could gain five or ten yards whenever they cared to. Even when the other team put two men on Raymond, he often slipped free with his quick moves. Unitas threw the ball while Raymond was halfway through his patterns. He knew precisely where Raymond would be when he completed the pattern.

Raymond's moves astonished even veteran pros. Once quarterback Bobby Layne watched Raymond walking through an airport lobby in his double-jointed, rolling gait. Layne shouted at Raymond, "Doggone it, Raymond, you even make moves when you walk."

Raymond Berry—he always hated the nickname "Ray"—had always been on the slight side. He weighed only 140 pounds as a junior in high school. The Berry family lived in Paris, Texas, and Raymond's father was the coach of the high school football team. Even that hadn't helped Raymond: he didn't make the team until his senior year. Raymond told *Sport* magazine writer Berry Stainback, "My mother and daddy never do a job halfway. I was brought up never to do anything sloppily."

At first no college was interested in the skinny Raymond. He went to a junior college in Texas, caught 32 passes in his first season and won a scholarship to Southern Methodist University. He caught 33 passes during his three years at SMU, but did not excite any pro scouts because he wasn't fast enough. The Colts made Raymond their 20th choice in the draft. He came to the Colt camp in the summer of 1955 tense and determined to succeed. He made the team that season, but only barely, and he worried from week to week that the coaches would cut him.

All that worrying made him jittery at the start of the 1956 season. "I am afraid for anybody to throw me the ball," he told a friend. "I keep thinking I am going to mess it up."

In one pre-season game he went out for a pass and saw the ball come toward him. "Don't miss it, don't miss it," Raymond said to himself. He stuck up his hands. The ball hit them and bounded away. He had

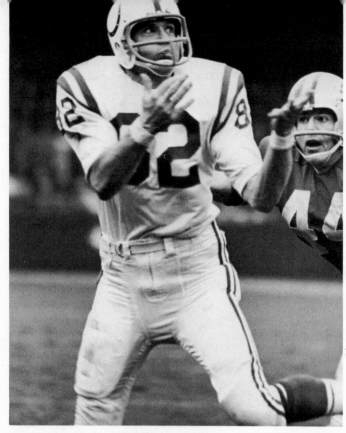

Berry waits for the ball (above) and gathers it in (right), staying one step ahead of Detroit's Dick LeBeau.

missed it.

Each night Raymond went to bed at eight o'clock, determined to get as much sleep as possible. One night he tossed and turned in bed for two or three hours, praying that he wouldn't be cut. "The Lord was good to me," Raymond said. "I caught a couple of passes a few days later."

In 1956 the Colts found the man who could throw the passes to Berry. That season an unknown named Johnny Unitas joined the Colts as their starting quarterback. Two years later Unitas was already recog-

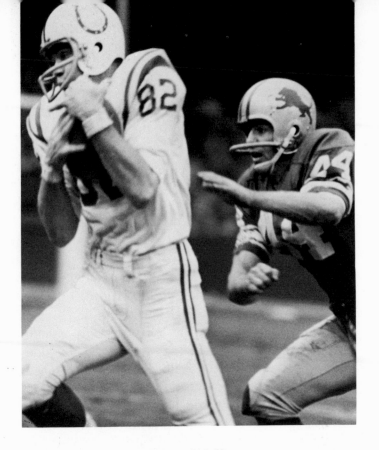

nized as a great quarterback and the Colts won the NFL championship. Raymond led the NFL with 56 catches, 794 yards gained and nine touchdown passes caught.

During that season he began to tip off Unitas on what the defense was doing. "I'll give you all the information I can get," Raymond told Johnny U. "Whether you want to use it or not is your business as the quarterback. If I see nothing then I'll keep my mouth shut. But I hate to come back silent. It's an end's job to go out and do reconnaissance."

Once, in a game against the Eagles, Raymond noticed that a cornerback was acting differently. At first Raymond couldn't identify the change. Then he suddenly realized that the cornerback was covering the sideline. He was afraid that Unitas would throw to the outside, toward the sideline.

Raymond trotted back to the huddle. With the cornerback favoring the outside, there should be room inside, Raymond realized. He said to Unitas, "Bend-in."

Unitas nodded but called another play. A minute later, though, with the ball on the Eagle 40, Unitas ducked into the huddle and said, "Bend in."

Raymond lined up on the left side. Sure enough, there was that cornerback edging toward the sideline. Raymond tried to keep his eyes straight ahead. He didn't want to look inside toward the middle of the field, where he would be running that bend-in pattern. He didn't want to tip off the play.

On the snap Raymond ran toward the cornerback. He saw the cornerback take a step that swayed his weight toward the sideline. Raymond cut toward the inside and each step widened the distance between himself and the cornerback, who recovered too late. Unitas pitched the ball into Raymond's hands. He caught the ball in full stride and ran all the way into the end zone for the touchdown.

One June day in 1961, Raymond and his wife, accompanied by writer Berry Stainback, climbed out of a Chevrolet at the practice field. Raymond jogged around the field, a football tucked under his arm, carrying it exactly as he would in a game.

"I do everything in practice exactly as I want to do it in a game," he told Stainback after he had finished jogging. "Then everything becomes a habit. In a game there's no time to think. Like I always try to keep my eye on the ball. If you've trained yourself properly, you do things like that without thinking about them."

Sally threw a couple of passes but they landed behind Raymond as he cut. "Lead me, honey," he yelled. The next pass bounced off Raymond's fingertips and he was angry with himself. "Oh, Raymond," he yelled, raising his eyes to the sky and shaking his head.

"Hit me with a post," he yelled at Sally. He faked inside, then turned and broke toward the imaginary goal posts. Sally arched the ball toward him.

The Colts are playing Washington in 1957. Unitas calls a pass to Berry on a post pattern. Raymond lines up on the right side. He runs down ten yards, fakes toward the sideline with his head and shoulders, does a little stutter-step, then jab steps with his right foot and takes off at an angle toward the goalposts, leaving the defender behind. Unitas throws. Raymond turns and sees the pass coming over his left shoulder. He reaches out, snares the ball and as the pass receivers say, he "breaks one," going 67 yards for a touchdown.

"An out pattern," Raymond shouted to Sally. He ran downfield eight yards, faked a move toward the inside, then cut outward at a sharp angle toward the sideline. Sally threw the ball, leading him.

One step inside the end zone, Berry makes the catch.

The Colts face Green Bay in 1960. Raymond runs the out pattern at the 16-yard-line. He catches the ball at the sideline, spins away from a tackler, and runs into the end zone for another touchdown.

"An in pattern," Raymond called to Sally. This was the seventh and last pattern he would run today. He ran downfield twelve yards, faked going toward the sideline, then cut inside. Sally lobbed the pass over an imaginary defensive line.

Baltimore is playing Detroit in 1961. The Colts are losing by three points late in the game. Unitas calls for an in pattern. On the snap Berry fakes going toward the sideline and cuts toward the "pit," that tangle of bodies around the line of scrimmage that Berry always tried to avoid. But now Berry sees daylight and realizes that one or two linebackers are gone. They're blitzing, he thinks. He turns and sees Unitas, about to be buried by the blitzers, snap that right arm. Here comes the ball. Raymond grabs it and runs 56 yards for the touchdown that beats the Lions.

Now, sweltering in the June heat, Raymond was ready for a final drill. Sally stood about ten yards behind him, Raymond with his back to her. Sally shouted, "Hey," and fired the ball at the back of his neck.

Raymond whirled and caught it. He flipped the ball back to Sally, again turned his back. She shouted, "Hey," and threw the ball at his feet. Again Raymond whirled like a dancer and grabbed the ball at his ankles. For 15 minutes they repeated this drill,

Sally hurling the ball to his left, his right, his feet and his head. Each time, he whirled and caught the ball —crouched low, feet spread, knees bent, hands poised ready to lunge in any direction.

Finally practice ended and a sweating Raymond walked slowly off the field, talking to Stainback. "Six to ten patterns is all you need," he was saying. "If you have a couple of sideline patterns, a couple of deep patterns, and a couple of inside patterns, and you and the quarterback are teamed up good on all those patterns, you've got all it takes to beat any defense. The more time you spend with a quarterback, the better you'll be."

Raymond Berry ran his last pattern as a pass receiver in 1967. He was 34 years old and had been slowed down by knee injuries. He retired to become an assistant Dallas Cowboy coach, to supervise various businesses in Texas and to write a book on pass receiving. He had every right to write *the* book on pass catching, said his Colt teammate, tight end John Mackey. "He had only two things," Mackey once said, "but those two things meant a lot. One, he was so dedicated. And two, he knew everything."

3. FRED BILETNIKOFF

WORRY,
WORRY,
WORRY

"Hey, Fred, how much of that stuff are you going to drink?"

Fred Biletnikoff ignored the question. He picked up the bottle and gulped down some more of the whitish liquid.

The other Oakland Raiders were pulling on their uniforms in the clubhouse before a game. They watched Fred drink. "I never saw anybody who drank so much of that before a game," a player said.

Fred put down the empty bottle. It was labeled Maalox, and was a medicine for soothing a nervous stomach.

41

Fred paced the room, a frown on his face. Tight end Billy Cannon turned to a rookie. "That Biletnikoff is a real worrier," Cannon said. "He chews his fingernails down to the elbows."

Big defensive tackle Tom Keating overheard what Cannon had said. Tom roomed with Fred. "He keeps a case of Maalox in his locker," Tom said. "He drinks at least two bottles, sometimes three, before a game."

Fred Biletnikoff never denied he was a worrier. "Look," he once told a friend, "I worry because when you are a wide receiver and you have any brains at all, you know that one mistake can hurt the whole team. If I drop a pass in the end zone with our team behind by three points, that wrecks what some 40 guys have been working hard to accomplish for a week. Who wouldn't worry?"

Fred Biletnikoff had other reasons to worry. When he was a rookie, some of the Raider coaches shook their heads when they saw him. "He's too slow to make it in this league," they said. For much of his rookie season Fred sat on the bench. When he got into a game he dropped passes. "What's the matter with you?" a friend asked him one day. "You caught all those passes in college, you were an All-American. Why can't you catch them in the pros?"

The sandy haired, 6-foot-1, 195-pound Biletnikoff frowned. "In college it was easy to run patterns," he said. "You ran out and cut left or right. The defensive backs were worried you would run deep for the long pass so they let you have those short ones. The pros don't give you anything, and it's hard learning to be at a precise place at a precise time. I make one false step and I'm too early or too late. Everything—all the patterns, all the signals—they seem so difficult. I never learned anything fast. When I go out to catch a pass I'm thinking too much about the pattern, I'm not concentrating on the ball and I drop it."

Fred shook his head. "I know they are going to cut me, I know it."

The Raiders didn't cut Fred. And by 1971 Fred Biletnikoff had caught more passes in his seven-year career than any Raider in the team's history. In that 1971 season he led the National Football League, both the American Conference and the National, with 61 catches, nine of them for touchdowns. But even when he was the league's top pass catcher, he worried. In practice he yelled loudly at himself when he dropped a pass. The day before a game he sat moodily, watching TV and talking little or not at all. The morning of a game he awoke complaining about the hardness of the bed and the noise in the hotel hallways during the night. "Two groans and a grumble," said his roommate Tom Keating. "That's Fred's idea of a good morning."

Then the game began, and the emotional Fred was feverishly eager to make his opponents worry about him. Once he was playing against the Jets' Johnny Sample, who liked to needle pass receivers with insults so they would be thinking more about Sample than the ball. "You'll drop it, you'll drop it," Sample shouted at Fred whenever he ran a pattern.

Fred caught a pass. He caught another pass. Then Sample was silent. "I like to play against guys like

In full stride and one step ahead of a San Diego defender, Fred Biletnikoff reaches for the ball.

that," Fred said after the game. "If you catch a few passes, suddenly they quit talking."

Fred dressed slowly after a game. "He's still worried," Tom Keating once said to a newspaperman. "It'll take him maybe eight hours to calm down."

Fred himself conceded that maybe he worried a little too much. "But look," he said, "I didn't have the speed when I came to the pros. I didn't have the natural moves to get open. And I always wanted to make good in this game. So naturally I worried."

His coaches agreed that Fred didn't have a lot of natural talent. "The thing that's impressive about Fred is that he is a man-made receiver," Oakland head coach John Madden told writer Glenn Dickey. "Some guys are just gifted. Like Warren Wells. Warren is almost animal-like in his movements. Fred isn't. He's had to work for everything he's got.

"His greatest quality is his ability to catch the ball. All pro receivers have good hands, but Fred goes beyond that. He can catch anything he can touch. And that's no accident. He has tremendous concentration. He doesn't think of anything but catching the football."

In a 1971 game against New Orleans, Fred ran deep for a long pass from Daryle Lamonica. He turned and looked over his shoulder and saw that the pass was going to be short. Fred slowed down. A defensive back, D'Artagnan Martin, cut in front of him and leaped for the ball.

Fred did not take his eyes off the ball. Fred thought that if Martin tipped the ball, there might still be a chance to grab it. But then Fred realized that Martin had gone up for the ball too soon. The

Biletnikoff gathers in the ball in a 1966 game against the Patriots.

ball floated over Martin's outstretched fingers. Fred grabbed the ball and galloped another ten yards before being tackled. By not giving up on the pass, following it every inch of the way, Fred had turned a near-interception into a completion and a long gain.

Once Kansas City coach Hank Stram was talking about Fred. "Because he doesn't have blazing speed," Hank said, "it's possible the defensive backs fail to respect him like they should. He has excellent moves and great concentration. He is probably the most underrated receiver in our conference."

Sixteen-year-old Fred Biletnikoff was strolling home from high school. A freezing wind whipped down the streets here in Erie, Pennsylvania, where Fred had grown up. Fred was daydreaming. He imagined he was running out for a pass, turning to look, seeing the ball come toward him, then grabbing the ball and running 75 yards for a touchdown.

Fred had always thought of himself as a pass receiver when he thought about football. As he often said, "I wouldn't know where else I'd play on the field if they put me out there and told me not to catch the ball. I've always liked catching passes. I never wanted to play anywhere but outside flanker. I guess that's the only position I can play."

Fred had been fortunate. His Erie High School team threw a lot of passes, operating out of a pro-type offense. However, while the team scored a lot on long touchdown passes, it gave up a lot of touchdowns on long passes. "We didn't win a lot," Fred once said, "but we sure were exciting."

When Fred was a senior at Erie High, a Florida State coach saw films of him catching passes. The school was switching to a pro-type offense. The coaches had obtained a long-throwing passer, Steve Tensi, and they thought that Fred had the good hands to hold onto Tensi's line-drive throws. Fred was happy when he got an invitation to go to Florida State. He hadn't received many scholarship offers because his grades were not very good. And he liked the idea of catching passes in balmy Florida after all those years of catching passes in Erie with frost-reddened fingers.

In Fred's senior year at Florida State, his strong hands had caught enough passes to rank him fourth in the nation among college pass catchers. He was picked for many All-America teams. In the 1965 Gator Bowl game he caught four touchdown passes tossed by Tensi as Florida State beat Oklahoma 36-19. Immediately after the game, standing under the goal posts, Fred signed a contract to play for the AFL's Oakland Raiders.

Almost immediately after reporting to the team that summer, Fred wished he had taken the offer from the NFL Detroit Lions, who also had wanted to sign him. He had thought that the Lions had so many young receivers he would have to sit on the bench. But now with the Raiders he was competing with Bo Roberson, a fast young receiver who could leave Fred in a swirl of dust. For the first six games of that rookie season, All-American Fred Biletnikoff sat on the bench.

"Everything seems so jumbled to me," Fred told his wife Jerrylyn one day. "The quarterback calls a new play at the line of scrimmage. I try to remember how it looks on the playsheets, and while I'm thinking, the play starts and I'm caught flat. By the time he's ready to throw the ball I'm out there running all kinds of crazy patterns not even in the playbook. Then if I do get to where the ball is thrown, I'm so upset I drop it."

For the first time in his life, Fred couldn't concentrate on the ball. But Bo Roberson, with all his speed, also had trouble holding on to the ball. Halfway through the season the Raiders traded Roberson and Fred came off the bench. In his first game he caught seven passes for 118 yards. Playing only the second half of the season, he caught a highly respectable 48 passes.

In 1966, however, Fred injured an eye. Then a tackler smashed into his knee and that winter surgeons operated to repair it. For a long time Fred favored the knee. Each time he ran he wondered if it would collapse under him. At camp before the start of the 1967 season he told the Raiders' other wide receiver, Warren Wells, "I'm afraid to plant the knee. I'm thinking so much about the knee I'm dropping passes."

Before a preseason game against San Francisco, Fred knew that the Raiders were going to cut eight players after the game. "They're going to cut me," Fred told a teammate. "Nobody told me, but I can just feel it in the atmosphere. You get that feeling when you've been a regular, when they're not playing you, and the coaches are hardly talking to you. . . ." His voice tightened. "I'm too fired up to talk about it."

When the game began Fred tried to forget his fears about being cut. Early in the game he was supposed to cut inside—toward the middle of the field —past defensive back Kermit Alexander. But Alexander was playing him inside, so Fred faked going inside, then veered to the outside—toward the sideline. He hoped that quarterback George Blanda would find him. Wily old Blanda saw the change. He threw the pass to Fred near the sideline and Fred galloped 41 yards for a touchdown.

The next morning the Raiders cut eight players. They kept Fred.

In 1967 Fred began a series of great seasons with the Raiders. Using his great hands, his concentration, and his inventive way of getting loose from defend-

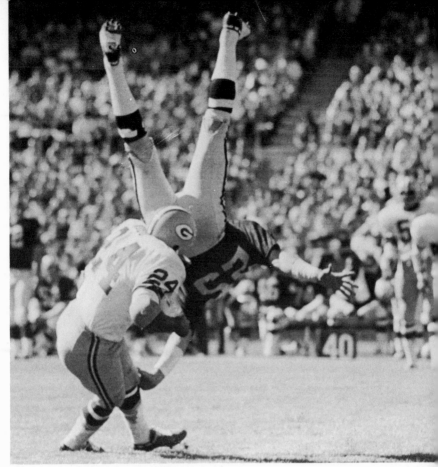

At left, Biletnikoff takes a touchdown pass. Above, he is upended
by Packer defender Willie Wood.

ers, he caught 40 passes in 1967, five of them for
touchdowns. The Raiders won the AFL championship. The next year, 1968, he caught 61 passes, third
highest in the AFL. In that season the Raiders lost to
the Jets 27-23 for the AFL championship, but in that
championship game Fred caught seven passes for a
total of 190 yards, tying two AFL records.

Fred kept up the good work in 1969, catching 54
passes and ranking second in the AFL behind Lance
Alworth. He caught 12 touchdown passes while the

other Raider wide receiver, Warren Wells, caught 14. People were calling them "The Touchdown Twins." In 1970 Fred ranked fifth in the AFC.

Then in 1971, Fred played without speedy Warren Wells, whose specialty was running the deep patterns. Fred began running long patterns as well as short. He had become a good deep receiver by polishing his moves to make up for his lack of speed. "He catches all of those passes because of the quickness of his moves," Raider general manager Al Davis said before the 1972 season. "He is not quick at the scrimmage line. But at a point some 15 or 20 yards downfield, he's feinting with his head, with his arms and with those crazy steps he takes. It's there he makes the moves which often leave faster men alone and wondering."

What Fred also needed was a strong-armed quarterback like Lamonica. "Tom Flores was our quarterback when Fred came to us," one assistant Oakland coach said. "Tom was accustomed to lobbing those soft passes to speedy receivers like Art Powell who could open up wide gaps between themselves and a defender. Flores would throw one of those soft passes to Fred and a defender would have the time to recover and bat down the ball before it came to Fred."

Lamonica zipped bullet-like passes. "Fred has great ability to cut left or right," Daryle once said. "He could lose his shadow for a second or two if he had to."

Fred told young players how he had taught himself to run sharp-cornered patterns. "I am able to get ahead of guys who have more speed because I challenge them with something else besides speed. I challenge them with the quickness of my moves. On a pattern what you try to do first is this: you try to convince the back that you are going deep. Then you make moves that force him to commit himself to going left, right or deep. Whichever way he goes, you go one of the two other ways.

"Pass catching is a matter of reflexes, the hands and eyes working together. For a few minutes before practice I spend several minutes punching a light punching bag to sharpen my reflexes. The bag comes back at different angles and I have to adjust to it. I think that helps the coordination between my hands and my eyes."

He showed that coordination in a 1971 game against the Eagles. The Raiders were losing 10-0 at halftime. Lamonica, who had sat out the first half, took over at quarterback as the second half began. "The first chance I get," Lamonica told himself, "I want to put Fred one on one against a cornerback."

With second and five on the Eagle 25, Lamonica told Biletnikoff to fake a short route to the sideline, then go deep. So far, Fred had been running a lot of those short patterns toward the sideline. As Fred lined up he saw Eagle defensive back Al Nelson edge toward the sideline, looking for that pattern to the outside. On the snap Fred ran toward Nelson, faked going to the sideline, then cut toward the middle of the field. Nelson had taken a half-step toward the sideline. Before Nelson could recover, Fred had opened up a gap between them.

That was all the room Lamonica needed. He fired the ball to Fred, who kept right on going into the

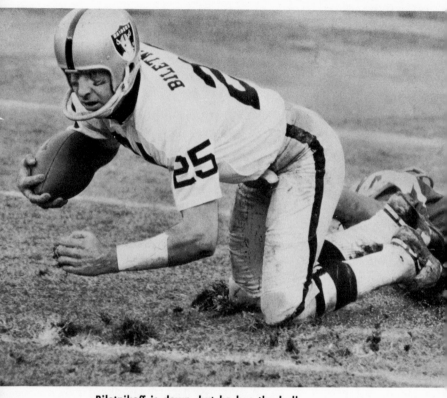
Biletnikoff is down, but he has the ball.

end zone for a 25-yard touchdown toss.

A few minutes later, the Raiders had the ball on their 44, third down and six to go. This time Fred ran straight at Nelson. Nelson came up to meet him, guessing that Fred was going left or right. Instead, Fred kept right on running, dashing by Nelson. The ball flew over Nelson's head. Fred caught it and ran to the Eagle ten before being knocked down. A minute later the Raiders punched over for a touchdown and were on their way to a 34-10 victory.

"Freddie turned the game around," Lamonica

said in the clubhouse. "Freddie makes the big plays. He's the kind of a player who can get a team going. I came into the game 10 points down and he was the guy I looked for. He's clutch."

Fred was pacing the locker room, still on edge. An interviewer asked him what he did during the off-season and Fred talked about a restaurant he owned.

"Business good?" the interviewer asked.

Well, business had been slow lately, Fred said. But he thought that it would pick up. Still, he said, he worried a lot about the place.

4. PAUL WARFIELD

*"HE'S
GOT
THE
NATURAL
MOVES"*

Paul Warfield stretched out on the bed in the motel room in Buffalo. He was relaxing the night before his Miami Dolphins met the Buffalo Bills early in the 1971 season. He was talking to a writer about Dolphin quarterback Bob Griese.

"Bob is a great thrower," Paul was saying. His bony, triangular face gave him an almost mournful expression. "He can thread that ball into a crowd of people and get it to his receiver. That's why I say he can get that ball to me even when I have two or three men covering me, as there are most of the time when I run out for a pass. When a team plays us, they say, 'Let's stop Warfield, let's make sure he doesn't even catch one pass.' But a good receiver can shake off two men covering him, and a good passer like Griese can zip the ball between those two defenders and into the receiver's hands."

Some two weeks later the Dolphins were playing the Pittsburgh Steelers, and the Steelers seemed on their way to a shocking upset, leading 21-3 early in the second period. But the Dolphins had a chance to score a touchdown, the ball on the Pittsburgh 12. Figuring that Griese would pass, the Steelers assigned two men to cover Warfield.

Griese took the snap and stepped into the pocket. He looked away from Warfield, seeing if his other wide receiver was open. No. He looked for a backfield man to be open. No. Warfield, meanwhile, had veered past one defender and was cutting toward the goal posts on a post pattern. He was rapidly outrunning the second defender. Griese suddenly turned and threw. Warfield caught the ball on his fingertips and danced into the end zone. Touchdown. Now Miami trailed 21-10.

A few minutes later the ball was way back on the Miami 14. Again Warfield shot by one defender and shook off the grasping hands of a second. He turned and saw the ball flying toward him, thrown between the two defenders. Warfield "looked" the ball into his hands. It hit his palm with a loud slap, and he took off. He outran two Steelers, racing some 80 yards for another touchdown. Score: Pittsburgh 21, Miami 17.

The two teams battled into the final period, Pittsburgh still ahead 21-17. Then the ball was on the

Against the Steelers in 1971, Warfield loses the ball. But he caught three touchdown passes later and Miami won 24–21.

Miami 40. Griese stepped into the pocket and looked for the open man. Two Steelers were dogging Warfield's heels. He ran left, then right, faked toward the sideline and took off on his favorite post pattern toward the middle of the field. He turned his head and saw the ball spiraling toward him. He caught the ball and ran some 50 yards for his third touchdown of the day. Miami went out in front 24-21 and held on to win.

For nearly all of his pro career, first with the Cleveland Browns and later with the Dolphins, Paul Warfield was shadowed by two or sometimes three defenders. "They'll usually double-cover me," he explained that night in the Buffalo motel room. "I'll run out a lot of times knowing the passer can't throw to me because I've got two men on me and that means someone else is open. I have learned you just have to be patient and wait to catch a pass when the opportunity presents itself."

Not surprisingly, Paul never caught a league-leading number of passes. But in 1968, while he was with Cleveland, he did lead the league in TD passes, catching 12. Paul might not catch a lot of passes but he caught the big ones and he caught the long ones. In fact, by the end of the 1971 season only two active receivers had caught more touchdown passes, and those two—Lance Alworth and Don Maynard—had played more seasons. And Warfield had gained an *average* of 21.4 yards per catch, topping all major active receivers.

BROWNS TRADE WARFIELD TO MIAMI DOLPHINS
That headline paraded across the front page of a

Cleveland newspaper on the cold and brisk evening of January 27th, 1970. Clevelanders rushing home from work stared at the headline, unbelieving. "It can't be true," they told each other. Paul Warfield's speedy legs and sure hands had helped the Browns win the NFL championship in 1964, his rookie year, and win NFL conference titles in 1965, 1967, 1968 and 1969. Not only did he catch passes, he intimidated all rival pass defenders because they knew he could go deep for the game breaking pass at any time. Worried that Paul would get behind them, they hung back, giving the Browns the room to throw short passes to other receivers.

"Good deep receivers are like long-ball hitters in baseball," former Cleveland coach Blanton Collier explained to Tex Maule of *Sports Illustrated.* "The outfielders have to back up against the fence when you have long-ball hitters. So a lot of those little hits over the infield drop in. If you know the hitter can't reach the fence, you play him up close and you catch balls that would be singles for a slugger. Same thing in football. If the defenses are deep, you have room over the line of scrimmage for the short pass to your tight end and to your backs."

Out of a football uniform, Paul Warfield certainly didn't look very fearsome. The official programs listed him as 6-foot and 188 pounds, but he seemed smaller and frailer. The face was bony, the torso almost sickly thin. But he had enormous sprinter's thighs, two pistons that could drive him through 100 yards in 9.6 seconds.

More important, Paul Warfield always knew the value of work, work, work. "In 20 years of coaching," his high school coach once said, "I've never seen another player like him. He is one of those rare people who doesn't compete with other people. He competes with himself.

"I can remember when he was only 13 or 14 years old. He'd be running out on that practice field in the dark, practicing moves, teaching himself how to catch the ball over his head, how to evade a block—all by himself."

Paul grew up in Warren, Ohio, where people take their high school football seriously. The 20,000-seat stadium was filled for every Friday night home game of the Harding High School Panthers. If you were good you played first string for the Panthers in your senior year. If you were super-good you might play first string in your junior year. Paul made the first team as a running back in his sophomore year. The first time a Panther quarterback handed off to Paul, he sped around end and left the other 21 players in the dust, scampering 60 yards for a touchdown.

By his senior year some 70 schools had offered him scholarships. But Paul already had decided on his football career plan. He would go to Ohio State and then to Cleveland to play for the Browns. The Browns were his favorite team and the star running back of the Browns, Jimmy Brown, was Paul's idol.

Paul was a running back at Ohio State, often running up the middle on quick-opening plays. Only occasionally did he run out for a pass. The Ohio State coach, Woody Hayes, didn't like to pass. "When you throw a pass," he often said, "only three things can happen and two of them are bad."

Pro scouts didn't think Paul was strong enough to

As a running back for Ohio State, Warfield carries the ball against UCLA.

be a running back in the NFL. But they liked his speed. One day a Brown scout said to an assistant Brown coach: "I've seen this Warfield at Ohio State only three times this year. In one of those games he only touched the ball three times. But I've noticed that the opposition seems to be afraid he'll break away and go for the long one. Several times he did get behind the defense but he was rarely thrown the ball. With his speed he could be a defensive back or a pass receiver."

The Browns drafted him number one in the spring of 1964. That summer Paul reported to the Browns' camp at Hiram, Ohio. He had been there before to watch his idols. But now he was running shoulder to shoulder with Jim Brown, Frank Ryan, Gary Collins and the other players he had once admired from the stands. Paul Warfield was a Cleveland Brown. Now if he could only stick with this team.

He stuck, not as a defensive back but as a receiver. Dub Jones, the coach of the pass receivers, saw Paul run one day. He turned to head coach Blanton Collier and said, "Look at those moves. He didn't learn those at Ohio State. They don't throw the ball that often. He's got the natural moves. This boy is a flanker."

Later Dub explained why he had known from the start that Paul would be a pass catcher. "He's the type, from the instant you look at him, see him run, catch a ball, see his fake, see his instincts. You don't have to be a genius to realize you have a natural on your hands. You say to yourself, 'If he has the other qualities it takes to be a receiver, you have a star.'"

"What are the other qualities of a star receiver?" Dub was asked.

"Ability to take punishment," Dub said. "And intelligence to understand the coverages being used against him. Also he has to have quickness to go along with his speed. This guy Warfield has that quickness."

Paul showed how quick he could be early in the season. He ran a hook pattern—running out, then hooking back toward the passer. But the passer, Frank Ryan, threw the ball far over Paul's head. Paul spun on his heels, and darted downfield for the ball. He caught up with the long pass and went all the way for a touchdown.

That kind of pass-catching helped the Browns win the NFL's Eastern Conference championship. In the 1964 NFL championship game, the Colts—led by Johnny Unitas—were heavily favored against the Browns. The Colt defense, looking at game films of the Browns, made a decision so many teams would make in the years to come: "We have got to put two

Warfield catches the ball against Detroit's Dick Le-Beau (right), but gets pulled down in a hurry (below).

men on Warfield on downs where the Browns are likely to be passing." The Colts did put two men on Paul, but that left only one man to guard the rangy Gary Collins. Collins caught three touchdown passes and the Browns were surprisingly easy 27-0 winners and NFL champions.

Over the next five seasons the Browns finished first in their conference four times and second the fifth season. The team never had an outstanding passer and Paul nearly always ran for a pass with two men on him. Yet every season he was among the top 10 or 15 in the NFL in pass catching, latching on to 50 in 1968 and 42 in 1969, and almost every season he averaged a whopping 20 yards a catch. He had learned how to sneak away from those two men who were usually shadowing him. "Paul runs the best and most precise, detailed patterns of anyone I know," said coach Blanton Collier.

In 1970, however, the Browns decided they needed an outstanding passer. They wanted to draft Purdue's Mike Phipps, and to get an early draft choice, they traded Paul to the Dolphins. Paul was surprised by the trade but he understood the reasons for it. He sold his Cleveland house and bought a 10-room mansion outside Miami, its lawn almost as wide as a football field.

Paul was still the small-town boy from Warren, Ohio. "I'm a loner," Paul once told writer J. K. De-Groot. "I guess I've always been one ever since I ran around in a backyard as a skinny kid. I'm not one you can get close to. But I'm human. And I love this game. I love what it has done for me and on Sunday afternoons I owe the public all I can give them."

In 1970, his first season as a Dolphin, he caught only 28 passes. But his average per catch—25 yards —was the best in the American Football Conference. Still, as the 1971 season began, Miami head coach Don Shula was telling an assistant he thought that Paul should be catching more passes from quarterback Bob Griese. "We didn't get the ball to Warfield near enough last season," he said. "We've got to concentrate on patterns that will put him in the open even when there are two men trying to cover him."

Paul himself thought he would catch more passes after he got to know Griese and Griese got to know him. "During the early part of last season," he said in the fall of 1971, "there were times when we weren't together on certain things. I would break one way and it would surprise Bob. He'd be throwing the ball the other way."

Early in the 1971 season the two were linking up in beautiful fashion. In a game against Buffalo, Griese walked to the line of scrimmage after calling a running play. But as he hovered over the center, calling the signals, Griese saw that the Bills were planning to blitz. With his computer-like mind, Griese calculated that with a blitz on, the Bills would have to cover Paul with one man. Griese knew that no one man could cover the slippery Paul.

Immediately Griese changed the play at the line of scrimmage with an "audible." He shouted out signals that erased the play he had called in the huddle, then he called out new numbers. Paul, standing wide of the line, knew that the new play was a pass to him.

Without his heavy equipment, Warfield works out in sunny Miami.

Paul streaked toward the defensive back, then veered inside on a post pattern. Just like that, he was open. But a blitzer had dashed through the line and was charging Griese. Bob threw the ball hastily, hoping Paul would turn and see it coming toward him.

Paul took three steps on his post pattern and turned his head. He saw the ball spiraling over the outstretched hands of the blitzer. Paul reached up, caught the ball, hugged it to his chest and ran some 20 yards into the end zone for a touchdown.

That was one of 11 touchdown passes for Paul in the 1971 season, the highest in the National Football League. All told, he caught 43 passes, ninth highest in the AFC, gaining a spectacular average of 23 yards a catch, tops in the AFC. Although he was usually double-covered, he caught more passes than any other Dolphin as the team finished first in the AFC's Eastern Division.

The Dolphins went into the playoffs, first opposing the Kansas City Chiefs. In the longest game ever played—it took 22 minutes, 40 seconds of sudden-death overtime to determine a winner—the Dolphins won when field-goal kicker Garo Yepremian kicked a 37-yard field goal for a 27-24 Miami victory. In that game the Chiefs gambled, putting their ace cornerback, Emmitt Thomas, on Warfield one-on-one. The gamble failed: Paul ran Thomas in circles and Griese threw him seven passes for 140 yards. Warfield's receptions kept three Miami touchdown marches alive.

The next week the Dolphins faced the Baltimore Colts for the championship of the AFC and the right to go on to the Super Bowl. All during the season teams had tried to throw long against the Colts and had failed. The Baltimore defensive backs were hanging back, allowing the short pass to be completed but refusing to give up the "big play" touchdown pass. Bob Griese went into the game with a plan to complete the "big play" pass.

Early in the game the Dolphins had the ball on

their 25, second down and five yards to go. Griese knew the Colts would be looking for one of the big Miami backs, Larry Csonka or Jim Kiick, to run through the middle for the five yards. "Play 119," Griese said in the huddle. The Dolphins clapped hands and flowed out of the huddle to the line.

Paul, lining up in his flanker spot, saw cornerback Rex Kern edging toward him and he thought he would also be covered by Rick Volk, the Colt safety-man.

Griese took the snap. He wheeled and pushed the ball toward Larry Csonka as the big back shot by him and into the line. Paul faked toward the middle of the field. Then he spun and started for the sideline. To his surprise, Rick Volk wasn't tailing him. Volk was rushing up toward the line, to tackle Larry Csonka.

But Csonka didn't have the ball. Griese had pushed the ball into his arms, then pulled it back. Griese was now looking toward the sideline. He saw Rex Kern backpedaling furiously, trying to catch up with Paul, the one-on-one situation that Griese wanted to see. Bob lofted the ball over Kern's head, and Paul caught it at the sideline at the 48.

Volk had seen his mistake, and was racing toward the sideline. When Paul caught the ball, Volk was only ten yards away. Paul turned and ran with Volk in pursuit, as some 78,000 people in the Orange Bowl roared.

Volk closed the gap to seven yards, then six yards and five yards. But the white-on-green yardstripes flew beneath Paul's feet. He could hear Volk's feet pounding behind him above the roar of the crowd.

The goalposts came closer and closer, then he was crossing the last stripe and running into the end zone. He had won the foot race and the Dolphins led the Colts 6-0.

In the fourth quarter the Dolphins were leading 14-0, the ball on their 45-yard-line. It was third down, only two yards to go, and again the Colts were looking for the run. Again Griese sent Paul out for the pass. Griese threw and Paul caught the ball and took it all the way to the five. From there

A few steps from the goal line in the 1972 championship game, Warfield has won his race with Baltimore's Rick Volk.

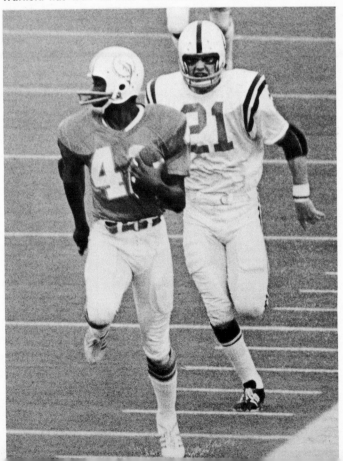

Csonka punched across for the touchdown that sealed a big 21-0 victory and sent Miami to the Super Bowl.

In the Super Bowl the Dallas Doomsday Defense rose up to throw back Csonka and Kiick. That same defense intercepted one Griese pass and limited Paul, with double coverage, to four catches for only 39 yards. The experienced Cowboys beat the young Dolphins 24-3. But after the game one Cowboy summed up what Warfield meant to the Dolphins and to any team he would ever play for.

"The only way to cover Paul Warfield," the Cowboy said, "is to stuff him in the garbage can and seal up the lid."

5. LANCE ALWORTH

*"WE'RE
GOING
TO
WIN
IN
THE
SUPER
BOWL"*

The Dallas Cowboys huddled, the ball on the San Francisco one-yard-line. A big Dallas substitute trotted in from the bench with the next play from coach Tom Landry. He leaned into the huddle and called the play. The Cowboys clapped hands and trotted up to the line of scrimmage.

The big San Francisco defensive line waited, determined to throw back the Cowboy attempt. They knew it would be a running play to gain that yard to the goal. The San Francisco 49ers *had* to stop this touchdown. Dallas was leading 7-3 early in the fourth period. Playing for the 1971 championship of

Showing his blocking ability, Lance Alworth (center) knocks aside a Cleveland tackler as Calvin Hill (35) goes for a big gain.

the National Football Conference, the 49ers still had a chance, but they could not afford to yield another touchdown.

Coach Landry had called a run to the left by back Duane Thomas. Now quarterback Roger Staubach took the ball, wheeled, and handed off to Thomas. The broad-shouldered running back broke toward the left. At the same time a 49er linebacker moved in the same direction on the other side of the line of scrimmage. In the footrace to the sideline, Thomas would have to reach the corner of the end zone before that linebacker knocked him down or forced him out of bounds.

A Dallas blocker, running in front of Thomas, headed for the 49er linebacker, but was suddenly bowled over by another 49er. Now Thomas seemed unprotected.

Suddenly the 49er linebacker was mowed down by a white-jerseyed Dallas blocker who seemed to come out of nowhere. Duane Thomas sprinted into the corner of the end zone. Touchdown. The Cowboys led 14-3 and were on their way to victory, the NFC championship and the Super Bowl game.

Up in the press box the reporters saw the white-jerseyed Dallas blocker get to his feet. They checked his numerals. It was Lance Alworth, number 19, the Dallas wide receiver. Instead of running out for a pass, he had run along the line of scrimmage, then upended the linebacker, clearing the route for Thomas into the end zone.

In this must-win game against the 49ers Lance caught only one pass. During the entire season he had caught only 34 passes, marking one of the few seasons in his ten-year career that he had caught fewer than 50. He had gained fame as a receiver, catching more than 500 passes, placing him second only to Don Maynard among all active receivers. But in this game, the 182-pound Lance had thrown a block on a 240-pound linebacker that had clinched the victory. For Alworth, applause from coaches and fans and the resulting chance in the Super Bowl was reward enough.

"Sure, anybody would rather catch than block," the skinny, sharp-featured Lance said after the game. "But there's one thing better than either, and that's winning and going to the Super Bowl. Nothing I have ever done, not even any pass-catching record I ever set, can be as important to me as helping us get into the Super Bowl. And we're going to win in the Super Bowl."

They called him Bambi after the famous deer in the Walt Disney cartoon. He leaped like a deer for passes. In his nine seasons with the San Diego Chargers, he caught short passes over the middle and went all the way for touchdowns. He ran deep on post and fly patterns and went all the way for touchdowns. He and passer John Hadl made the Chargers famous as the "big play" team. At any moment, from anywhere on the field, Hadl would step back and throw to the fleet Lance and—*bingo!*—a quick touchdown.

He and John Hadl worked together like two scientists, testing carefully and patiently to find a weakness in the defense. Then Lance took advantage of the weakness, caught the quick pass and flew toward the end zone with the speed of a sprinter.

In one game against Oakland that the Chargers needed badly to win, Lance noticed that a safety man was inching up closer than usual to the line of scrimmage. "I think I can take him," Lance told Hadl in the huddle. "He's so close I think I can run right by him."

Hadl nodded, but then called a running play. As the San Diego ball carrier ploughed into the line, Hadl sneaked a look at the safety man. He *was* up awfully close.

In the next huddle John turned to Lance and said, "I think this is the time." He called the pass to Alworth. As Lance lined up he saw the safety creep closer to the line. Hadl took the ball from the center. Lance burst toward the safety man and shot right by him. Hadl arched a long pass that floated down in front of Alworth. Lance reached out and pulled the ball to his chest. Ahead of him were only empty space and the goal line, behind him the helpless Raider defenders.

From 1962 to 1969 Lance played for the Chargers in the old American Football League. During much of this time, National Football League fans scorned AFL players as bush leaguers. But even NFL fans agreed that there were some AFL players who would be stars in the NFL. One was Joe Namath. Another was Lance Alworth.

Alworth, with his acrobatic leaps to snare passes, thrilled fans and helped to make the new AFL exciting and spectacular, a league where the next-to-impossible happened nearly every game. One of Lance's earliest leaping catches was in the 1964 AFL championship game. Early in the game he glided down the sideline with Buffalo defensive back Ron Hall a step behind. The ball, thrown short, floated down between them. Lance soared high into the air and plucked the ball away from Hall's reaching fingers. Then he ran the rest of the way for a touchdown. San Diego finally won 20-7.

"What does he do?" muttered Hall after the game. "Train on a trampoline?"

"I don't really understand it myself," Alworth said. "I can't really jump very high when I am not leaping for a football. For instance, I played basketball in high school and I could never stuff the ball into the basket during practice. But I've seen pictures of myself going up for rebounds with my hands above the rim. I guess when I'm concentrating real hard on a ball, I don't realize how high up I've gone."

In the 1966 season he showed courage as well as talent. In one game he chipped a bone in his right hand. The Chargers kept the injury secret, and the next week Lance was used as a decoy while Hadl threw to receivers who could hold onto the ball. But on one play, Alworth ran out for a long pass, leaped for the ball, and fell heavily on his left wrist. He walked slowly off the field, grimacing, holding the wrist. At a hospital doctors took a look and told him, "Now you've broken bones in both hands."

The doctors told him they could put a cast on the left wrist, keeping him out of action for eight weeks. Or they could put it in a leather brace and he might be able to play.

Lance chose the brace. When a ball hit that frac-

Playing for the Chargers, Alworth leaps between two Kansas City defenders, but this time he misses the ball.

tured wrist, Lance winced with pain. He figured out a way to catch passes with his elbows, cradling the ball to his chest. And he went right on playing—and catching passes. That year he led the league in pass catches and in touchdown receptions.

He led the AFL almost every season in one pass-catching department or another. One reason was that he seldom missed a game, often playing under hardships that would have stopped lesser men. He led the league in pass catches in 1966, 1968 and 1969. In 1964, 1965 and 1966 he led in touchdown passes.

The hand injuries in 1966—his best year—were not even the most serious he received that season. In a late-season game Kansas City's big Bobby Bell crashed into his knee, ripping ligaments. For the rest of the season Lance could run only at three-quarter speed. Without his breakaway speed, Lance could no longer outrun defenders on dashes down the side-line. Yet he claimed that this injury turned him into "a professional receiver."

"Before, I would just run right at a defender, make a quick fake and depend on my speed to beat him," he said. "Heck, in college, I didn't know what a move was. After I got hurt I ran moves like they are supposed to be run. And I caught more short passes and they set up the long ones."

Lance set almost a dozen AFL pass-catching records. He set one record that stopped a game. In the 1930s and 1940s the long-striding, lean Don Hutson had caught at least one pass in 95 straight games for the Green Bay Packers. That record, unbroken after 25 years, seemed unbreakable.

From 1962 to 1969, catching at least one pass a game, Lance slowly crept up on that record. By December 14, 1969, Bambi had caught a pass in every game of every season since 1962, a total of 95 games, tying Hutson's record.

Don Hutson was invited to see the game against the Buffalo Bills in which Lance would try to break the old master's record. John Hadl wanted to get the record early in the game for his old passing partner. The first time he handled the ball, John stepped back to pass, looking for Lance.

Two Bills converged on Lance as he ran toward the sideline. Reluctantly John looked away, saw big Gary Garrison cutting down the other sideline, forgotten by the Bills in their double-coverage of Alworth. Hadl threw. Garrison caught the ball over his shoulder and galloped into the end zone for a 41-yard touchdown play.

At the sideline a coach said to Lance, "They'll be double-teaming you on every play."

"So?" said Lance, a grin on his long thin face. "That'll leave Gary or someone else open. And I'll get that one pass. They're not going to stop me even with two or three guys on me. John will get one to me. Just wait."

A few minutes later the ball went over to the Chargers again. On the first play Hadl ran back to pass. Again he saw two men sandwiching Alworth.

Hadl turned to look for someone else, but saw no one free. At that moment Lance made a move and got away from his two bodyguards. Seeing him open, John threw. Lance leaped, caught the ball and tumbled to the ground.

Alworth looks for running room against the Buffalo Bills.

Whistles screeched, and officials stopped the game. A public address announcer told the fans that Don Hutson's record had been broken by Lance Alworth. Don Hutson trotted onto the field and congratulated Lance. Later he said, "Lance deserves the record. He is unbelievable."

Certainly Lance had been lucky. His father had been an oil executive and as a boy Lance had everything. He was born in Houston on August 3, 1940. The family moved several times, and when Lance was ready for high school, the family was living in Brookhaven, Mississippi, a town of 6500 people.

By the time he was a senior, everybody in town knew who he was. Lance ran on the track team. He hit home runs and roamed center field for the baseball team. He punted, ran back punts and carried the ball through the line for the football team. The New York Yankees offered him $25,000 to train him as a shortstop. But Lance and his dad decided he should go to college.

Lance chose the University of Arkansas. He was a running back who also caught passes and returned punts. In his senior year he gained nearly 1,000 yards rushing and during his three years at Arkansas, the Razorbacks won 24 of 30 games and went to three post-season Bowls.

Lance was happy when the Chargers, after signing him in 1962, converted him to a wide receiver. "I've always worried that I'm too small and fragile to be a running back," he said. "Especially in the pros. I could be a running back in pro ball, but I don't know how long my body would stay in one piece."

Alworth makes a diving catch as he crosses the 10-yard-line.

Indeed, even among pass receivers, most of whom are slim, the 180-pound Lance looked like a rail. San Diego coaches winced when linebackers ran into him. But nearly always he bounced right back up. His leaping helped Bambi to keep in one piece. "If they hit you when you're up in the air like that," he often said, "it doesn't sting."

In 1969 the San Diego Chargers played their last game in the AFL, the old AFL teams becoming part of the American Football Conference. Lance celebrated that last AFL game by breaking Hutson's consecutive-game pass-catching record, going over 1,000 yards for the season in pass-catching yardage, and winning his second straight AFL pass-catching title. A few months later *The Official History of the American Football League—1960–1969* was published by *The Sporting News.* On the cover was a color photo of Lance Alworth catching a pass.

Alworth was being acclaimed as pro football's top receiver and he was also considered pro football's only millionaire ballplayer. He had invested in a number of enterprises, including dry cleaning stores in some 12 states. But then his luck suddenly turned. The stock market fell, money became scarce, and his businesses began to fail. Soon Lance had to declare himself bankrupt. Then he had a dispute with Charger general manager Sid Gillman, saying he had been promised money and had not received it. He quit the team, then returned. But the coaches told him to stop suggesting plays to John Hadl. Hadl was told to throw to the other receivers. Lance had the feeling he no longer was wanted.

At the start of the 1971 season Lance was traded to the Dallas Cowboys. People raved about the Cowboy pass-catching combination of Bob Hayes and Lance Alworth. But Cowboy coach Tom Landry had other ideas. He also had a spectacular running team, led by Duane Thomas, Calvin Hill and Walt Garrison, and assisted by one of the best offensive lines in the business. Ironically, Alworth made his big play of the season as a blocker for running back Duane Thomas.

"Many linebackers today weigh 240 pounds," Los Angeles writer Bob Oates reminded Lance one day. "At 180, you're giving them 60 pounds. How can you block a man that much bigger?"

Lance grinned. "You can't unless you spend a

week thinking about it. You have to make up your mind to give each block a good honest 95 percent effort."

"A 95?"

"With 100 I'd get killed."

"Even so, how do you do it?"

"For one thing, most defensive players don't respect wide receivers. They don't expect to get blocked by a flanker, and that gives me the advantage. The other thing is that I had enough brains to realize there's no way I'm going to knock down a 240-pound linebacker. The trick is to get in his way."

"Do the larger linebackers ever speak to you about this?"

"Well, the other day I had to block the same guy three times. I didn't get him off his feet, of course, but he didn't make the tackle, either. The last time, he looked around and said, 'You gnat. Keep away from me, you gnat.'"

"All things considered, wouldn't you really rather be catching touchdown passes?"

"Sure, anybody would rather catch than block. But there's one thing better than either, and that's winning. Here I am, 31 years old this year, and I've never been to the Super Bowl. Nothing I've ever done compares with the glow of being on a team with a shot at the Super Bowl."

Winning nine straight games, the Cowboys marched into Super Bowl VI. The Cowboys were playing a smart, aggressive Miami Dolphin team. The big Cowboy running backs, bursting through holes in the middle of the Miami defense, marched

50 yards to the Miami nine-yard-line late in the first period. There the advance stalled. Kicker Mike Clark came onto the field and booted a field goal to put the Cowboys ahead 3-0.

In the second period the Cowboys started another drive into Miami territory. On the Miami 47, quarterback Roger Staubach got a message from coach Tom Landry: throw to one of the wide receivers. On the snap, Lance ran up the middle. He saw cornerback Curtis Johnson veer toward the inside. Lance cut toward the outside. Staubach, in the pocket, saw that Lance was a step ahead of Johnson. He threw and Lance took the ball to the Dallas 32 for a 21-yard gain.

Lance trotted quickly to the huddle. He'd seen something, and just as he had always told John Hadl how he thought he could get loose, now he told Roger Staubach. "That cornerback wants to play me to the inside. I think I can beat him going to the outside."

Staubach nodded. That information was relayed to coach Landry. On the next play, when Lance ran out, the Dallas coaches noticed that Johnson, the cornerback, indeed was playing Lance too much to the inside.

The Cowboys marched to the seven. With a minute left in the half, Landry didn't want to settle for another field goal after grinding out so much yardage. He sent in a play: a pass to Lance Alworth.

Lance lined up, eyeing the cornerback. Sure enough, he was edging toward the inside. On the snap, Lance darted straight ahead, faked toward the inside, then cut outside toward the flag at the corner

In the 1972 Super Bowl, Alworth steps into the end zone with the ball. Dallas won 24–3.

of the end zone. Staubach threw a quick lead pass. Running right at the flag, Lance snatched the ball and hugged it to his chest, scoring his first Super Bowl touchdown. The Cowboys led 10-0. They went on to win decisively 24-3.

Continuing to frighten rival teams with his ability to break away and gaining new distinction as a blocker on a crucial play, Alworth remained one of the most exciting performers in football. An old AFL receiver, Charley Hennigan, once said, "A player comes along once in a lifetime who alone is worth the price of admission. That player is Lance Alworth."

6. CHARLIE SANDERS

"ANOTHER IMPOSSIBLE CATCH"

Charlie Sanders glided some ten yards downfield, then cut toward the sideline. He looked over his left shoulder. He saw the ball hanging in the clear October sky. Now it was dropping toward him, seeming to get bigger and bigger.

Charlie reached out for the ball. It hit his fingers and bounced away. Charlie stared at the ball, frowning, as it bobbed along the grass.

A coach was standing on the sideline watching as Charlie, a junior here at the University of Minnesota, trotted over to pick up the dropped pass. The coach turned to someone with him. "I think," the coach

Charlie Sanders catches the ball . . .

said, "we've seen enough of Charlie Sanders to know he is not a pass catcher."

Charlie Sanders, the hulking 6-foot-4 tight end for the Detroit Lions, took his stance. He leaned for-

. . . and comes down hard.

ward, shoulder to shoulder with the Lions' offensive right tackle. A Philadelphia Eagle defensive back, only two steps away, warily eyed Charlie. On the snap Charlie ran straight at the defender, then wheeled in a tight arc toward the sideline. An Eagle defender and Charlie leaped for the high pass. Charlie started to fall backward. He stuck up both hands and snared the ball. He landed on his head, the ball secured in his hands.

"Impossible," said a Lion coach. "Charlie Sanders has made another impossible catch."

In only a few years Charlie Sanders changed from someone who couldn't latch on to the easiest pass to someone who could make impossible catches. What happened inside Charlie Sanders was both physical and mental. The physical problem was easy to fix. After that disaster of a junior year, when Charlie dropped so many passes he was switched from offensive end to defensive end, surgeons repaired torn ligaments in the thumb of one of Charlie's hands. Before the operation Charlie hadn't been able to hang onto passes. After the operation he was able to pull down the ball with one hand.

The mental problem took a longer time to solve. When Charlie came to the Lions from the University of Minnesota, he was making a lot of those one-handed spectacular catches. But he sometimes let the easy-to-catch passes slip through his fingers.

One day, sitting in the living room of his brick two-story house near Detroit, Charlie leaned back in a chair and tried to explain to writer Don Kowet what the mental problem was with those easy-to-catch passes.

"Catching is psychological," Charlie said as he sneaked a glance every now and then at a college football game on TV. "When I have to make a difficult catch—one that I know is going to be difficult—I relax. My mind is relaxed, my body's at ease because I know the people think there's no way I'm gonna get it. And I'm thinking: they *know* I can't get it, so if I don't get it, it's no big deal. I usually come up with those because I am relaxed.

"But when I'm running down the field and I know I'm wide open, the next thing that goes through my mind is: How will I catch it? Will I catch it over my shoulder or will I turn my entire body? And next I'm thinking how far is the guy behind me, how will I score? . . ."

Charlie would be thinking about everything except the football. He wasn't "looking" the ball into his hands, as the receivers say, and the ball would bounce off his fingertips.

With experience, however, Charlie learned to concentrate on the ball and to forget the other distractions. Nearly every season Charlie caught at least 40 passes to lead the Lions in pass-catching—an unusual accomplishment for a tight end, because quarterbacks usually throw more often to their wide receivers.

Times are changing, however. Pro offenses are changing, and one of the biggest changes is the role of the tight end. A decade ago a tight end was a big, solid man who lined up next to the tackle and had to be big enough and strong enough to do much the same kind of work. His primary job was to throw blocks, knocking people down. The classic tight end of this type was Green Bay's 6-foot-3, 240-pound Ron Kramer. In 1960, when the Packers won the Western Conference title, Ron caught only four passes.

The next year Ron caught 35 as the role of the tight end began to change. Teams began to pass over the middle to these big men, who could bowl over tacklers like a fullback. There came a string of these big tight ends who could catch the ball and run with it, notably Mike Ditka and, perhaps the best of them all, Baltimore's John Mackey.

Still, up to 1970 most teams used their tight ends to keep defenses off-balance: throwing short passes to the tight end to suck the defense in toward the line of scrimmage and set up the long pass to the wide receivers. But in 1970 and 1971, more and more NFL teams were employing zone pass defenses, which succeeded in reducing the number of long touchdown passes. With the long-pass routes cut off by the zone, many coaches began to throw short passes in front of the zone—and a lot of these passes were being aimed at tight ends. As a result, 1971 was the first time ever that a tight end—New York's Bob Tucker—won the NFL pass catching championship. The runner-up was San Francisco's Ted Kwalick—also a tight end.

Charlie Sanders wasn't near the top of the list in 1971 because he had been hobbled by leg injuries. But around the league the coaches were saying that Charlie Sanders was the best all-around tight end in the league, the successor to the great John Mackey. For while Charlie could catch the ball with any receiver—he was called Charlie Deep by his teammates because of his ability to go deep for a long pass—Charlie did the other job of a tight end, throwing blocks, as well or better than most offensive linemen.

Sanders lines up for a play.

"Sanders is a better blocker than some tackles," insisted Don Shinnick, the former Colt.

"Sanders is comparable to Ron Kramer as a blocker," said former Bear coach Jim Dooley. "And Kramer was probably the best blocking tight end ever." An assistant at the University of Minnesota, Mike McGee, said, "I consider Charlie the best downfield blocker I ever coached."

A good tight end like Charlie, then, must have many talents. He must be big enough and strong enough to block, fast enough to evade quick defen-

sive backs, and durable enough to absorb punishment from 250-pound linebackers who wallop him
when he catches those short passes.

Charlie learned in one game just how tough a job
he had. The Lions were playing the Falcons early in
the 1971 season. During the first period Charlie axed
a linebacker with a block across the knees. The linebacker flipped backward; one of his cleats struck
Charlie across the knee, sending pain shooting from
head to toe. Charlie limped off the field. But a few
minutes later, when the Lion offense trotted onto the
field, Charlie was back in the game with the rest of
his unit.

Now it was the second period. On the snap a defensive end charged across the line of scrimmage,
aiming for the quarterback. Charlie cut down the
end with a block. Charlie got up slowly. Someone
had kicked him in the hip. He felt the pain, but this
time he didn't allow the pain to show through the
face mask. He stayed in the game. "After all," he
said later in his quiet way, "I'm paid to play when
I'm hurt."

The Lions and Falcons battled into the third period, the score seesawing back and forth, first one
team ahead by a touchdown, then the other. Halfway through the period, Charlie dashed at a linebacker as though to block him. The two collided.
Then Charlie spun off the linebacker's shoulder and
veered into the end zone. Lion quarterback Bill
Munson floated a pass high over Charlie's head.

Charlie sped for the ball and so did a Falcon defensive back. Both went up for the ball. Charlie
grabbed it, held it, and the two of them crashed to

Sprawled on the ground, Sanders clutches the ball.

the ground, first Charlie, then the back. The defender landed on Charlie with body-jarring impact.

The defender got up. Charlie didn't. He lay face-down in the end zone. A trainer ran out. Although he was unconscious, Charlie still gripped the ball that had given the Lions a touchdown. The trainer carefully turned Charlie over onto his back. Charlie's eyes blinked open; he began breathing again after having the wind knocked out of him. He stood up slowly, shaking his head. For the second time he left the field injured.

He came back in the fourth period. The Lions were leading 41-38, hoping to control the ball and run down the clock. Bill Munson called for a sweep to the right.

Charlie lined up next to the tackle. On this play he was to "block down" on the defensive end, John Zook—knock him toward the center of the field. At the snap Charlie bolted forward, aiming at the end. Zook whirled and one of Zook's fingers plunged into Charlie's eye.

"I'm blind," Charlie thought. "I'm blind." He didn't want to open the eye, fearful he would see only blackness.

This time the Lions' team physician, Dr. Richard Thompson, ran onto the field. He examined the eye, then started to lead Charlie off the field. "I don't want to go," Charlie shouted, in a state of shock at this point. "I don't want to go."

The doctor and the Lions convinced Charlie to come out. The shock of the eye injury, which did no permanent damage, soon began to wear off. But Charlie watched the final minutes of the game from the bench. The Lions held on to win 41-38.

In the clubhouse Charlie slumped on a stool, his uniform soaked with sweat. His teeth were clenched, eyes squinting with pain. He tugged at a shoe, trying to pull it off, then gave up. The effort was too much. He looked up at a friend. "That was the worst beating I've ever taken," he said, gasping out the words.

Charlie could hand out beatings as well as absorb them, even though he had to try to outmuscle men much bigger than he. He battled toe to toe with defensive linemen like Alan Page and Jim Marshall, both of whom outweighed Charlie by at least 25 pounds.

"Hey, Charlie," a reporter said to Sanders one day. "How do you prepare yourself to take on those big guys?"

"I don't build myself up to hate them or anything like that," Charlie said. "My way is to know as little as possible about the guys who'll be covering me. I figure the less I know about the guy, the less attached I can get to him, the less I care about him. Of course sometimes I do know a guy. Like we'll be playing the Vikings. I know Carl Eller. I know Alan Page. I know Jim Marshall. They're friends of mine. I know those guys well. But once that game starts, Eller, Page, Marshall, I don't know you!"

A few weeks later the Lions clashed with the Vikings. Early in the game Charlie tried to stop Marshall on a pass rush. Marshall flailed fists and elbows at Charlie—and Charlie flailed right back. The reporter, watching from the press box, said to someone next to him, "That's Charlie slugging his friend Jim Marshall because this is game day and on game day Charlie Sanders doesn't know anybody."

Charlie Sanders walked into the Lions' dressing room on this Tuesday afternoon, a smile on his impish face, his Afro bushing high on his head. One of the Lions said something and a soft smile crept over Charlie's face, but there was a tough, alert look in his eyes.

He sat down to talk with a visitor. Even sitting

down he looked big, with long arms and legs. "You look taller than 6-foot-4," the visitor said.

"That's all I am," he said. Again he smiled. "I was about two inches short of being big enough to be a college forward in basketball, and I was too big to play guard. I had always liked basketball better than football or any other sport, but my high school coach told me I ought to concentrate on football."

He talked about his youth. "I was born in a little town called Richland in North Carolina. When I was eight my father and mother moved to Greensboro. My father is a professor in a college in Greensboro and my mother taught in the public school. I had it a lot easier than the average black guy in the South. I never really had to struggle for material things.

"Anyway, when we moved to Greensboro I met this boy Kenny Henry and we became close friends. He was about four days younger than I was. But I was a country kid and he was from the big city: Greensboro. As far as I was concerned, he knew everything. He took me under his wing. We started out playing Little League baseball. Then Pony League. Then it was basketball. In the tenth grade we started playing organized football. And everything we did, we did together. We always promised we were going to stick together in athletics.

"In our senior year Kenny was the quarterback and I was a flankerback. We got scholarship offers from Wake Forest, the first ever offered a black athlete. Then the University of Minnesota sent someone down to look at us. Kenny hurt his elbow and didn't play. I did, and they offered me a scholarship. I said yes because I wanted to leave the South and Kenny and I broke up. He now works for an airline.

"At Minnesota I started out my sophomore year as a flanker. But I was dropping all those passes. I didn't know I had hurt the thumb when it got stuck under someone's shoulder pads and got pulled. So in my junior year they switched me to defensive end. Then I had the hand operated on and I showed them I could catch the ball. But they said they had plenty of wide receivers. What they didn't have was a tight end. So I became a tight end.

"I wasn't heavy enough at two hundred pounds to play tight end in the Big Ten. I began to drink a lot of malted milks. Seven to eight malteds a day. I went from two hundred to two-thirty-five in two and a half months."

As a tight end in his senior year, Charlie led the team in pass catching with 21 catches for 276 yards and two touchdowns. The Lions picked him as their number-three draft choice. In the summer of 1968, thinking about those big NFL linebackers he'd have to knock down as a Lion tight end, Charlie decided to pack on more weight. He gulped down more malteds and came to camp a blimpy 255 pounds.

Head coach Joe Schmidt frowned when he saw Charlie. "Fella," growled Schmidt, "either you lose that extra weight or you're gone from here."

Hastily Charlie began to shed weight, skipping fatty foods. His weight spiraled down: 235 . . . 225 . . . 215. And it kept on dropping, all the way to 200.

"You're too thin," a coach screamed at him. "You

Sanders reaches for the ball as he crosses the goal line.

gotta put on weight. Those linebackers will take you over their knees and snap you in two."

Charlie went back to an old friend: his malteds. This is his recipe for those who want to gain weight: "Start out with a couple of raw eggs. Then add some honey, a bunch of bananas, some Karo syrup, some malted milk, some dry milk, some regular milk, and a couple of scoops of ice cream. Throw it all in a blender and goosh it up pretty good. Then drink it. I've worked myself up to two quarts a day."

Charlie filled out to 225 pounds. But the extra weight didn't slow him down. He was as elusive as he had been when the players at Minnesota called him Charlie Deep. During the 1971 season the Lions scored more points than any Lion team in history. Charlie helped lead that touchdown parade with five touchdown catches.

The Lions are behind 31-27 midway through the fourth period. The ball is on their opponents' 16. In the huddle Landry calls for a pass to tight end Charlie Sanders in the right corner of the end zone.

On the snap Sanders runs to the center of the end zone, fakes going one way, then cuts toward the right corner. The defensive back tries to cut with Charlie but now he's a step behind Charlie, then two steps behind. Charlie turns and sees the ball coming over his shoulder. He reaches out and snares the ball for the touchdown.

The defender is angry with himself. He tries to make himself feel better by ridiculing the Lions' dependence on that corner-of-the-end-zone pass.

"I *knew* you were going to the corner of the end zone," the back says to Sanders.

Charlie doesn't reply, he just grins. Detroit goes on to win.

"When the Lions get within the 20-yard-line," Charlie says later, "the opposition knows what we are going to do. It's going to be a Greg Landry to Charlie Sanders pass in the corner of the end zone. They know what's coming but they can't stop it because no one is going to stay with me one on one."

7. BOB HAYES

*"HE
NEVER
LET
UP"*

The rookie receiver ran out for the pass, curling toward the sideline. The quarterback stepped back and threw, the ball speeding toward the receiver on a low arc. The rookie reached for the ball, grabbed it in both hands—and dropped it.

The Dallas coach, watching the practice from the sideline, shook his head. "That kid," he said, "has 9.1 speed and 12-flat hands."

That kid was Bob Hayes, Olympic 100-meter champion, who had set a world record of 9.1 seconds in the 100-yard dash. Like dozens of other sprint champions, he was trying to be a football pass catcher. And like many of those sprinters, he could run away from defensive backs, but he couldn't hold on to the ball. Speedy feet, the coaches said, but slow hands.

"He doesn't hold his hands right," said Dallas pass catcher Buddy Dial, who was watching Hayes in this practice session. "He doesn't spread out his thumbs and they get in his way. He bats down the ball instead of catching it." Dial laughed.

A little later Bob lined up for another pass play. "C'mon," roared assistant coach Red Hickey, "show me what you can do. On this next play run so you get inside the middle linebacker."

Hayes nodded. The quarterback, bending over an imaginary center, slapped the ball in his hands, and Bob took off. He cut toward the linebacker, who outweighed him by 40 pounds. Bob tried to shove his way to the middle of the field. The linebacker pushed Bob aside. The pass, thrown down the center of the field, landed 15 yards from where Bob was standing.

"I can outrun that linebacker," Bob thought to himself, "but there is no way I can outshove him to get inside."

He walked slowly to where Red Hickey was standing.

"Coach," Bob said, "I can't get inside of him."

"You have to."

"There's no way."

"Find a way or I'll send you home," Hickey said.

Hayes' eyes widened. He was going to be cut from the Cowboy squad if he didn't improve. Later that day Bob met Mrs. Jake Gaither, the wife of his college football coach. Mrs. Gaither had been a second mother to Bob. "Coach Hickey says he may have to send me home," Bob told Mrs. Gaither.

"Coach Hickey is a good man," Mrs. Gaither snapped. "You're a professional now; you're not running past all those college boys. You're just going to have to work harder."

Bob Hayes went on to become one of the most feared pass catchers in the NFL. "Hayes is our game breaker," coach Tom Landry once said. He meant that Hayes could catch a pass and score from any point on the field, even 95 yards from the goal line. On a typical catch he would streak straight at a defensive back, fake to the left, then the right, and then "turn on the afterburners." With that extra speed, he would shoot past the defender, turn and catch the pass. Then there was no one who could catch him. The "world's fastest human" would outrace the defenders to the goal line. Of every five passes he caught, he carried one all the way for a touchdown.

How did Bob Hayes turn those 12-flat, all-thumbs hands into a pro receiver's hands? Red Hickey explained it this way: "He had to learn football discipline." That may be another way of saying that Bob came to pro football thinking he could be a success with speed alone, but he learned he had to work and work hard.

One day Bob ran out to catch a pass. He leaped high into the air to catch the ball, even though he could have caught it much more easily on the ground. He thought he would impress Hickey.

Bob Hayes seems to have his eyes closed as he pulls down the ball.

Bob trotted back to where Hickey was standing. "Why did you jump for that ball, Hayes?" Hickey asked. Other players stopped to stare and listen. "You could have caught that ball without jumping."

Bob gulped. "Yeah, I know," he said.

"Look," Hickey growled, "I don't care how fast you are. I don't care how many Olympic medals you've won. You're not going to outrun anybody with both your feet in the air."

The other players laughed. Bob walked away, head down. He was learning to forget the frills and concentrate on the basics of pass catching.

Somewhat to Bob's surprise, he got help on the basics from Frank Clarke, who had been the Cowboys' top pass catcher. With Hayes coming to the team, Clarke was being moved to tight end. But he didn't sulk after losing his job to the rookie. Instead he offered to help Bob.

One afternoon after practice Clarke showed Bob how to hold out his hands to catch the ball, spreading the fingers wide, with the thumbs pointing away from the ball rather than toward it. "You don't want to fight the ball," Clarke told Bob. "You just want to let it come." And he showed Bob how to turn to catch a ball over the shoulder, again with the thumbs flared out away from the ball.

Bob was the starting wide receiver for the Cowboys when they opened their 1965 season against the Giants. Early in the game he ran a square-out pattern, turned and caught a short pass from Don Meredith. Bob turned and sped some 37 yards down the sideline before being knocked down when he ran by his wall of blockers. A few minutes later he caught another short pass and this time he passed up all his blockers and all the Giants, racing some 40 yards for a touchdown.

The next week Washington assigned the veteran Johnny Sample to cover Bob. On one play Bob cut to the sideline, then broke inside and caught a quick pass over his shoulder. He ran away from Sample for a 40-yard touchdown play—the first time that anyone had caught a touchdown pass against Sample in more than a year.

"What impressed me," said Sample after the game, "wasn't his speed because I'd expected that. But I didn't expect his moves to be so great."

Rival coaches began to study Bob's moves. "Hayes is no superman," one coach told his players. "I only hope some of you give him a rap in the mouth and we'll see how he does."

One of his players decided to act on the coach's suggestion. During the game he "accidentally" swung an elbow into Bob's face. Bob jabbed an elbow into the player's side. And then he ran deep and caught a pass.

In a game against the Giants, Bob threw a block that flattened defensive back Dick Lynch. "I didn't know you could hit like that," Lynch said, staring up in surprise at Bob's barrel-chested 185-pound frame.

"You're on the ground, baby, right?" Bob said, grinning.

After that game with the Giants, Bob was chatting with some friends. "I've always had to know how to handle myself in a fight," he said. "That's why I think I can take the physical punishment a receiver has to take. I know that some sprinters who try football, they've never experienced being hit. They're contact-shy. If you're afraid to be hit, it's all over for you as a receiver. You start hearing footsteps when you're looking to catch a ball and you're going to miss it. I don't like being belted but I've come to accept it."

Bob had learned to accept being hit as a boy growing up in a tough neighborhood in Jacksonville, Florida, where gangs pummeled each other on street corners. Bob was fast even then, but as he told his friends, "You can't run from trouble. You have to make a stand."

Bob's mother and father broke up when he was seven. Bob stayed with his mother, shining shoes to bring in some money. But he wasn't the hardest-working boy on his block. "My mother used to say I was the slowest dishwasher in northern Florida," he said.

A friend once asked how he became the fastest sprinter in the world. "I wasn't the biggest boy in high school," he said. He was about 5-foot-6 and 120 pounds as a freshman at Matthew Gilbert High School. "But I always could run. I won a lot of nice bets racing in the streets.

"Anyway, one afternoon at school we had an activity period and the teacher had us running down a blacktop road. The track team was working out in a field along the road, and somebody told me which one on the team was the fastest. When he came over I told him, 'I can beat you.' Naturally he didn't put up with that, so we got it on, right there in the road.

And I did beat him. The track coach saw the race and he got all excited. 'You've got 9.6 speed,' he said."

Bob did have 9.6 speed, running the 100-yard dash in 9.6 while still in high school. He was growing, too, filling out, with muscled arms and legs. When he barreled down a track, arms flailing, he didn't seem to be running a race, writer John Underwood said. "He seemed to be trying to beat the track to death."

Hayes breaks the tape in a heat of the 100-meter dash at the 1964 Olympics.

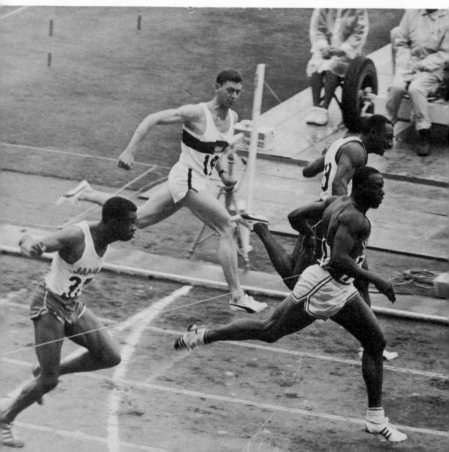

Bob was the fullback on his high school football team, charging through lines and running away from pursuers. Nearly 100 college football coaches offered him scholarships. But Bob didn't want to leave Florida and his mother. He chose Florida A & M.

Coach Jake Gaither used Bob as a running back. He was a good running back, gaining almost five yards every time he ran with the ball. But he became nationally famous as a trackman. In 1961 he tied Jesse Owens's world record by running the 100 in 9.3. Later he set world records for the 60-yard and 70-yard dashes. And in 1963 he ran the 100 in 9.1 to set a world record.

In 1964 he flew to Tokyo to run in the Olympics. He won a gold medal in the 100 meters, winning in 10 seconds flat, also a world record. A few days later he ran the anchor leg of the U.S. 400-meter relay team. When he took the baton his team was sixth. He flew by five of the world's fastest sprinters to finish first and go home with his second gold medal.

Back home, the Cowboys discussed Bob as a football prospect. They knew that when other teams had tried to turn sprinters into pass receivers, they usually failed. But when Bob finally made the Cowboys as a pass catcher, his old college coach, Jake Gaither, wasn't surprised. "Bob was always a football player first and a sprinter second," Gaither said. "He just happened to be fast enough to run 9.1 in his spare time."

In 1965, his rookie season, Bob led the league with an average gain of 21.8 yards a catch. Of his 46 catches, 12 went all the way for touchdowns—also a

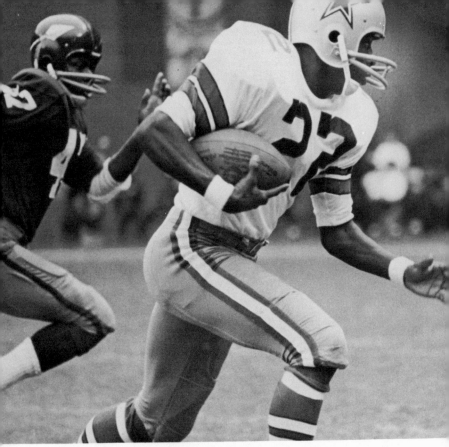

Running with the ball, Hayes outraces the opposition . . .

league high. He led the league the following year
with 13 touchdown catches.

In 1966 and 1967 the Cowboys went all the way
to the National Football League championship game
and both times they lost bitterly fought games to the
Green Bay Packers. In 1968 the Cowboys finished
first in their division but were beaten by Cleveland
for the Eastern Conference title. In 1969 the same
thing happened, the Cowboys finishing first in their
division and then losing to a Brown team they had
beaten during the season. By 1970 the same com-

. . . **and receives blocking help from his teammates.**

plaint was heard over and over: the Cowboys can't
win the big games.

Coach Tom Landry made some changes at the
start of the 1970 season. For one thing, he put Bob
Hayes on the bench. But when the team was playing
poorly, Landry started Bob in a game against Kansas
City. Early in the game Dallas took the ball on its
eleven. Quarterback Craig Morton threw a pass to
Bob, who caught it over the middle and turned on
the speed, scoring an 89-yard touchdown, the longest of the season in the NFL. And the Cowboys won

27-16. After that game Bob once again was one of the Cowboys' starting wide receivers.

On Thanksgiving Day the Cowboys met an old antagonist, the Packers, in a game that Dallas had to win to keep alive their hopes of going to the Super Bowl. It was a typical game for Bob, one in which he touched the ball only a few times. But almost every time he did touch the ball, he changed the character of the game.

He ran back a punt 34 yards to the Packer 32, then caught a pass from Craig Morton that set up a Dallas field goal to tie the game 3-3.

A little later, with the Cowboys deep in their territory, he caught a pass over the middle and zigzagged 38 yards to propel the Cowboys out of dangerous territory.

Then he caught a pass over his shoulder and galloped 55 yards to the 7, from where Dallas kicked another field goal to take a 9-3 lead.

In the fourth period he wheeled around behind the line of scrimmage to take a handoff on the end-around play, dashing into the end zone to score a touchdown. The Cowboys won 16-3.

The Cowboys won the last five games of the season, battled through the playoffs and entered their first Super Bowl—against the Baltimore Colts. Early in the game Bob streaked down the sideline, turned to look for the pass and saw it was going to be short. He stopped and leaped back toward the ball and caught it on the twelve, where he was wrestled to the the ground by a Baltimore defender. But the Cowboys could not push into the end zone for a touchdown, settling for a field goal, and that failure proved to be a grievous one. With only seconds left in the game and the score tied 13-13, the Colts' Jim O'Brien kicked a field goal to defeat the Cowboys 16-13. The Cowboys still seemed to be unable to win the big one.

In 1971 Landry had a new starting quarterback, Roger Staubach, an artful dodger who could throw a ball so hard, said Cowboy back Dan Reeves, "that it could go through a car wash without getting wet." With Staubach throwing to Lance Alworth and Bob Hayes and sending his big backs—Calvin Hill and Duane Thomas—plunging through defenses, the Cowboys made it to the postseason playoffs. They opposed the Purple People Eaters—the Minnesota Vikings—in the first round of the playoffs, and in the week before the game the Cowboys heard the old whispers: Dallas can't win the big ones.

At the half the Cowboys led 6-3. In the third period Duane Thomas ran 13 yards for a touchdown for a 13-3 lead. But a ten-point lead, the Cowboys knew, might not be enough against this big Viking team. The Cowboys marched from their 48 to the Viking 9. Now the Cowboys had to try to score the big touchdown, the one that would clinch this victory.

Back went Staubach to pass. He looked, then ran to his left, slipping past a tackler. Down in the end zone he saw Bob Hayes feint one way, then another. Then he was standing alone, arms high. Staubach threw one of his bullet-like passes. Bob reached out for the pass, caught the ball and held on to it. The Cowboys were ahead 20-3 and on their way to Super Bowl VI. And that was a big game they would win,

Hayes relaxes by the swimming pool in New Orleans before the 1972 Super Bowl.

decisively beating Miami 24-3.

Bob caught only two passes in that Super Bowl game for 23 yards, but he played a role in the final Dallas touchdown. He drew off two Miami defenders, freeing tight end Mike Ditka for a catch in the end zone.

On every play, running or passing, Bob was going "flat out," as the sprinters say. "Don't give up on even a pass you think you'll never get to," he once told a group of youngsters. "Keep on running for it, don't let up, and you just might run under it. I want people always to say, Hayes doesn't let up. That's what I want on my tombstone some day, 'He never let up.'"

8. DON MAYNARD

*"BE
A
LITTLE
DIFFERENT"*

The Jet players lounged on chairs by the side of the motel pool, talking about the thick sirloin steaks they had enjoyed at dinner. Tomorrow, here in Oakland, they would play the Raiders. A breeze rippled the water of the pool and one player said, "It's so pretty somebody ought to dive in."

Don Maynard, who had been dozing, jerked up his head. "Put up some money and I'll do it," he said quickly.

"All right," one player said, laughing. "Let's make up a pot of money by passing around the hat. But, Don, you've got to jump into the pool with all your

119

clothes on. And you've got to jump in off the diving board."

"Well," drawled Don slowly, the twang of Texas in his voice, "I don't know about that. I don't think I'd want to jump in with these cowboy boots on. They're mighty expensive and I could ruin 'em."

"OK," said another player. "You jump in with all your clothes on except the boots."

The players collected $57. "Now *that* makes it worthwhile," Don said, eyeing the money. He slipped off the boots, then stepped onto the diving board, hardly looking like a swimmer in his brown slacks and tan sportshirt. But he bounced high into the air, then leaped gracefully off the board and knifed into the water, the cuffs of the brown slacks disappearing in a splash of white. He surfaced, then swam the length of the pool. He clambered out, water sluicing out of his trousers, his wet socks tracking the floor. He picked up the $57 and stuffed the bills into a watery pocket.

"Hey," he said, "did I ever tell you fellers I was on the diving team in college?" And then Don, laughing, went off to change into a dry suit.

Don Maynard was always doing rather unusual things. When Don got on a bus and dropped a quarter into the coin box, he flipped open a little black book and jotted down, "25¢ for bus ride downtown." When he got up in the morning, he jumped into his cowboy boots. Once a teammate who roomed with Don said, "It's a heck of a sight waking up in the morning and seeing a guy cook eggs in his pajamas and boots."

Way back in 1958 Don came to the training camp

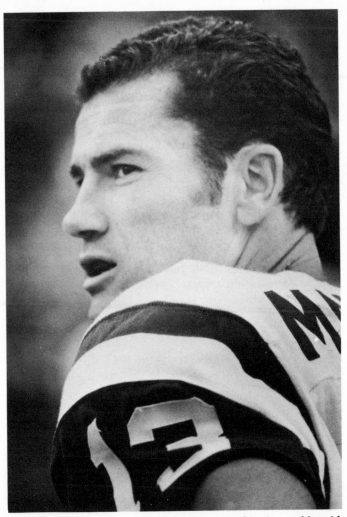

Don Maynard displays the sideburns that got him in trouble with the New York Giants.

of the New York Giants. In those days all the players had their hair cut so short that the tops of their heads looked like toothbrushes. Long before it was in fashion, Don liked long hair, and his sideburns curled halfway down his cheeks.

"Shave those sideburns off," growled Giant head coach Jim Lee Howell.

"Yes, sir," Don said.

The coach saw Don the next day, and his sideburns were still long. "I thought I told you to shave those sideburns off," he snapped at Don.

"Yes, sir, you did."

"Why didn't you do it?"

"I like them."

"You'd better have them trimmed tomorrow."

"Yes, sir."

The next day the sideburns were still long—and they stayed long. The fast-stepping Don had impressed the Giant coaches with his speed and they made him a substitute running back. Two years later the new Giant head coach, Allie Sherman, saw Don running a play in practice in his long-striding way. "Run!" Sherman shouted. "This isn't a track meet."

Maynard yelled back in his independent way, "I can cover more ground than any two backs you have here."

Two days later Don was an ex-Giant. He played in Canada for a year, then joined the New York Titans of the new American Football League in 1961, their first season. The coach was Sammy Baugh, the former quarterback, whose idea of an offense when he was a passer was, "Everybody run downfield and jump around. I'll hit somebody."

Don, who had caught passes in college as a running back, liked that idea when Baugh decided to make him a wide receiver. At a gangly 6-foot-1 and 185 pounds, Don was as hard and lean as whipcord, but he didn't have the size to run through the line as a running back. Soon he was yelling at quarterback Al Dorow in the huddle, "Throw the ball to me."

The Titans didn't win very often. They played in the huge old Polo Grounds before crowds as small as 4,000. And when the team didn't win, the quarterbacks and the coaches often blamed Don. Don ran patterns the way he wanted to run them. "My job is to get loose," he said, "and I'll get loose whatever way I can figure. Then, after I get loose, it's up to the quarterback to find me."

The coaches didn't buy that. "Run the patterns," they told Don.

"They wouldn't let up on me," Don once told writer Maury Allen. "Every bad pass was my fault. Every broken play was my fault."

In the 1965 season Joe Namath joined the team, which had changed its name to the Jets. In one game Joe threw a long pass to Don, but Don turned the wrong way and missed the pass. When Don came to the sideline, head coach Weeb Ewbank and the other coaches were screaming at him.

Don had swallowed all the abuse he could hold. "Trade me or shut up," he shouted. "I don't want you guys on my back all year. I'm not a kid. If you got to chew somebody, chew somebody else. How am I going to concentrate on catching passes when I have to worry about being yelled at all the time?"

The coaches were shocked into silence. They stopped yelling at Don and he began concentrating better, turning to the correct side to catch passes. And, for the first time, Don was working with a quarterback who could throw the long pass, dropping it into a receiver's palms 50 yards away. Joe Na-

Maynard leaves the last tackler in the dust as he goes for a touchdown.

math was Don Maynard's kind of passer. Now Don could do what he liked best: race downfield, slow down a trifle, then suddenly burst ahead of the defender, turn and grab that perfect pass.

In 1966, his first year catching the passes of Broadway Joe, Don caught 68 passes for 1,218 yards. His 14 touchdown catches led the league. In 1967 he led the AFL in total yardage with 1,434 yards and in 1967 and 1968 his average per catch—over 20 yards —led the league. By 1972 Don had caught passes for a total of more than 10,000 yards—more than anyone in the history of pro football. With a career total of some 600 catches, he ranked second behind Raymond Berry as the top pass catcher of all time. Although Don was now 35 years old, he still had a chance to top Berry's 641 catches and become the leading pass catcher of all time.

The free-wheeling Don liked working with an independent spirit like Namath, who also was a nonconformist. "I had trouble with Don my first year," Namath said later. "But I know him now and sense what he can do. He doesn't run a pass pattern with the perfect precision of a George Sauer. Sometimes Don will run a square-out that looks more like a round-out. But he's usually there, just where he is supposed to be. He reads defenses so well that he'll signal me with his hand when he's breaking the pattern. Then I look for him somewhere else."

Most of the time Joe was looking long distance for Don. If you watched Joe and Don during their best years, you remember scenes like this.

Joe is standing in the pocket, hands high clutching the ball, looking . . . looking . . . looking. Around him rages the hand-to-hand battle between his blockers and the pass rushers. Now a big tackle gets loose and closes in on Joe, towering above him.

But Joe lets fly the ball a split-second before he is dashed to the ground. The ball wings downfield 30 . . . 40 . . . 50 yards.

Far downfield, the skinny legs of Maynard are whirling underneath him like the spokes of a wheel, racing slightly ahead of a defensive back. Maynard reaches out his long arms, like a prisoner asking mercy from a judge. The ball angles downward into those big hands and he takes it in and speeds into the end zone. Namath and Maynard have completed another 50-yard pass.

No Namath-to-Maynard long pass was more important than one they completed against the Oakland Raiders in the 1968 AFL championship game. The winner of this game would go on to play the NFL champion in the Super Bowl. The Raiders led

23-20 with only eight minutes remaining in the game.

The Jets had the ball on their 32, a long 68 yards from the goal. Joe decided to try to cover that distance with one thrust. He stepped back into the pocket and looked for Don. Racing along the sideline, with Raider defensive back George Atkinson at his heels, was Maynard. Atkinson turned and saw the pass was going to be short. He tried to brake to a stop but Maynard was already wheeling around and coming back toward the ball.

Namath, watching from more than 50 yards away, saw that the ball was going to be short. Just as Maynard turned, the ball arrived. With hands as quick as a cat's paws, he reached out and snatched the ball. Atkinson saw he was too late to reach for the ball. He knocked Maynard down on the Oakland 6. But Don held on to the ball, and a Jet touchdown seemed sure.

But knowing the toughness of the Oakland line, Namath decided he would have to pass for the TD. These were the toughest passes to complete—the short ones into the end zone. The defenders did not have to fear that a receiver would go deep; he could go only 10 yards into the end zone.

"When you're on that goal line," Maynard said later, "your man is practically shaking hands with you. He's kind of like your shadow and you try to lose the shadow."

On the snap Joe took the ball and ran to his left. He looked for halfback Bill Mathis. Covered. He looked for wide receiver George Sauer. Covered.

Maynard lies in the end zone after scoring the winning touchdown against Oakland in the 1968 AFL championship game.

Then he saw Maynard's back, the green 13 gleaming on the jersey. In desperation Namath threw at Maynard's back, hoping that Don would turn and look back in time.

At that moment Maynard wheeled and saw the ball streaking toward him. He dived, his hands brushing the grass tops. The ball thudded into Don's calloused palms. Up went the referee's hands. Touchdown. The Jets had won 27-23 and were on their way to the Super Bowl.

In the clubhouse, hands wrapped around a bottle of champagne, Broadway Joe grinned at Don and said, "Are you going to be ready for Baltimore?"

"Joe," Don said, "I'm always ready."

Joe turned to newsman Milton Gross. "Don must have 92 bruises all over him right now," Namath said. "But he's a skinny fellah. He gets hurt and it goes away fast."

Not always, not this time. Don was still limping, both knees aching, as the Jets trotted onto the field for the start of Super Bowl III in Miami's Orange Bowl. In this game Don Maynard would show how he could help his team without catching a single pass. Early in the game Namath wound up and threw one of those long passes to Don down the right sideline.

Don reached for the ball, fingers straining, but the ball dropped a foot in front of his fingertips. The crowd sank back into the seats, still *aaaaahing* over how close the Jets had come to a quick touchdown. The Colt defensive backs stared at one another. They had been told that the injured Maynard could run at only three-quarter speed. Yet he had outrun a defender on that play. The Colts began to rotate a second defender toward Maynard's side whenever he lined up in a passing situation. Joe, meanwhile, began to throw to George Sauer on the other side. Sauer caught eight passes for 133 yards, several of them on important third-down plays. "I believe that one pass put some fear into them and they began to watch Don too closely," Jet assistant coach Clive Rush said later. "While they were looking at Maynard, Joe was passing to Sauer."

The Jets won 16-7 and Don Maynard, the tall guy from Texas who liked cowboy boots and long sideburns, was a member of the world champions. He had come a long way from Crosbyton, Texas, a little cotton-growing town of some 10,000 near Lubbock. The son of a cotton dealer, Don moved with his family from one Texas town to another during his early years. He attended eight different grade schools and five high schools. "Just when I got to know some kids," he said, "my family would move and I had to go."

He was on the football and track teams at Colorado City (Texas) High School when one of his football teammates, Charles Smith, broke a leg. Charles had worn the number 13 on his jersey.

When other members of the team refused to wear "unlucky 13," Don agreed to take it. Someone asked him why and he said, "Because it's a challenge." From then on Don always walked onto a football field with the number 13 on his back. He may also have felt that people would notice the man wearing

number 13. "Wear cowboy boots," he once told a
friend. "Do something different to get yourself noticed. You've got to be a little different."

"But I'm no cowboy," his friend replied.

"I'm no cowboy, either," Don said, "but I wear
cowboy boots."

Don attended Rice University for a short time and
then went to Texas Western. One day he saw a
pretty cheerleader, Marilyn Weaver, fondling a
stuffed monkey. "Why don't you name that monkey
Shine?" Don asked the cheerleader.

"Why should I name him Shine?" Marilyn said.

"That's my nickname, Sunshine," Don said. "But
everybody calls me Shine."

Marilyn later became Don's wife.

In his early years in the pros, Don often found it
difficult supporting himself, Marilyn and their two
children. He learned to count his pennies. He got
into the habit of noting how he spent each dime by
marking the sum in a notebook. One year he left
Marilyn at home in El Paso, Texas, while he roomed
in an apartment house near New York's Shea Stadium with two other Jets.

"Once we sent Don to the grocery store," one of
the roommates recalled. "We thought he would
bring back some steaks. He brought back a couple of
cans of beans."

Jet coach Weeb Ewbank was always amused by
Don's carefulness with a dollar. Don worked for a
company that made Swipe, a cleaning fluid. "The
stuff cost $3.02 a bottle," Weeb says. "Someone
once asked me how many free bottles of the stuff

Maynard gave me. I said none. The price is $3.02—not $3 even but $3.02—and you better believe that Don collects the two cents."

The Jets had a nickname for Don—Country—because of his cowboy boots and drawling manner, but he was no country bumpkin in the big city. He liked New York's boldness and he could match it with a boldness of his own. "I was kind of shy with my southern accent and all," said Bill Mathis, who was from Georgia. "But not Don. He would hitch up his pants, pull on his boots, polish his buckle, and march downtown."

As the years went by and his pay went up—to more than $50,000 a year—Don kept busy even when he was away from football. In the off-season he taught mathematics in an El Paso high school. He owned a cleaning business, a golf cart business and a credit card business, and he sold the cleaning fluid. And he was also a licensed plumber.

"Down home," he once told writer Milton Gross, "you need five years and hundreds of hours of plumbing to become licensed and I worked in the off-season whenever I could to get that license."

With his football and non-football earnings Don bought "a little old spread" high in the mountains of New Mexico some 80 miles from El Paso. "It's a nice spread for me, Marilyn and the kids," he said. "Five acres, right in the middle of the pines. The other day I was up there and I saw seven wild turkeys, first time I've ever seen one. I was riding around and I counted 52 deer. They've got sheep up there and probably wild hogs and two lakes full of trout."

Don liked that clean mountain air after the season

Posing with his famous quarterback, Joe Namath, Maynard lowers his eyes.

ended and he had escaped the smoggy fumes of New York. But those fumes never slowed him down when he dashed along the Shea Stadium sideline after a long Joe Namath pass.

"He's one of the fastest receivers I've ever seen," Jet assistant coach Walt Michaels once said. "And he's got good hands. But the biggest thing is his change of pace. When many guys come down the field, they're going all out. But while they're going all out, Maynard is going at three-quarter speed. When you think he's going all out, he turns it on. Fast, slow, fast, slow. Then he makes his moves."

"He's deceptive," said head coach Weeb Ewbank. "He has a gait that makes him look like he's coasting and then he turns it on, goes into overdrive and leaves you there. He just explodes."

Several years earlier when Don dropped two touchdown passes in the end zone, Weeb said bitingly, "The quarterback wasn't very good. He hit Maynard in a bad place. Right in his hands."

Maynard shrugged. "Coaches never bawl out the quarterback," he said, "only the receivers." The next week Maynard went back to catching touchdown passes. "That's what being a pro pass receiver means," he said, "knowing how to come back after a miss."

9. DANNY ABRAMOWICZ

*"MILLION-
DOLLAR
HANDS
AND
TEN-CENT
FEET"*

Danny Abramowicz sat by the telephone, staring glumly out the window. A cold, steady rain was falling on the green campus of Xavier University in Cincinnati, making him feel even gloomier. "The phone has got to ring," he thought to himself. "That Dallas Cowboy scout said they were interested in me."

Danny knew he wasn't the fastest college pass receiver. He had set a lot of pass-catching records here at Xavier, but Xavier was a small school—hardly a football powerhouse. He knew he wasn't the biggest pass receiver at 6-foot-1 and 185 pounds and he knew he didn't have all the moves of a Raymond

135

Berry. But he *knew* he could catch passes in pro football just as he had caught them at Xavier— passes over his head, at his shoetops, to his left or to his right, diving, leaping and maybe somersaulting for passes. Danny had "the soft hands," and he could catch almost any ball he could put a finger on.

Danny looked at his watch. He switched on the radio to hear the news.

"And now for the sports news," the announcer was saying. "In New York the NFL is conducting its annual draft of college players and. . . ."

The announcer named some of the college players who had been drafted in the first round. They were the names of famous All-American stars. He went on to say that the teams were now in the 17th and final round—they were choosing from the bottom of the barrel. He pointed out that the NFL and AFL teams had already picked more than 400 players and that few players who are below number 300 ever become successful in pro ball.

Danny switched off the radio. He looked at his wife Claudia, who had come into the room from the kitchen. "I can't believe no one wants me, Claudia," he said. "The Dallas scout had said they were interested."

"Get some sleep," Claudia said. "If the phone rings I'll call you."

Danny could not fall asleep for a long while. If he wasn't picked, he would have to forget what he'd dreamed of being since he was a boy back in Steubenville, Ohio. He hadn't been the biggest or the fastest pass catcher at Steubenville High School either. The school sent dozens of football players to

Big Ten schools, but none of the Big Ten schools even invited Danny to their campuses.

When coach Ed Biles of Xavier showed up in Steubenville and offered Danny a scholarship, Danny said, "I'm sure happy to see you show up." Xavier wasn't the most famous football school, but Danny saw himself as a pro football pass receiver, and even playing for Xavier put him a little closer to that goal.

He broke many receiving records at Xavier, but few thought of him as a pro prospect. "He is never flashy," said coach Biles. "But he plays with a recklessness that makes you worry about his safety. And he works hard. He is the kind who enjoys staying after practice to work with the quarterback, running patterns and catching the football. He has had to work to develop the only God-given talent he has as a receiver—a sure pair of hands. Danny has always been so terrified at the prospect of not playing well that he always gives you 500 percent."

The coach used Danny as an end on defense as well as a receiver on offense. Danny weighed only 175 at the time, but he could spill 220-pound fullbacks with his low, jarring tackles. Still, his first love and biggest talent was pass catching.

In one game he hurt his back. Doctors decided he could play for only a few plays in the next game. Danny was so frustrated when he heard their decision that he smashed his fist into a Coke machine, bruising his knuckles. Coach Biles sent Danny into the game only on third-down-and-long-yardage situations. The opposition knew Xavier was going to pass and they knew Xavier was going to pass to

A jarring tackle knocks the ball from the hands of Danny Abramowicz.

Abramowicz. The Xavier quarterback did throw to Danny eight times and Danny caught all eight passes for first downs. Xavier won.

Only one pro scout, from Dallas, came to watch Danny play at Xavier. He told Danny the Cowboys were interested in him. Now, trying to sleep, Danny remembered that conversation and wondered why he hadn't gotten a phone call telling him that the Cowboys had drafted him.

Early the next morning the phone rang. He ran to the phone, picked it up and gasped, "Hello?"

"Hi, Danny!" a voice yelled. It was Danny's father, calling from Steubenville. "Just heard it on the radio this morning," his dad shouted. "We were listening down at the firehouse. You were picked on the 17th round by the New Orleans Saints."

Danny breathed a sigh of relief. *Someone* had picked him; that was the big thing. And he didn't mind being picked from the bottom of the barrel. He was the 420th college player to be picked of a total of 445. You couldn't get much closer to the bottom than that. But he had a chance to make the pros and that was what he had always wanted. "I have to make it," Danny told his father that morning. "I just have to."

He and his father talked about the Saints. It was a brand new team that would play its first game in this upcoming 1967 season. It had drafted a lot of tested veterans from other NFL clubs, as well as rookies like Danny. There would be a lot of good players trying hard to win jobs on the new team.

Danny's big problem was speed. "Maybe we can make you a little faster, Danny," coach Biles suggested. "Try this. Put a towel at the foot of your bed. Every day, work at picking it up with your toes. That might strengthen the tendons and give you a quicker takeoff."

For weeks Danny picked up towels with his toes. One afternoon he went out to a track with a friend.

"I'm going to see if I can do better than 5.1 for the 40-yard dash," he told a friend. "Even the pro linemen can run the 40 in 5.1."

Danny sprinted the 40 yards with his friend clocking him. His time was 4.9. Still not fast for an NFL receiver, but he was improving.

A few days later Danny sat down with his cousin, Tom Franckhauser, who had been a defensive tackle with the Rams and the Vikings. "You'll have to fight to catch the coach's eye," Tom told Danny. "Run and never stop running. When they say, 'Hit the blocking sleds,' you be the first one on line. Always do something in a way that will stand out."

A few days later Danny was flying from Steubenville to San Diego, where the Saints had their training camp. On the plane Danny met another rookie on his way to camp. He was halfback Charlie Brown, a number ten choice from Missouri. As casually as he could, Danny asked the halfback how fast he ran the 40. "Four-six or four-seven," Brown said. Danny knew he couldn't run four-six with a hurricane at his back. Yet a wide receiver was supposed to be *faster* than a halfback.

At camp Danny wrote on a form that he was 6-foot-1 and 195. Then a doctor weighed and measured him, smiled and wrote down 6-foot-1 and 185. Danny dreaded the morning the coaches would test his speed. That happened on the second morning at camp. Assistant coach Ed Khayat stood at the finish line for the 40-yard sprint, a clock in hand.

As Danny got set at the start, a voice within him kept saying, "I've got to run this in 4.9, I've got to, I've got to!"

Abramowicz (left) chats with another great receiver, Dave Parks.

He leaped off the starting line and sprinted down the track. As he crossed the finish line he knew he'd run that 40 in 4.9.

He turned to look at Khayat. "You're gonna have to run that over," Khayat said, scowling. "My watch got stuck."

Breaking into a nervous sweat, Danny walked slowly back to the starting line. He ground his teeth, determined to run that 40 just as fast a second time. But he couldn't. As he finished he heard Khayat yell, "Five-one."

"Are you sure?" asked Bob Shaw, the coach of the receivers.

"That's what I got, five-one on the button," Khayat said, looking with surprise at Danny. Ashamed, Danny wanted to crawl off somewhere and hide. It seemed that others must be laughing at him. "Runs like he had a piano on his back," they seemed to be saying.

There were 100 rookies and some 40 veterans in camp. The coaches had to start cutting the squad to 40 or 45. Each day a half-dozen players were called into coach Tom Fears' office and told to pack their clothes to go home. Each night Danny slept fitfully in his room, worrying that he would hear a knock on the door. Late in the evening "the Turk" made his rounds. The Turk was an assistant coach who brought players to Tom Fears' room, where the coach told them they were being cut.

One day, with the squad down to 70 men, Danny asked veteran linebacker Steve Stonebreaker what happened when players were cut. "They hand you a plane ticket and you get out," Stonebreaker said.

"But what happens if you refuse to go?" Danny asked.

Stonebreaker stared at the rookie. "I never heard of anyone getting cut and refusing to go."

"Well, you're looking at the first guy, Stoney, because I'm not leaving. I'm going to stay here and follow the team around if they cut me."

Stonebreaker laughed. Then he noticed Danny's grim face and suddenly realized he was serious. "Somehow," Stonebreaker said, "I don't think you're going to be cut."

And Danny wasn't, even after the Saints broke camp and started their preseason games. But with eleven pass receivers on the squad, Danny didn't get many chances to catch the ball. Instead, coach Fears put Danny on the "suicide squad."

The members of the suicide squad dash downfield on kickoffs and punts. When the Saints kicked off, they tried to nail the other team's kickoff-return man inside the 20-yard-line. And when the other team kicked off to the Saints, they blocked for the New Orleans kickoff-return man, trying to spring him loose for a long gain. The suicide squad gets its name because it carries out the most dangerous assignments in football. If a pursuer meets a blocker head-on, their collision speed may be 30 miles an hour. A suicide squad man must be fearless.

In the Saints' first game of the season St. Louis kicked off to the Saints' Jon Gilliam. Gilliam raced up the right sideline with Danny running in front of him. Danny hit a man, knocking him aside. Gilliam burst through the hole and ran 94 yards for a touchdown. In another game Danny mowed down an enemy kickoff-return man on his six-yard-line. "Hey," said Tom Fears after the game, "that kid Abramowicz is a real headhunter on those kickoffs. We sure could use a few more like him."

Once in a while Danny also filled in as a wide receiver. One day early in the season the Saint coaches were looking at statistics. "Hey," one said, "you know that we've thrown eleven passes to that kid Abramowicz so far, and he's caught all eleven."

"He has only one strong talent as a receiver," Tom Fears said, "and that is his hands. But he's been making some unbelievable catches with those hands. And he is great on that short pass to the sideline. He knows just where to look for the ball."

Midway through the season a Saint tight end was hurt. Wide receiver Ray Poage took over at tight end and Danny started at wide receiver in Poage's spot. In his first game, against the Steelers, Danny caught twelve passes for a total of 156 yards. The next week he caught two against the Eagles and then seven against Dallas, one for a touchdown.

Little by little, he was picking up little tricks to get him free from quicker defensive backs. He learned to make his move when a defender crossed his feet and couldn't move one way or the other for a second. And he spent hours with Saint quarterback Gary Cuozzo looking at films of Raymond Berry. Cuozzo had thrown to Berry when both were with the Colts. "See that?" Cuozzo said one night. "See how Raymond makes his defender turn? When the defender turns, he takes his eyes off you for a moment and that's when you can make a cut and get away from him."

With those tricks, those soft hands, and that determination to excel, Danny soon ranked as the Saints' number one pass catcher. In his rookie season he caught 50 passes, ranking 13th in the league, and he caught six passes for touchdowns. He ran one into the end zone on an 80-yard touchdown play. "Abramowicz ran so slow on that long touchdown play," said Norm Van Brocklin, then a TV commentator, "that the officials almost called him on a delay-of-the-game penalty."

Danny only grinned when he heard about Van Brocklin's wisecrack. "I'm no speed demon," he said. "But I have found I don't need straightaway

This diagram shows some of Danny's favorite pass patterns.

speed. You do a lot of zigzagging out there. I think I can get away from most people one on one if I don't have to run in a straight line."

Zigzagging and diving for passes, Danny ranked among the league's top pass catchers during the next three seasons, ranking first in 1969, third in 1970, and 14th in 1971. In New Orleans they still talk about two of his acrobatic catches. In one game he dived through the air and snared a sinking pass only a foot off the grass. In another game he leaped between two taller defenders and snatched a high throw in the corner of the end zone.

"He knows exactly where that line is behind the end zone," said one of his coaches. "He knows just how deep he can go. At least twice officials have nullified touchdown passes he has caught deep in the end zone. They said he stepped over the line. But then we looked at the films and they showed Danny catching them in-bounds."

Danny wrote a book, *Pass Catching,* showing youngsters how to catch passes. A diagram, which he called his "tree," shows the patterns he ran from his wide receiver spot. Two of his favorites were the slant and the five-yard square out.

On the slant, wrote Danny, "I must come off the line real hard so the defensive man thinks I'm going to go deep. When I've gone about four yards out, I push off on my right foot. Then I start driving toward the middle. . . . There is no faking on this pattern. The quarterback releases the ball quickly as I maneuver between the linebackers."

On the five-yard square out, Danny angled toward the sideline. "As I make my fourth step," he said, "my left foot has hit the ground and my move has begun. This will give me the necessary sharp right-angle pivot. The head and arm movement is especially important because it brings the body around to the proper position to make the catch. As my right foot hits the ground, my arms and head swing around to pick up the flight of the ball, which is usually released the moment I start making my turn. . . ."

Late in 1969, Danny caught a couple of his most important passes. He, the Redskins' Charley Taylor and Roy Jefferson of the Steelers were tied with 65

On his way to leading the league in 1969, Abramowicz catches a pass against the Steelers.

catches apiece on the final Sunday of the season. The Saints were playing the Steelers, so Danny would be competing directly with Roy Jefferson. Yet he told Saints quarterback Billy Kilmer, "Don't throw to me unless you're sure of it. I don't want catches just to boost my total."

Early in the game he ran out on a slant. Kilmer saw him open and threw. Completion number one. Taylor would catch six passes that afternoon, and Roy Jefferson only two. So Danny would need seven to win the title. He caught another pass on a slant pattern and another on a square out. He caught a fourth pass.

Now it was the fourth period, the Saints ahead 27-24. Danny ran out on a short zigzag pattern, turned and caught the ball. He'd caught five. More important, he had caught a pass for a first down. The Saints still had the ball in this close game.

Again the Saints had to throw. Danny wheeled and ran toward the sideline. Kilmer zipped him a pass. He'd caught six. He didn't know it then, of course, but he had tied Taylor for the league pass-catching championship.

The Saints called another pass play. Danny was cutting over the middle. Kilmer threadneedled the ball into Danny's hands, those sticky fingers wrapping around the ball, and Danny was the league pass-catching champion. The game ended a little later, the Saints 27-24 victors.

"Yeah, I've got good hands," Danny said in the clubhouse. "Most pass catchers like to lock the ball in on their chest when they catch it, but I've got good enough hands to catch a ball like you'd catch a baseball."

A Saint overheard. "That's right," he said, grinning, "Danny's got million-dollar hands and five-and-ten-cent feet."

INDEX

Page numbers in italics refer to photographs.

Ancient Peoples and Places

THE CRUSADERS

General Editor

DR GLYN DANIEL

ABOUT THE AUTHOR

On completing his schooling at Christ's Hospital, R. C. Smail entered Sidney Sussex College, Cambridge, in due course becoming a Fellow and Director of Studies in History there. In addition to being a University Lecturer in History at Cambridge, Dr Smail is a Fellow of the Society of Antiquaries. His main historical interests have been in the crusading movement, and in 1956 he published a book titled Crusading Warfare 1097–1193, *since 1972 available in a paperback edition. He has also contributed articles to a variety of learned journals.*

THE
CRUSADERS
IN SYRIA AND THE HOLY LAND

R. C. Smail

70 PHOTOGRAPHS
33 LINE DRAWINGS
3 MAPS
2 TABLES

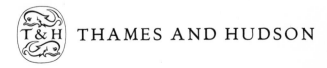

THAMES AND HUDSON

THIS IS VOLUME EIGHTY-TWO IN THE SERIES

Ancient Peoples and Places

GENERAL EDITOR: DR GLYN DANIEL

CONTENTS

List of Illustrations

Preface

Nearly all historical writing involves its author in problems of selection, and these are particularly severe when he is dealing with a subject such as the crusaders and the space available is limited. This book has been written to fit into the series of which it is part. It is therefore short, though I am grateful to the editor and publishers for allowing me to exceed the length originally stipulated, as I am for their unexampled patience in waiting for the manuscript. Like other volumes in the series it is chiefly concerned with visible remains, in this instance of the crusader settlement, which are discussed against a background of the society which produced them, and of some main changes to which that society was subject through time. These are immense subjects on which there is a very large body of literature, and at every stage of writing this book rigorous selection has therefore been necessary. As its title makes clear, it does not deal with the crusaders who settled in Cyprus and Greece. Where the monuments are concerned, coverage has had to be restricted to the castles, to churches and their decoration and to miniature painting.

While it is hoped that the book will be of value to students, and specialists in related fields will find it of interest, its main purpose is to introduce the general reader to its subject-matter, and perhaps to draw that reader to a deeper interest and to a knowledge of some of the books and articles set out in the bibliography. These again are a small selection from many hundreds of relevant publications, but they are the work of scholars on which this book is mainly based and to whom I am most deeply indebted. My particular thanks are due to Mr C. N. Johns, formerly of the Palestine Department of Antiquities, under whose guidance I first studied crusader monuments on the ground; to Professor Joshua Prawer and two of his young colleagues at the Hebrew University of Jerusalem, Dr Benjamin Kedar and Dr Amnon Linder, for their unfailing kindness and help during my visits to Israel; to Dr Jonathan Riley-Smith, whose reading of the book in manuscript led to the removal of many errors. I take sole responsibility for those that remain.

R.C.S.

The Historical Background

Of all the crusades to the Holy Land, from that preached by Pope Urban II in 1095, to that which the Lord Edward, heir to the English throne, led to Acre in 1271, the most successful was the first. It achieved a brilliant and astonishing climax by its conquest of Jerusalem in mid-July, 1099. Some of the leaders had already made conquests further north, before the crusade had reached the Holy City, and they had come no further; there were always to be many crusaders for whom material acquisitions were the main consideration. But for the great majority of those who took part, and especially the rank and file, the only goal which mattered during their three-year journey eastwards was the Holy City. They regarded themselves not as immigrants or colonists, but as pilgrims; and once they had stormed the walls of Jerusalem and massacred the population, and walked in procession through the bloodstained, corpse-strewn streets to make their devotions at the Holy Sepulchre, they regarded their pilgrimage as accomplished and nearly all of them returned to the West. (So much for the fashionable theory that the crusades were a kind of mass emigration imposed by the pressure of a European population which had grown too great for its resources.) Only a handful remained as settlers. The control they proceeded to establish over parts of the eastern seaboard of the Mediterranean was to last for nearly two hundred years.

In the years 1098 and 1099 the crusaders made three major conquests: Edessa beyond the Euphrates, Antioch on the Orontes, and Jerusalem. Within ten years Provençal crusaders who had remained in the country had forced the surrender of Tripoli. These were the centres from which the original settlement was expanded. Jerusalem became the capital of a newly-founded kingdom, Antioch of a principality, Edessa and Tripoli of counties. These were the four Latin states in Syria. There were to be many links between them, though each was to be always legally independent of the others. Edessa remained in European hands until 1144, Antioch until 1268, Tripoli until 1289. Jerusalem was lost to Saladin in 1187, but its kingdom remained, mainly in the coastal plain until Acre, its thirteenth-

Fig. 1

century capital, was lost in 1291. In that year the crusader states in Syria and the Holy Land were finally extinguished.

The lands over which the Franks established their control extend some four hundred miles from the Gulf of Alexandretta in the north to the edge of the Nile Delta in the south. From west to east, from sea to desert, the habitable area is nowhere much more than seventy miles wide. Physically the area is divided into four zones, each of which is continuous

Fig. 1   The Middle East in the twelfth century

through the whole length of the country from north to south. First, the coastal plain, narrow and sometimes interrupted by mountain spurs in the north, continuous and ever broadening south of Mount Carmel. Second, the foothills and mountain ranges which overlook the coastal plain. In the north, the Amanus range and the Jabal Ansariyah, much of it nine to twelve hundred metres above sea level, with peaks above fifteen hundred. Further south, the true mountain wall of the Lebanon,

Fig. 2

11

with summits three thousand metres high. In the Holy Land itself, the mountains and hills of upper and lower Galilee, the hills of Samaria and Judea.

To the east of these ranges is the third natural feature, a rift valley extending from Turkey to the Red Sea, which carries the main rivers of the country: the Orontes which flows north and the Litani, south, before they turn through the mountain range towards the Mediterranean; and the Jordan, flowing south through Lakes Huleh and Tiberias before it empties itself into the Dead Sea. In Galilee this rift valley is some two hundred metres below sea level, and in the Dead Sea, 'the lowest point on earth', over three hundred and seventy. Beyond the Orontes and the Jordan there is open, habitable plateau country, and beyond the Litani, the anti-Lebanon range, with the snow-covered peak of Hermon rising to eight thousand feet. East of this fourth and most easterly natural region lies the desert. A large oasis on the western edge of that desert is the site of one of the great cities in human history, Damascus, the natural capital of all Syria.

The physical conformation of the country offered certain advantages to the Frankish settlers. Based as their settlement was on the sea-shore and the coastal plain, they had every facility for maintaining the all-important communications with the West. It will be seen that the Syrian Franks were always aware of their isolation and of their dependence on Europeans in the western homelands. Italian mastery at sea and the many Syrian ports at their disposal kept Europe and Latin Syria closely linked. There was a further advantage. If the Franks, based on the coast, could extend their control over the comparatively short distance eastwards to the edge of the desert, then the possibility of joint action between the Moslems of Iraq, Egypt and Asia Minor could be made more difficult, and the crusader occupation correspondingly more secure. For a time they achieved this in the south, and the desert route from Damascus to Egypt was under their control. But further north there was always a Moslem as well as a Latin Syria. Neither Damascus nor Aleppo ever fell to the Franks, nor the main towns on the middle Orontes.

These lands have rarely, if ever, been the home of one people, one religion, one government. They have been a cross-roads and a meeting place where ideas from East and West have fertilized each other. It is no accident that they have been the birthplace of alphabetic writing and monotheistic religion. The earliest crusaders found a mixture of peoples, languages and religions. Then, as now, they could hear spoken Arabic, Turkish, Armenian, Syriac and Hebrew. Of the world's great religions, not only had Christians and Moslems been living there side by side for centuries (together with small Jewish communities) but within themselves they were deeply divided. Among the Moslems there were, besides the orthodox Sunni, many sects of the Shi'a, including that most extreme group of the Isma'ili, the Assassins. Amongst the Christians there were, and are, Greek Orthodox, Armenians, Jacobites, Maronites, Nestorians and Copts, each of them a distinct Church, with its own hierarchy, liturgy and canon law. It was a situation that assisted the Franks in two ways. The ethnic and religious division, especially when joined with political division, weakened resistance to the crusaders. And the eastern Christians, so far from opposing fellow Christians from the West, were in some instances ready to support them.

The region has been the meeting place not only of cultures but of governments. Marked by so many kinds of diversity, it has generally lacked political unity and political independence. During much of its history it has been a province in a great empire, the Roman, the Byzantine, those of the Caliphs and the Ottoman Turks; or it has been a battle-ground over which imperial governments have fought, and especially empires based on the Nile on the one hand and on the Tigris-Euphrates on the other. No one knew this better than the Israelites of old, crushed as they often were between the upper and nether mill-stones of Assyria and Egypt.

In the tenth century AD this ancient historical situation was renewed when the 'Abbasid caliphs of Baghdad were challenged by the establishment of an heretical Shi'a Caliphate in Egypt. Even while the forces of the First Crusade were besieging Antioch in 1098, the Egyptians captured Jerusalem, reasserted their hold on Palestine and so far misunderstood the character of the crusade as to propose a partition with the Franks. There were other divisions besides that between Baghdad and Cairo. During the tenth century authority in the lands of the 'Abbasid Caliphate had become fragmented and the effective power of the caliphs shrank to within Baghdad and its immediate neighbourhood. This decline was arrested by the advance of the Seljuk Turks, to whose leader the caliph, in 1055, gave the title of sultan and in whose hands he placed the direction of temporal affairs. For forty years the lands of the caliphate were largely reunited, and even extended; the defeat of a Byzantine army at Manzikert in 1071 enabled the Turks to overrun the Byzantine provinces in Asia Minor. But when Malik-Shah, third and greatest of the Seljuk sultans died in 1092, there was a disputed succession, and the unity achieved since 1055 was lost. No province was more fragmented than Syria. At the time of the First Crusade, a nephew of Malik-Shah ruled in Damascus, another in Aleppo. Other Syrian cities and the district immediately surrounding them were each subject to a different magnate who, for the time being, was subject to no superior power. In 1098 the Egyptians held Palestine, but not so firmly that they could prevent the first crusaders from taking Jerusalem.

It will be seen in the rest of this chapter how the situation of the crusader states was always to be closely affected by the unity or disunity of their Moslem neighbours. The initial disunity, which was unchecked until about 1130, made possible the success of the First Crusade and the extension of the Frankish conquests. Zengi and Nur-ad-Din reunited Moslem Syria and then joined it with Egypt. By succeeding to this inheritance Saladin almost destroyed the crusader kingdom of Jerusalem. After his death in 1193 his empire was divided among members of his family, and during the first half of the thirteenth century the Syrian Franks were helped by the resulting disunity. It removed the acute pressure once exerted by Saladin. But after 1250 such pressure was restored. In that year the sultan of Egypt, a descendant of Saladin, was overthrown by a revolt of those regular regiments of Turkish slaves known as the Mamluks. The rulers they set up consolidated their power, won Damascus in 1260 and thereafter became masters of Moslem Syria. It was they who set on foot the final assault on the crusader states, so that by 1291 the Franks were finally expelled from Syria and the Holy Land.

It must not be thought, however, that the existence of Latin Syria was wholly determined by the political state of its Moslem neighbours; there were times when it could count on powerful assistance from fellow Christians. During the first three-quarters of the twelfth century the Byzantine emperors were able to reconquer from the Turks much of southern Asia Minor, and once again to play a major part in Near Eastern politics. The fear of provoking the intervention of Byzantium caused some Moslem rulers, for a time, to reduce their activities against

Latin Syria. After 1175 the Byzantine protectorate ceased to exist, but the possibility of aid from western Europe, in the form of a new crusade, always existed during the twelfth and thirteenth centuries and was from time to time fulfilled. Considered in their Levantine setting, the Latin states were small and weak organizations which clung precariously to a narrow fringe of the Asian mainland. But they were also part and outpost of the western world, and in that world they held a unique position. Every year, almost without exception, thousands of pilgrims from Europe were drawn to the lands of the Bible, especially to the Holy Places. When they returned home, as nearly all of them did, they carried news of Latin Syria with them. Histories written in western Europe during the twelfth and thirteenth centuries show how widely that news was disseminated. No part of Christendom was better known or attracted more general interest, and there was not only knowledge but concern. The establishment of a new Christian kingdom in 1100, with Jerusalem as its capital, was regarded as an achievement of all western Christians. All of them, without exception, were held to bear a continuing responsibility for its maintenance and defence and, after 1187, for its recovery. Sir Maurice Powicke has written that 'the recovery of the Holy Land, whether as an ideal, a symbol, or an immediate duty, pervaded the minds of men in the thirteenth century. It was inseparable from the air they breathed. However indifferent or sceptical they might be, they could not escape its influence. "If I forget thee, O Jerusalem, may my right hand forget her cunning." It was a constant preoccupation of the papal curia.'

Such preoccupation meant that secular rulers were never allowed to forget their duty towards the Holy Land. Although many of them never went on crusade, pressure on them to do so was constantly renewed, and sometimes was so strong that monarchs as unwilling to leave their realms as Philip Augustus and the Emperor Frederick II could not resist it. Not only magnates but ordinary folk in their tens of thousands were moved to take the cross. Historians are sometimes too ready to state or imply that they did so not from religious but from secular motives and the prospect of material gain. There were those who reaped handsome, visible profits on crusade, but they were the exceptions. For the great majority the situation was very different. To leave homes, goods and families for months or years meant an accumulation of problems, dangers and expense. Yet appeals for a crusade were constantly answered, and a long succession of armed expeditions, some great, some small, to certain of which historians have allotted numbers and to others not, made the journey to the East. It is often said that enthusiasm for the crusade waned in the early thirteenth century, and that this is to be explained by the limited success of the Third Crusade in the years 1189–92, by the tragic events of 1204, when the Fourth Crusade conquered Christian Constantinople, and the mounting criticism against the whole crusading idea. Such a verdict is not borne out by the facts. At no time in the history of the crusading movement did expeditions follow each other so closely as in the sixty years after 1189. It is true that during this period the Latin states in Syria became weaker and still more divided. Yet however crippled and attenuated they were by civil war, city state politics and lack of effective government, they still held the power to move western Christians, great and small, to come to the rescue, and this western aid helped to prolong their existence. Here a more detailed historical sketch of Latin Syria may help the reader.

The immediate task of the earliest settlers and their leaders was to expand the areas under their control and to defeat the counter-attacks sent against them. Both kinds of activity were intermingled during the first thirty years of the occupation. Fresh conquests were made partly because of those divisions among the Syrian Moslems already discussed, but also because of the energy and ambition of the earliest Frankish rulers, both of which were on a truly heroic scale. The count of Edessa, established with a tiny following in an exposed outpost far to the east of the Euphrates, was ready to thrust even further to the south and east towards the heartlands of the 'Abbasid Caliphate, and in 1104 was defeated near Harran in an attempt to do so. He did for a time establish a strong-point at Qala'at Ja'bar on the Euphrates, in the neighbourhood of the river port of Raqqa, where Moslem merchants dealt in commodities of Far Eastern trade, brought upstream from the Persian Gulf by way of Baghdad. The princes of Antioch, not content with subduing much of northern Syria and mounting a challenge to Aleppo, at the same time disputed the Cilician plain with Byzantium and campaigned against the amirs of Danishmend. As for the king of Jerusalem, as early as 1103 he granted a charter to the Genoese which envisaged the future conquest of Egypt.

Such men as these lost little time in carrying the attack into all those natural regions of the country to which reference has been made. The area in which success mattered most was the coastal plain. The seaports were needed for communication with the West and for the development of that commerce on which Frankish government and the economy were so heavily to depend. Since a successful siege of such places needed to be mounted from the seaward as well as from the landward side, the mastery soon established in Syrian waters by the fleets of Genoa, Venice and Pisa was of decisive importance. Even so, Tyre held out until 1124, and Ascalon, efficiently supplied and reinforced from Egypt, managed to resist until 1153. But the rest of the coastal towns were in Frankish hands by 1110.

By 1130 the Frankish conquests had reached their maximum extent. They were masters of the coastal plain, from the Gulf of Alexandretta to Egypt, with the exception of Ascalon. They effectively occupied the coastal hills and mountains, save for an area in the Ansariyah range, where in the 1130's the sect of the Assassins established themselves in a number of castles; their occupation was to outlast that of the Franks in Syria. The Biqa', between Lebanon and Anti-Lebanon, was still disputed with the Moslems of Damascus, but the Franks controlled the rest of the rift valley, except for the big towns on the middle Orontes; they also occupied much of the country to the east of that river, as well as all that beyond Lake Tiberias and thence continuously southward to the Gulf of 'Aqabah. Aleppo and Damascus still eluded them, although in the late 1120's Baldwin II of Jerusalem threatened both as never before. He pressed on Aleppo so severely, that the citizens looked to the east for salvation, and their saviour was 'Imad-ad-Din Zengi, from Mosul.

Fig. 2

He was not the first to launch a counter-attack against the Franks. The Fatimid government in Egypt had begun the process while the first crusaders were still besieging Jerusalem in 1099. The army they then sent was too late to save the Holy City; but in each of the following six years they sent an army, or fleet, or both, against southern Palestine, using Ascalon as a base. Even when these intensive attacks achieved no permanent success and became less frequent, raiding parties from Ascalon still made the country unsafe for travellers between Jerusalem and Jaffa, and a full-scale campaign might always be mounted if the Franks were

Fig. 2 *The crusader states* c. *1130. Inset: the southern desert drawn to the same scale*

in difficulty elsewhere, as they were in 1123. From 1110 it was the turn of the 'Abbasid-Seljuk government in Baghdad. In nearly every year for a decade they despatched a magnate from Iraq, often the amir who held Mosul, to attack the Franks, generally those of Antioch and Edessa.

The first thirty years of the Latin occupation were thus full of wars, both of attack and defence, and in both the Franks were generally successful. Even when they were few in number they found that the furious cavalry assault by their knights brought them quick victory against the static Egyptian forces. The mobility of the Turkish archers presented more difficult problems, but the Franks could usually contain the attacks in the north by skilful manoeuvre rather than by pitched battle. Sometimes they were beaten in the field, as was King Baldwin I of Jerusalem by the Egyptians in 1102, and by Maudud of Mosul in 1113. Six years later Roger, Prince of Antioch, died in a lost battle. The crisis which followed each of these reverses was met by mutual help, and a cautious defensive strategy. The prince of Antioch and count of Edessa twice brought forces four hundred miles south to aid Baldwin I. After Roger's death, Baldwin II was more often in the north than in his own kingdom. In the early 1120's the Franks survived a regency in Antioch and the captivity of Baldwin II of Jerusalem; and when in 1124 Baldwin was set free, he was soon leading attacks against Damascus and Aleppo.

Then came Zengi. Until his death in 1146 he had possessions both in Iraq and Syria, and therefore needed to divide his activities between the two regions. Nevertheless he was still able to inflict lasting damage on the Syrian Franks. He deprived the princes of Antioch of virtually all their lands east of the Orontes; from the counts of Tripoli he reconquered bases from which they were threatening Homs; and in 1144 came his greatest success, the recapture of Edessa. None of these losses was ever to be recovered by the Franks. Besides striking these blows against the Christian enemy, Zengi began the process of reuniting Moslem Syria. From Aleppo he extended his power to Hamah and Homs; he began to threaten Damascus which drove its rulers into alliance with the Franks of Jerusalem. During Zengi's career in Syria, the expansion of the crusader states was at last halted, their reduction was begun, and so was the process of reuniting Moslem Syria.

Zengi's work was continued, and some of it completed, by his son Nur-ad-Din, Noradinus to the Franks, among whom his fame was second only to that of Saladin. This prince succeeded only to his father's Syrian lands, and he was thus able to concentrate on Syrian affairs. By 1150 he had driven the Franks to abandon the rest of the county of Edessa; he had further reduced the size of the principality of Antioch; and in 1154 he triumphantly completed the reuniting of Moslem Syria by his acquisition of Damascus. At the same time he survived the temporary reinforcing of Latin Syria from the West. In Europe the loss of Edessa had been regarded as so great a calamity that a new crusade had been organized. Its two main contingents (there were many others), respectively led by Louis VII of France and Conrad III of Germany, were seriously weakened in Asia Minor before they reached Syria. Once in that country, it was difficult to select an objective, since Jerusalem, the goal of all other crusades, was already in Christian hands. After a number of interested parties had competed for the crusaders' services, a decision was taken to attack Damascus, which was not as foolish as many modern historians have asserted, but which was controversial. Damascus and Jerusalem had been for some time past in alliance against Zengi, and many Syrian Franks thought that they should remain so. As a result the attack was delivered without unity or conviction and was given up after a few days.

Six years later, in 1154, it was Nur-ad-Din who held Damascus, and the crusader states were then faced for the first time by a united Moslem Syria. Their only consolation was the conquest of Ascalon in 1153, which provided them with a base from which to exert pressure on Egypt. In mid-century the government of that country was weakened by faction and by literally cut-throat competition for the office of vizier. A position was reached in which the two contending candidates looked for help outside the country; one called in King Amalric of Jerusalem, and the other Nur-ad-Din. From 1164 until 1170, Moslem and Latin Syria continued their battles in the Nile Delta. Nur-ad-Din was never in Egypt himself; in command of his expeditionary forces he appointed a tough Kurd named Shirkuh who took with him a young nephew, Saladin. Amalric always led his knights and their auxiliaries in person on five Egyptian campaigns. The early encounters were drawn; Amalric and Shirkuh reached stalemate and both agreed to evacuate the country.

In 1167 the Franks seemed to be getting the upper hand. The vizier whom they supported was in power; a formal alliance was made with the Fatimid Caliph; they were well subsidized for their services, and for a time western knights garrisoned certain gateways in the capital as a guarantee of payment; Shirkuh was made to fight in Upper Egypt and Saladin was besieged in Alexandria. So small a body of Europeans, alien in language and religion, could not finally establish their control over so rich and populous a country; the changes and chances of Egyptian politics provided too unstable a foundation. Even with Byzantine assistance they could not prevent Shirkuh assuming power there in the name of his master, and when Shirkuh died, Saladin was able to succeed him. In 1171 the young ruler suppressed the Fatimid Caliphate, and for the first time in 200 years Egypt returned, however nominally, to its 'Abbasid allegiance.

It was even longer since the same man had ruled both in Damascus and Cairo and, as time was to show, it was a situation which represented the deadliest threat of all to the existence of Latin Syria. The Franks must have hoped to escape from it in 1174, when Nur-ad-Din died, leaving only an infant son to succeed him. Such hopes were soon dashed. Saladin, with outstanding political skill and a measure of good fortune, was able to establish himself as independent ruler of Egypt, then quickly to occupy Damascus and, from 1174 to 1183, to acquire the rest of Nur-ad-Din's Syrian lands. Against all odds (for Moslem régimes were then particularly vulnerable to changes of ruler and to minorities) Moslem Syria remained united within itself and to Egypt.

During the fifteen years after 1174 the balance tilted even more sharply against the Franks and led to unprecedented disaster. Latin Syria became progressively weaker not only in relation to the mounting strength of Saladin, but absolutely. Edessa was no more, and Antioch was gravely weakened by the defeat at Harim in 1164 and by conflict between prince and patriarch. Byzantine support, continually in evidence during the third quarter of the century, was no longer forthcoming. In 1175 a great Turkish victory at Myriocephalon in Asia Minor had been comparable in its effects with Manzikert a century earlier. The death of the Emperor Manuel Comnenus in 1180 had meant the end of his francophile policy, and this was soon followed by an anti-European reaction in Constantinople. The Latin kingdom of Jerusalem, deprived of these sources of external support, unable despite repeated efforts to rouse a new crusade in the West, was left to face Saladin not only alone, but divided by faction.

Amalric had died only a few weeks after Nur-ad-Din, and he too had left a child to succeed him. Baldwin IV, only thirteen years old, was also a leper, who would be incapable of begetting children. Two problems were thus raised which were state business of the first magnitude: who should be regent, and who should in due course succeed Baldwin as king. In 1174 the immediate conflict for the regency was settled, ominously, by murder, and the office was held for two years by the king's cousin Raymond, Count of Tripoli by hereditary succession and, in the kingdom, Prince of Galilee in right of his wife. Thereafter Baldwin, an exceptionally gifted young man, who in 1177 inflicted on Saladin the heaviest military defeat of his career, was able to assume power himself, but only for a time. In the early 1180's his illness was depriving him progressively of sight and the use of his limbs, so that a regent again became necessary. It seemed possible that the marriage of his elder sister, Sybil, might solve both problems. Her husband, besides fathering an heir, could also be regent. By her first husband, William of Montferrat, heir to one of the greatest of European titles, she bore a son who was to be the last in the direct male succession in the royal house of Jerusalem but William, who was acceptable to the baronage of the kingdom, died before his son was born. In 1180, Sybil married again. This time it was to Guy, a cadet of the Poitevin house of Lusignan, who was not generally acceptable. Many of the baronage, always ready to resent newcomers to the kingdom, especially when they married an available heiress, judged him insufficient to bear rule in the kingdom either as regent, or eventually as king, in right of his wife. In 1183 Guy was ousted as regent and replaced by Raymond and a scheme of succession was devised with the sole purpose of excluding Sybil and Guy.

As Saladin increased his pressure on the kingdom in the mid-1180's, the ruling group were deeply divided, and the divisions were envenomed by personal vendettas. The two years which followed the death of Baldwin IV in 1185 were crucial. In 1186 the kingdom was rent by an exclusion crisis, and in 1187 Saladin mounted a major attack. Baldwin IV was followed by his eight-year-old namesake, the son of Sybil and William of Montferrat. Under the anti-Lusignan scheme for the succession, Raymond of Tripoli was regent, and if the boy were to die young, Raymond was to remain in office until an *ad hoc* committee of the Pope, the western emperor and the kings of England and France had chosen the next ruler. In 1186 the child king did die; but by a skilfully engineered coup Sibyl succeeded by hereditary right and crowned her husband. The thwarted barons, and especially Raymond, brought the country to the brink of civil war, and this was the situation in the spring of 1187 when Saladin prepared to invade Galilee. In face of this crisis, a reconciliation was patched up; but the deep-seated differences could not be concealed for long, and they bedevilled the council of war held to plan the approaching campaign. Should the army remain in its well-supplied base at Saffuriya and cautiously watch Saladin's movements until his army dispersed at the end of the campaigning season, or should it risk marching through miles of waterless country to attack him as he besieged Tiberias? King Guy was persuaded, against Raymond's advice, to adopt the second course. Saladin gave battle, and the Christian army was annihilated at Hattin.

Measured by its consequences, this was a battle of major importance. In order to muster an army large enough to oppose Saladin, the Franks had drawn heavily on the garrisons of castles and walled towns. When the army was destroyed, many of these places were left defenceless. By the autumn of 1187 the kingdom of Jerusalem was reduced to the city of Tyre and a few isolated castles. All other places, including the capital, had in the space of a few weeks surrendered to Saladin. In 1188 he went north, did little damage to Tripoli, but inflicted further and permanent losses on Antioch. He still further separated it from the rest of the Latin states by conquering Latakia and Jabala, and so driving a wedge into the coastal plain, hitherto held entirely by the Franks.

The loss of Jerusalem at last moved the West to a new crusade, and in the period from 1188 to 1191 contingents of armed pilgrims moved from all parts of Europe towards the Holy Land. The focal point was Acre which Guy, a prisoner after Hattin, but released in the following year, began to besiege in August, 1189. This operation was not only strongly resisted by the garrison of Acre, but was hampered by Saladin's army in the open field, so that although the weight of reinforcement from the West at length forced the surrender of the town, the siege had lasted only seven weeks less than two years.

The crusade was a major European enterprise, led by some of the greatest rulers of the day, but its results were disappointing. The Emperor Frederick Barbarossa was drowned in Asia Minor while still on the way to the East, and only a fraction of his fine army seem to have continued the journey. Philip of France and Richard Coeur de Lion, at war immediately before the crusade, brought their enmity to the East with them. Soon after the fall of Acre, Philip returned to Europe. Richard was left in imperfect command of forces rent by divisions of many kinds. Pisans and Genoese were rivals for commercial opportunity; Guy's claims to the throne were challenged by determined opponents, especially after the death of Sybil, the heiress who had brought him the royal title. The French contingent, now led by the duke of Burgundy, were not always disposed to fall in with Richard's plans, and conflicting advice was offered as to what those plans should be. Finally Richard marched down the coast from Acre to Jaffa, and from the base he established there tried to force his way inland to Jerusalem. Opposed by Saladin he twice failed to achieve this objective and by the late summer of 1192 he saw that there was no alternative to negotiation. In September he and Saladin concluded a treaty by which the Franks retained the coastal strip won back by the crusade. In other words, they now held the territory which could be controlled from the seaside towns of Tyre, Acre, Haifa, Caesarea, Arsuf and Jaffa.

The results of the Third Crusade were modest, but they gave a further century of life to an attenuated Latin kingdom, with its capital at Acre. Further north, those parts of the county of Tripoli and the principality of Antioch which Saladin had not been able to conquer remained in Christian hands until the latter half of the thirteenth century. But Latin Syria after 1192 was different in many ways from the Latin Syria of the years before 1187. It was so much reduced in physical area that its foothold on the edge of western Asia was far more precarious. It was overlooked by its Moslem neighbours as it had once overlooked them. Furthermore, the fortunes of the Latin states had been directed in the early and middle years of the twelfth century by rulers of high personal quality who, as leaders of a conquest, acquired wide powers. This was particularly true of the Latin kings of Jerusalem, who ruled not only in the kingdom, but who in times of crisis temporarily assumed control in Tripoli, Antioch or Edessa, and coordinated the joint efforts of all the

Latin states. The attenuated Latin Syria of the thirteenth century had just as great a need of decisive leadership, especially as divisions among neighbouring Moslems created opportunities of which a resolute government could take advantage. In fact, the monarchy first declined and then withered away. For forty years the succession passed through heiresses, first Sybil, then her younger sister Isabel, then Isabel's daughter, then that daughter's daughter. Power, while it could still be exercised, was in the hands of their husbands, who might replace each other in rapid succession. The first Isabel, for example, was married in 1190, 1192 and 1197. Finally, the marriage of her grand-daughter in 1225 brought the crown to Frederick II, the Western Emperor, in whose family it remained by male succession until 1268. Frederick was in the country as a crusader from September, 1228 until May, 1229, but he never visited Syria again, and neither did any of his successors. Forty years of heiresses were succeeded by forty years of absentee kings. After the extinction of the Hohenstaufen succession in 1268, the monarchy of Jerusalem became a matter of dispute, and even a commodity offered for sale. It is not surprising that it ceased to have any effective existence.

Beset by such weaknesses, how did the Latin kingdom survive for nearly a century? Partly because of divisions and rivalries among Saladin's descendants and partly because of continued help from the West. When Saladin died in 1193, his empire was immediately divided. One of his sons took power in Egypt, another in Damascus; and although in a few years they were supplanted by their uncle, al-'Adil, who thus reunited Egypt and Syria, these lands were in turn divided between his sons on his death in 1218. This weakening of Ayyubid power gave the Franks two advantages. First, it enabled them to negotiate truces; it has been calculated that, of the fifty years after 1192, only eight were not covered by such agreements. Second, the Ayyubid princes often went to war with each other, and sometimes looked for allies. There were times when the rulers in Cairo and Damascus, in particular, competed against each other for Frankish support, and the payment they might be ready to offer was to restore some of the lost lands of the crusader kingdom. In 1229, and again ten years later, visiting crusaders were able to take advantage of Ayyubid rivalries to negotiate the restoration of lands which had been part of the Christian kingdom during the twelfth century.

Fig. 3

The crusades of the thirteenth century, together with other forms of help from the West, also helped to keep the Latin states, and especially the kingdom, in being. Crusading activity was never higher than during the sixty years that followed the Third Crusade. In the 1190's the Emperor Henry VI was planning to attack Byzantium as well as the Moslems in the Holy Land, and it was while a German crusade was in the country in 1197 that Beirut was retaken. In the same decade Pope Innocent III preached a crusade to recover Jerusalem, but the expedition then launched conquered Byzantium. This did not deter him from putting in hand the preaching of a new crusade in 1213 – the Fifth – which in 1218 invaded Egypt, and attempted to force a decision there until its final defeat in 1221. For a few months in 1228 and 1229 the Emperor Frederick II was in the Holy Land. He recovered Jerusalem by negotiation; while from 1239 to 1241 successive expeditions led by the king of Navarre and the earl of Cornwall also prevailed on the Ayyubids to restore important territories to the Latin kingdom. In 1249 and 1250 Louis IX of France headed a major crusade in the Nile Delta; after its failure he spent more than four years in the Latin kingdom.

The truncated kingdom therefore survived into the last decade of the thirteenth century, and the two smaller crusader states for nearly as long. Like the kingdom, they were for a time helped by having not too hostile Ayyubid princes as their neighbours. Tripoli, firmly based on its fortified coastal towns and its control of the coastal plain, always enjoyed a measure of protection from the height and steepness of the Lebanon ranges and from the strength of the Military Orders in the county, their power based on such strongholds as Krak, Safita (Chastel Blanc) and Tartus (Tortosa). Count Raymond III died without heirs soon after the disaster of Hattin. He bequeathed the county to the younger son of Bohemond III of Antioch, who eventually succeeded his father also in the principality, so that Tripoli and Antioch were joined under the same ruler until their reconquest by the Moslems. These princes chose Tripoli as their principal residence and their visits to Antioch became increasingly rare. No one acquainted with the physical amenities of 'cette belle corniche libanaise' will feel surprised at their choice, though their northern territories would perhaps have been a more appropriate field of action for princes who, down to the loss of Antioch and beyond, bore the great name of Bohemond.

Fig. 3 Sites named in the text. Insets: the neighbourhood of Tripoli (a), of Jerusalem (b)

Certainly the existence of the principality was more precarious than that of the county and the kingdom. From the early conquests of Zengi beyond the Orontes it had been the first to suffer serious and permanent losses of territory, and the process had been continued by Nur-ad-Din and Saladin. In the Cilician plain it had been replaced, first by

27

Byzantium, then by the kingdom of Armenia. Such losses had not been recovered, as they sometimes were in the kingdom, by new crusades from the West. After 1188 Antioch's physical links with the rest of the Latin states, already impeded by the Assassins in the Jabal Ansariyah, were further severed by Saladin's conquest of Jabala and Latakia which, except for their brief restoration to the Franks by the Mongols, were to remain permanently in Moslem hands. Shorn of its former possessions, partially isolated, neglected by its princes, Antioch in the thirteenth century was more exposed than Tripoli and Acre to pressures from a wider world; it could be more directly affected by the balance of power between more powerful governments in Mesopotamia and Asia Minor. Its relations with Armenia were particularly close, largely through interpenetration. There had been large communities of Armenians in the principality of Antioch from the time of its foundation. There were Franks in Armenia, especially in the upper strata of society. Frankish barons, some of them exiles from Antioch, held lands there, and there was much intermarriage across the border. Furthermore, at the turn of the twelfth and thirteenth centuries the ruler of Armenia sought inter-national political advantage by aligning himself with the western world; for a time he gave his ecclesiastical allegiance to the Pope and sought the authority of the western emperor when elevating himself to royal rank. Western influences became strong in Armenia; some evidence of this is provided by the form of the castles built there at this time; by the translation of the laws of crusader Antioch into Armenian; by generous endowment of the Military Orders, especially the Hospitallers.

Intermarriage between the ruling houses led, in the last decade of the twelfth century, to Armenian intervention in the succession problems of the principality, even to an attempt to take control of the city of Antioch itself. This found support among the Armenians who lived under Frankish rule, but was strongly resisted by the large Greek community in Antioch. It was in this crisis that a commune was formed in the city, of which the Greeks were an important element. So too were the Frankish burgesses, but the Frankish lay and ecclesiastical aristocracy were divided among themselves on this issue.

In the kingdom proper there was less danger of communal strife, but more of conflict between king and baronage. Such a situation had arisen in 1186, and was repeated at least twice before the end of the century.

Henry of Champagne and Aimery of Lusignan, respectively the third and fourth husbands of Queen Isabel I and who successively ruled in the kingdom, each tried to discipline a baronial magnate without reference to the High Court composed of their feudal tenants-in-chief, and on each occasion the court asserted its right to be the ultimate authority in these matters. Such difficulties did not arise again during the first quarter of the thirteenth century. Isabel and Aimery both died in 1205, and were succeeded by Maria, still a child, the daughter of Isabel by her second marriage, which had been to Conrad of Montferrat. A regent was necessary, and that office was filled by John of Ibelin, the greatest baron of the kingdom. In 1210 Maria was married to John of Brienne, a baron from the county of Champagne, who was first king in right of his wife and then, after her early death, was technically regent (although he kept the title of king) for his infant daughter, Isabel II, until her marriage in 1225. Thus for twenty years men born into the feudal nobility were at the head of the government; just as, in England during the years after 1216, a leading baronial figure, William Marshal, Earl of Pembroke, was *rector regis et regni*. In neither kingdom was there, in these circumstances, a clash between government and baronage.

A new situation arose in the Latin kingdom as a result of the marriage of Isabel II. On many occasions during the twelfth century the Latins in the Levant had attempted to strengthen their position by attracting a wealthy magnate from the West to take charge of their affairs. The hand of an heiress had sometimes been offered as an inducement. In 1222, the year after that final failure of the Fifth Crusade to which reference has already been made, King John of Jerusalem undertook a journey to the West to find a husband for his daughter Isabel, Queen of Jerusalem in her own right. Through the good offices of Pope Honorius III a marriage was arranged with the head of the Hohenstaufen house, Frederick II, King of Sicily, King of Germany, Western Emperor. The marriage, celebrated in 1225, was to have such disastrous consequences for Latin Syria that it is easy to overlook how brilliant a match it seemed to contemporaries. What better solution could be imagined to the problem of the crusade and the Latin East than to involve in them, as king of Jerusalem, the greatest secular ruler of the West. And within four years of the marriage he had led a crusade to Syria, and had regained for Christendom most of the city of Jerusalem.

Table I

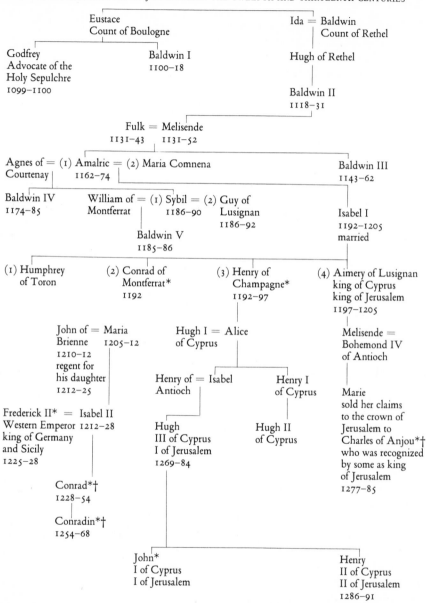

Eustace
Count of Boulogne

Ida = Baldwin
Count of Rethel

Godfrey
Advocate of the
Holy Sepulchre
1099–1100

Baldwin I
1100–18

Hugh of Rethel

Baldwin II
1118–31

Fulk = Melisende
1131–43   1131–52

Agnes of = (1) Amalric = (2) Maria Comnena
Courtenay   1162–74

Baldwin III
1143–62

Baldwin IV
1174–85

William of = (1) Sybil = (2) Guy of
Montferrat   1186–90   Lusignan
                             1186–92

Isabel I
1192–1205
married

Baldwin V
1185–86

(1) Humphrey
of Toron

(2) Conrad of
Montferrat*
1192

(3) Henry of
Champagne*
1192–97

(4) Aimery of Lusignan
king of Cyprus
king of Jerusalem
1197–1205

John of = Maria
Brienne   1205–12
1210–12
regent for
his daughter
1212–25

Hugh I = Alice
of Cyprus

Melisende =
Bohemond IV
of Antioch

Frederick II* = Isabel II
Western Emperor 1212–28
king of Germany
and Sicily
1225–28

Henry of = Isabel
Antioch

Henry I
of Cyprus

Marie
sold her claims
to the crown of
Jerusalem to
Charles of Anjou*†
who was recognized
by some as king
of Jerusalem
1277–85

Conrad*†
1228–54

Hugh
III of Cyprus
I of Jerusalem
1269–84

Hugh II
of Cyprus

Conradin*†
1254–68

John*
I of Cyprus
I of Jerusalem

Henry
II of Cyprus
II of Jerusalem
1286–91

*Never crowned as king
†Never in the Latin kingdom

The dates, from 1100 onwards, are of the reigns of
the kings and hereditary queens of Jerusalem.

Frederick's crusade brought added weakness to the Latin East. The expedition had been preceded by so many years of delay that Pope Gregory IX had lost patience with Frederick and after a false start to the crusade in 1227 had excommunicated him. When the emperor finally arrived in Acre in 1228 the sentence had not been lifted, so that Frederick had a mixed reception. He himself had created distrust and opposition by his behaviour in Cyprus, which he visited on his way to the East. He claimed special rights in the island because his father, in his capacity as emperor, had raised to royal rank the Lusignan who ruled there. In 1228 the Lusignan king was a minor, and effective power was in the hands of that John of Ibelin to whom reference has just been made. He was head of the greatest baronial house in the Latin East, kinsman of the royal family of Jerusalem, with wide estates both in Cyprus and on the mainland. Frederick seems to have decided that he could best establish his power in the East by asserting his authority over such a man. With a show of force, he called on John to render account of the revenues he had received as regent in Cyprus, and to give up his fief of Beirut in the kingdom of Jerusalem. John refused to be browbeaten and replied that he would answer any charges brought against him only before his baronial peers in the High Court of Nicosia or Jerusalem. An open breach was somehow avoided; John and his supporters accompanied Frederick to Acre; but Frederick had raised a matter on which the baronage of Jerusalem were particularly sensitive. For sixty years past one formerly royal power which they had sought to limit was the king's right to deprive a vassal of his fief by his own arbitrary decision, rather than by judgement of the High Court. Frederick's attempt to disseise the kingdom's greatest vassal of his principal fief aroused the fears of the whole baronage.

Paradoxically enough, his success in regaining Jerusalem made matters worse. He achieved this by peaceful, even amicable, negotiation with the Ayyubid sultan of Egypt, and this new method of crusading undoubtedly shocked large sections of Christian opinion. He gave further cause for offence because he had to agree that the Dome of the Rock and the Aqsa Mosque should be left in Moslem hands. It was also held that he had made no satisfactory arrangements about rebuilding the city's fortifications. Frederick's excommunication, the opposition of the Pope and the Latin Patriarch of Jerusalem, the controversy about his treaty with the sultan, the fears of some of the barons about the style of his government and the security of their tenures, all these things divided the Frankish community in the East and weakened the emperor's authority there.

When Frederick left Acre to return to Italy he was never again to set foot in the Levant, but he bore the title of king of Jerusalem for the rest of his life and tried to regulate the kingdom's affairs by remote control. In 1231 he sent a marshal of the empire, Richard Filangieri, at the head of a small army and fleet, to re-establish imperial authority both in Cyprus and in Acre. But since Filangieri's first action was to lay siege to Beirut, thus seeming to renew the earlier threat against John of Ibelin, a baronial opposition came into the open. The Ibelins and their supporters formed a sworn association in Acre – yet another commune in Latin Syria – and were able to prevent Filangieri from establishing himself there. He was forced to use Tyre as a headquarters, and so began a situation, which was to persist for all but the last five years of the kingdom's history, in which Acre and Tyre were the seats of rival powers. In 1232 there was brisk campaigning both in Cyprus and on the mainland; but while in the island the imperialists had the worst of the exchanges, between Acre and Tyre there were years of stalemate. At length, in 1243, Conrad, Frederick's son by Isabel of Jerusalem, reached his fifteenth birthday. Even by the emperor's most determined baronial opponents in Acre, this boy was accepted as their lawful king, and by the laws of the kingdom, fifteen was the age of royal majority. It was put to the barons that, since Conrad's personal rule had now begun, his father no longer held authority, and his father's agent, Filangieri, had no further standing in the kingdom. Tyre was therefore attacked and taken, and the imperialists expelled.

In their own eyes, these barons had won a famous victory. They had upheld the law, and those liberties which the law protected, against a tyrant who would have trodden them underfoot. But they had also repulsed, for better or for worse, the one ruler who might have brought strong government to the kingdom, and when a people is threatened by an external enemy, strong government has its virtues. As it was, the once effective monarchy of Jerusalem was lost beyond redemption. Until 1268 it stayed in the Hohenstaufen house, but none of those who bore the title ever came to the East. Authority should have been exercised on their behalf by regents but, as will be seen, that office too became the focal point of disputes and subject to the control of the baronial High Court.

The last occasion on which the Franks were able to take advantage of Ayyubid divisions was in the years 1239–41, when two minor crusades brought temporary strength to Acre. The first was led by Theobald, Count of Champagne and King of Navarre; the second by Richard of Cornwall, brother of Henry III of England and brother-in-law of Frederick II. By one of the historical accidents of which there are so many in crusading history they came at a time when the Ayyubid house was in the full throes of a succession crisis, so that both Damascus and Cairo, needing allies, were prepared to do a deal with the Franks. As a result the crusading leaders were able to regain by negotiation much of the territory west of Jordan – Nablus and Hebron were the main exceptions – which had formerly belonged to the first Latin kingdom. But the fact that both Damascus and Cairo were bidding against each other sowed division among the Franks. With whom should an alliance be made? In 1244 the Franks of Acre were persuaded mainly by the Templars, to join forces with Damascus and to invade Egypt. They made a major effort, and the army they put into the field was the largest they had assembled since the Hattin campaign. Old times were still further recalled by the presence of a contingent from Antioch-Tripoli, and by the fact that the main clash with the Egyptians was on the southern coastal plain near Gaza. And for the Franks it was indeed another Hattin in the comprehensiveness of their defeat.

The Egyptian victory at Gaza had many consequences. In the first place, the Ayyubid Sultan of Egypt, alarmed by the coalition formed against him, had himself looked for allies, and had called into Syria the Khorezmian Turks. These were the survivors of a people whose empire had been broken by the Mongols and who were available as mercenaries. As they swept southward to link up with their new employer, they not only sacked Tiberias and Nablus, but briefly occupied Jerusalem and expelled the Franks, this time for good. The Holy City was not again to be under Christian rule until General Allenby entered it with his troops in 1917.

The final loss of Jerusalem in 1244 was not the end of this sequence of events. The victorious Egyptian Ayyubid became master of Damascus and, from this position of strength, deprived the Franks of nearly all they had recovered in 1239–41. Military defeat, the loss of Jerusalem, other Moslem reconquests, all these recalled the days of Saladin. And just as his successes had provoked a new crusade in the West, so did the Egyptian victories of the mid-1240's. In 1248 St Louis sailed from Aigues Mortes for Cyprus and in the following year disembarked before Damietta.

This brilliant expedition was in vain. As in 1219, Damietta was taken. As in 1221, an attempt was made to invade Egypt in depth, and once again the attempt ended in the surrender of a Christian army. St Louis was a prisoner, and although he was soon ransomed, his crusade was a failure. After these events of 1250, he remained in Latin Syria for four more years, during which the kingdom had its last experience of masterful government. But while he had been a prisoner in Egyptian hands, there had been one momentous change which, as time was to show, sealed the fate of Latin Syria. The Ayyubid regime was over-thrown by the Mamluks.

Successive Egyptian governments had relied on slave regiments, mostly Turkish. The commanders of these troops assumed growing importance in the official hierarchy, and in 1250, taking advantage of the uncertainty of a succession crisis, they seized power. When one of their leaders, Aybeg al-Turkmani, was proclaimed sultan, he inaugurated a regime which was to survive until the Ottoman conquests in the sixteenth century. In contrast to the conditions of the first Latin kingdom, the Egyptian armies were now to be those whom the Franks had most need to fear; in forty years they destroyed the Latin settlement.

The Mamluks quickly became a Near Eastern power; but in that same decade, the 1250's, a world power briefly intervened in Syria. During the first quarter of the thirteenth century Genghis Khan had led the Mongols in conquests which established one of the greatest Asian empires of all time. His armies invaded China and annexed territory in Korea and Manchuria; they had fought in the Punjab; in Central Asia they had broken the power of the Keraits and Khorezmians; further west they had defeated armies of the Christian Georgians and the Christian Russians. After the death of Genghis Khan in 1227, they came to be feared as a threat in western Europe. In 1240 they destroyed the armies of the Poles and the Teutonic Knights; they passed through Silesia and Hungary and reached the Adriatic.

In 1258 the Mongol leader Hulagu (his brother Kubla Khan was then ruling in China) invaded the heartlands of the 'Abbasid Caliphate. He took Baghdad and hanged the caliph. It was something of an event in world history. The Abbasid caliphs had held their office for five hundred years. Baghdad was one of the world's most famous and ancient capitals. Now it had fallen, little more than half a century after that other old and long inviolate capital, Constantinople, and neither has since recovered its former glory.

From Iraq Hulagu passed into Syria. Among the clients who came to join him were the King of Armenia and his son-in-law, Prince Bohemond V of Antioch. And so, for the first and only time in crusading history, a Frankish prince was present at the two conquests which the Syrian Franks could never themselves achieve: Aleppo fell to the Mongols in February, 1260 and Damascus a month later.

Mongol power seemed irresistible; but one government was not afraid to challenge it. In disputing control of Syria with invaders from the north, the Mamluks were following an ancient tradition in Egyptian foreign policy. Their task was made unexpectedly easier by the death of the Mongol Great Khan. The succession crisis demanded the presence of Hulagu, who withdrew from Syria with a large part of his forces. Kitbogha, his Christian general, was left behind with a much reduced army, which was destroyed by the Mamluks in a battle fought a few miles southwest of Lake Tiberias on 3 September, 1260. The victory gave Damascus to the Mamluks. Once more Latin Syria had as its strongest and most hostile neighbour a power which was established in both Syria and Egypt.

As Mamluk power rose, so the ability of the Franks to resist it declined. In the late 1250's, when Syria became a battle-ground for major forces in western Asia, Acre became the battle-ground in the Latin kingdom's worst and most damaging civil war. It began with a dispute between the privileged Venetian and Genoese trading communities in Acre over property belonging to the monastery of St Sabas. Both sides used force, constantly augmented by naval reinforcements despatched from the West by the respective mother cities, and were supported by allies. In the years 1256–58 nearly all the main groups in the kingdom, Hospitallers, Templars, Catalans, the communities of Marseilles and Ancona supported one side or the other or, like the Pisans, backed each in turn or, like the baronage, were divided between the two. Acre was in a turmoil. It had all the highly coloured character of a great cosmopolitan seaport. It was a centre for men who had been banished from Europe, or sent overseas to expiate a crime or to relieve harassed families. It was a city of narrow lanes, of houses, private and corporate, strengthened for defence, of whole quarters enclosed by walls and towers. In those years it was the scene of street fighting, arson, bombardment and counter-bombardment by the stone-throwing artillery of the day between one fortified centre and another. Nor were hostilities confined to Acre. The Genoese were supported by Philip of Montfort, Lord of Tyre. When the Genoese were forced to abandon Acre, Philip established them in Tyre; and since the war at sea between Venice and Genoa continued long after the cessation of hostilities on land, Acre and Tyre once again assumed the role of rival centres in the kingdom.

It is necessary to emphasize the lack of an effective monarchy in the thirteenth-century kingdom. Government may not have been the most important aspect of the society of Outremer, nor was all government concentrated in the king's hands; but if the Latin kingdom was to survive on the edge of western Asia in the conditions which developed there after 1250, some agency was needed to organize its resources and to apply them to solving the problem. Given the contemporary forms of government and society, only the monarchy could undertake this role; but after the failure of Frederick II to establish his authority and the ending of the *de facto* rule of Louis IX, the Latin monarchy withered away.

Isabel II, Queen of Jerusalem, married to Frederick II in 1225, had died in 1228, ten days after giving birth to their son Conrad. The baby at once became lawful king of Jerusalem, and remained so until his death in 1254, the year in which St Louis returned from Acre to the West, leaving the Latin kingdom to its own devices. Conrad, who had never seen his kingdom, was succeeded by Conradin, a child of five. Since the child monarch was in Europe, it was necessary to appoint a regent, and by this time the law of the kingdom decreed that the office be filled by the king's next-of-kin, the heir apparent, who was present in the Latin East. In 1254 this was Hugh, king of Cyprus, a descendant of Isabel I's marriage with Aimery of Lusignan. But he too was a little boy of five, so he, the regent, in turn needed a regent, an office which was claimed by his mother, Queen Plaisance. She came to Acre to make her claim before the High Court in 1258, at the height of the war of St Sabas, and it became yet another issue which divided the main groups in the kingdom. Plaisance succeeded in establishing her claim, but decided not to rule in person. She therefore appointed as executive head of her government John of Arsuf, a member of the Ibelin family. A child as absentee king, another child as absentee heir, a woman as absentee regent, a baronial administrator whose family was involved in an unsettled civil war, such was the situation of the monarchy at a time of great events and great changes in the Levant, which included the Mongol invasion and the rise of Mamluk power.

Through the 1260's and beyond the position continued to deteriorate. The monarchy remained Hohenstaufen until Charles of Anjou executed the last of the line in 1268. Meanwhile regents were still needed, and on the death of Queen Isabella of Cyprus in 1264, rival claimants argued their case with a wealth of legal and genealogical learning before the baronial High Court, which took the final decision. In many ways there is much to admire in this elaborate demonstration of the rule of law, but it was all a far cry from the masterful government of Fulk, Amalric and the Baldwins. Worse was to follow. In 1269 the monarchy passed to the Lusignans; Hugh III of Cyprus became Hugh I of Jerusalem as well. But in his new kingdom he could not impose his authority. He was flouted and defied by his vassals, and still more by the Master of the Templars. In 1276 he abandoned all attempts to rule. He withdrew to Cyprus and left the mainland kingdom without effective government.

Hugh's title to rule then came under challenge from yet another quarter. Mary of Antioch was the grand-daughter of Isabel I's youngest daughter, and was therefore in a line of succession junior to that of Hugh; but she was a generation nearer than Hugh to their common ancestress and claimed seniority to him. It was a situation to which feudal law and custom gave no clear answer, so that although Mary's claims were rejected by the High Court of Jerusalem, she felt justified in pursuing them at the Papal Curia. Finding no satisfaction there she finally sold her claims to Charles of Anjou, the younger brother of St Louis. Charles had completed the destruction of the Hohenstaufen. King of Sicily by conquest, he followed his predecessors in pursuing large ambitions in the eastern Mediterranean, and he assumed the kingship of Jerusalem not by marriage or succession, but by the purchase to which reference has been made. In 1277 he sent his representative to Acre to assume authority in his name and, with Hugh still refusing to act as king, that representative was accepted. This bizarre interlude came to an end in 1282, when Charles' power was broken by the Sicilian Vespers. For the last nine years, until Acre fell in 1291, the kings of Cyprus once more ruled on the mainland as kings of Jerusalem. But until 1286 they had no power in Acre, which should have been their capital, while Tyre and Beirut were never brought under their effective control. As for Antioch-Tripoli, that was equally torn by faction and vendetta. The last princes lived in Tripoli; even before Antioch was lost in 1268, they left that city to its own devices. A succession of minorities and of disputes for the office of regent removed any possibility of organizing effective resistance to the external enemy.

Especially when that enemy was Baybars. The assassination of his predecessor had enabled Baybars to become sultan of Egypt in 1260, soon after the Mamluks' victory over the Mongols and their conquest of Damascus. From that year the Franks had as their nearest neighbour not the tolerant and chivalrous Ayyubids, who in pursuit of their family quarrels would make treaties with the Franks of Tripoli or Acre, but a genius in politics, warfare and government who was implacably bent on their destruction. In four campaigns, the first in 1265 and the last in 1271, Baybars reduced Latin Syria to a few strong places on the sea-shore, from Latakia in the north to Château Pèlerin in the south. His conquests included Antioch in 1268 and, in 1271, Montfort, the headquarters of the Teutonic Knights, and the Krak des Chevaliers, a provincial headquarters of the Hospitallers. Their northern bastion, Marqab, fell to Kalavun, successor to Baybars, in 1285. So, before 1290, did Latakia and Tripoli. Kalavun prepared the destruction of Acre, but this was achieved by his successor in 1291. With that loss, the Franks abandoned for ever their other possessions on the mainland – Tartus, Sidon, Tyre and Château Pèlerin.

Crusader Society and Institutions

Western Europeans were able to control Syria for nearly two centuries because they devised forms of government which were sufficiently strong and workable, and sufficiently acceptable to the majority of the inhabitants. Such government was monarchic, even though in a limited sense, in that one man was recognized as its head and principal director – a king in Jerusalem, a prince in Antioch, a count in Tripoli and in Edessa.

In the Middle Ages the legislative function in government was far less prominent than it has since become. There was then a far greater degree of respect, even veneration, for the law as it had come down from the past. Medieval governments did not regard it as their main task to amend and revise it (though this sometimes happened), but to make it work, and the fundamental power in government was that of holding a court, in which the law was interpreted, applied and enforced. This power was not monopolized by the ruler, but was divided among many agencies. Important areas of the law were regarded as the responsibility of the Church and its hierarchy of courts; these included, for example, all those legal problems arising from the state of matrimony and its dissolution, from the testamentary disposition of personal property and from criminal proceedings taken against heretics. Other areas were the concern of landlords, who could hold court for their tenants, and there were other privileged bodies with the same all-important right.

This diversity was reproduced in the crusader states. There was in particular a profusion of ecclesiastical courts, since the Christian subjects of the crusader rulers included not only European settlers who were members of the Roman Church, but indigenous Syrians divided among a number of eastern Churches, each with its own canon law and, presumably, its tribunals in which that law could be applied. On the secular side an important group of courts existed because of the right of any landlord to hold a court not only for villagers who cultivated the land they held from him, but also for his feudal tenants, those tenants, that is, who were personally free, who were bound to the lord by personal ties of fealty and homage, and who as a condition of their tenure rendered services to their lord which included military service. Any lord with such tenants, from the king downwards, could hold a court for them; there was a hierarchy of such tribunals, of which the summit was that High Court summoned by the ruler himself in his capacity as the principal feudal lord, and attended by his direct tenants who included the greatest men in the land. There were, however, many Frankish laymen who held their property neither on feudal nor on servile terms, but usually by a money rent, and with a freedom to alienate that property which went with their freedom of status. Such Franks, who varied widely in wealth and social standing, were known in the Latin East as burgesses. The affairs of this group, too, were regulated by a separate body of law and customs in special burgess courts, presided over by an officer known as the viscount, of whom more will be said in the course of this chapter.

So much for the Europeans; what of the affairs of the native Syrians? Since the Franks were always a small minority of the population and, after the manner of their age, respected existing custom, it is not sur- prising to find that they left in existence arrangements and institutions which they found already in operation when they first occupied the country. The rural population lived in village communities, in each of which disputes were settled and decisions on matters of common concern were taken in a village court presided over by one of the older and more substantial members of the local community, who nowadays would be called the mukhtar, but then the rays. Not that the rays, or the courts over which they presided were confined to the countryside. There were similar arrangements for those Syrians who lived in towns. Both in town and country these courts exercised minor jurisdiction. Criminal charges which might involve a penalty of death or mutilation were passed to the burgess courts, and so were civil causes concerning property held by burgess tenure.

These courts for Syrians, together with those for ecclesiastics, for feudal tenants and for burgesses, covered the bulk of the population. There were as well courts with a more limited jurisdiction, especially in the seaports. There were privileged merchant communities, mainly Italian, with limited powers of jurisdiction, and the bodies which administered the harbours and some of the urban markets held courts to settle the disputes that arose there. The market court in Acre, indeed, came to absorb the court of the rays and this may have happened in other towns as well. The president of such a court was a Frank, and its decisions were taken by a mixed body of two Franks and four Syrians.

It is not easy for the general reader to form a picture of the courts in action. In the Law Books written in the thirteenth century, some by members of the baronage of Jerusalem and Cyprus, the specialist can find plentiful information about procedure and forms of pleading in the High Court and the burgess court. There has survived also an almost verbatim record of the learned arguments presented to the High Court when in 1264 it sat in judgement on a dispute relating to succession to the regency. The fundamental importance of the doctrines stated on this famous occasion was immediately recognized; hence their careful preservation. The famous History by William, Archbishop of Tyre, includes an account of the procedure followed in a major treason trial which came before the High Court in the 1130's. The court decided that the issue should be put to the proof of battle between accuser and accused.

We know from another impeccable source that the Franks brought many of their judicial procedures to the Levant. Usamah ibn Munqidh was born in 1095, the year in which Pope Urban II began to preach the First Crusade; when he died as a very old man, Saladin had reconquered Jerusalem. He was a cadet of a noble Arab family which ruled in Shaizar on the Orontes from 1081 until they were virtually wiped out in the shattering earthquake of 1157. From childhood therefore the Franks of Antioch were his neighbours, established as they then were in Qal'at al-Mudiq (Apamea) and in other places east of the Orontes. When as a teenager he first saw military action, they were the enemy. In times of truce, however, he met his social equals among them on friendly terms, and these occasions increased in number when he moved to Damascus. He served the rulers of that city in the years on either side of 1140 when they were in alliance with King Fulk, and Usamah was sent on more than one mission to the Latin kingdom. He knew the king, his court and his capital. The Franks interested him, and he had many friends among them. In old age he recorded his reminiscences, which can still be read with pleasure today, because they are based on his own keen observation of the world he knew and give us an insight into the character and customs of the Franks. Among the many lively anecdotes he relates, one describes a judicial duel which he had witnessed, another concerns a Moslem who had been subjected to the western ordeal by water.

In Latin Syria, therefore, as elsewhere in Latin Christendom, many agencies were engaged in operating the law. In some medieval western monarchies the king or prince became the most powerful of these agencies, and ultimately subordinated the rest to his control. England, Sicily and later, Capetian France, all provided royal success stories of this kind; Germany, Jerusalem and the other crusader states did not. This failure to set up effective monarchic government in the East was due mainly to the chances of politics and war. Edessa was destroyed and Antioch was progressively weakened not only by Turkish and Byzantine pressure but, in the early thirteenth century, by a long succession dispute. In Jerusalem, too, monarchy was weakened in the 1180's by conflicts about the succession and by the conquests of Saladin, then by a period of forty years of queens regnant and their various husbands, and finally by a further forty years of absentee Hohenstaufen kings.

In the East, therefore, monarchic government was not effectively established in the long run, but its eventual failure was not evident from the beginning. It began with many of the advantages possessed by successful monarchies in the West. Like those established by the Normans in England and of which they laid the foundations in Sicily during the thirty years which preceded the launching of the First Crusade, it was based on conquest. Those who became the first rulers of the Latin crusader states took the lead in the work of conquest and in organizing defence against Moslem counter-attacks. This enabled them, as it enabled the Conqueror in England and Count Roger in Sicily, to retain in their own hands lands and revenues to a degree which made them far wealthier than any of their subjects. This was particularly evident in the ample demesne reserved by the Norman princes of Antioch, while the kings of Jerusalem, in retaining Acre and two-thirds of Tyre, assured themselves of a large money income. Furthermore, they inherited and continued to use institutions which had proved themselves in the past. The courts of the rays, to which reference has already been made, provide one example. The office of dux in Antioch and in other towns in the north was taken over from the earlier Byzantine administration. Just as the Normans in England continued to operate the Anglo-Saxon courts of shire and hundred, and the Normans in Sicily to use Byzantine and Moslem officials, so did the crusaders in Syria and the Holy Land continue to use machinery and officials already available to deal with technical and sophisticated matters of which they had no experience, the administration of thriving seaports, for example, with all the complex business this entailed of fixing and collecting duty and customs payments, often reckoned *ad valorem*, and of providing judicial remedies for the disputes that inevitably arose.

With advantages of this kind, it is not surprising to find that monarchic rule was highly effective in the Latin East during the early and middle years of the twelfth century. In all four crusader states, the ruler played a masterful role in extending and defending the area under European control. In this early period they were less affected by rebellion and civil disorder than was any contemporary western ruler. They built up specifically monarchic powers which, in the Latin kingdom, were already formidable by the reign of Baldwin III, and perhaps even thirty years earlier in the reign of his grandfather. We know, for example, that the law recognized his power to deprive of their fiefs, without a court judgement, vassals found guilty of certain crimes. And it exercised this authority not in autocratic isolation, but in frequent consultation with the great vassals assembled in the High Court. It was medieval royal government as it was meant to work: strong direction from the top, yet collaboration with the people who mattered most.

Government in the Latin East failed to build on these promising foundations partly because of the political setbacks to which reference has been made, and partly because of its failure to develop at important points. Medieval government was widely decentralized. Not only the ruler but also feudal landlords and ecclesiastical dignitaries wielded enforceable authority, and reference has already been made to the wide dissemination of power to hold a court. The ruler, however, also had means to govern which were at his direct disposal. The household which served his domestic needs helped him also to meet his public responsibilities; and since these responsibilities were usually greater than those of even his greatest subjects, his princely household adapted themselves more rapidly and more extensively to meet them. Such growing activities in the public sphere could lead, as in England and Sicily in the twelfth century, and in France in the thirteenth, to a growing degree of specialization and professionalism in royal households, and even to the appearance of embryonic executive departments, especially for the transaction of financial and judicial matters. The English exchequer, the Sicilian *duana* and the French *parlement* and *chambre des comptes* are all cases in point.

Improved apparatus for the exercise of royal power developed not only in the central household, but also in the localities. Kings had always needed stewards and reeves on their estates, if only to collect their rents and other dues, and these estate agents could also be given public duties. In kingdoms where there was a close network of such officials, presiding over the king's courts and executing his commands, royal authority visibly existed everywhere side by side with the feudal. It could also compete with it, especially in the all-important field of jurisdiction. If kings reserved certain judicial matters for their own courts, as they did in France, or devised and monopolized better legal procedures, which were most attractive to litigants, as they did in England, then they competed with their feudatories for the powers and profits of jurisdiction from a position of strength.

None of these conditions ever worked, in the long run, to the advantage of rulers in the crusader states. They were each attended by a household, members of which were used in the work of government. To the highest offices in the household, which were often filled by the greatest men in the land, executive duties came to be attached. The seneschal was concerned with judicial matters, and the ruler's revenue; the constable, assisted by the marshal, held the highest military responsibility and, in the absence of the ruler, commanded the army; the chancellor presided over the secretariat which specialized in the production of formal written instruments – charters and treaties – at the highest level. All this closely resembled the apparatus then available to magnates, royal and non-royal, in western Europe. As already mentioned, some of the most precocious developed by way of specialization of function and growing professionalism, but those in the crusader states were among the many which did not. It is possible that, given time, they might have done so. Institutional advance at the centre of French royal government, to which that of Jerusalem is often compared, belongs to the thirteenth century, but by that time princely government in the crusader states had been bled by those political and military wounds to which reference has been made.

Nor were local conditions more favourable. The viscount in the kingdom of Jerusalem presiding over the court of burgesses has been compared to the English sheriff in the shire court. But there was a decisive difference. Every sheriff was a royal official and every shire court was an assembly which lay outside the feudal dimension, and for the working of which the king had made himself responsible. In Jerusalem, how-ever, the burgess court was a royal court and the viscount a royal officer only when these were established on royal demesne. A list given by the thirteenth-century baronial jurist, John of Ibelin, shows only four royal viscounts. The other thirty-three, together with the courts of burgesses over which they presided, were the responsibility of those feudal mag-nates in whose fiefs they lay. The network of royal officials, working in parallel and in competition with feudal officers was not available in the Latin East to promote the interests of kings and prince. Nor were those special royal procedures which elsewhere weighed in favour of the ruler competition for judicial business. After a promising beginning, the possibility of developing as other successful western monarchies developed withered away, and the reasons for this were partly political, partly institutional. As a result a state of affairs was reached in which crusader governments could neither control nor even hold their own against other organized groups in the community.

Such groups did not include the most highly organized of all in medieval society, the Roman Church. It is true that during the months which followed the conquest of Jerusalem by the First Crusade, a Latin Patriarch made a powerful bid to take over the Holy City and to found an ecclesiastical principality; but this attempt was scotched by King Baldwin I and was never effectively revived. Thereafter, in all the crusader states, there was in the main a long record of cooperation between *regnum* and *sacerdotium*. The part played by secular rulers in ecclesiastical appointments probably exceeded what was acceptable to the best churchmen of the day; but the clergy in the Levant accepted it, and the full theocratic claims of the Church were never consistently pressed in any of the crusader states. Sometimes there was friction, even violent quarrels, between individual princes and patriarchs, especially in Antioch in the time of Bohemond III and IV, and Frederick II in conflict with Pope Gregory IX met uncompromising opposition from the Latin Patriarch of Jerusalem. These, however, were all exceptions from the normal *modus vivendi.* Nor did Syrian Christians or Moslems threaten the ruler's authority except at times of successful Moslem invasion. The Frankish burgesses, too, were usually dependable as subjects, except during certain political episodes when some of them allied with baronial opponents of the government. The groups which gave rulers the greatest difficulty, and which they ultimately failed to master, were to be found among the baronage, the Military Orders and the privileged communities of foreign merchants. Something will be said of each in turn.

Every medieval ruler needed to maintain a balanced relationship with his greatest subjects. In a society in which land was the principal source of wealth and status, these were the major landlords, lay and ecclesiastical, who as a group could command resources which might challenge those of the ruler. And there was not only the ability to make such a challenge; in a feudalized society, law and custom gave the magnates, in certain circumstances, the right to do so. As vassals of the ruler, holding their lands as fiefs, they had obligations towards him as their lord; but feudal law and custom also gave them rights against him which he was bound to respect. If these rights were overridden, the vassals could lawfully take action to restore them. Most medieval government was limited, constitutional government, with a well-developed right of resistance.

The balance of power between the ruler on the one hand, and his principal tenants-in-chief on the other, was often a cardinal fact of medieval politics. It was a balance which could differ between one realm and another, and within any one realm could change through time. It has been emphasized already that in the crusader states the early rulers enjoyed some of the same advantages as had the Norman conquerors of England and Sicily, and signs appeared in the first half of the twelfth century that these rulers were masterful overlords with effective control over their vassals.

In the middle years of the century there was some evidence that the balance was changing. Baronial rebels more often challenged the ruler's authority; there were important changes in the law which favoured baronial interests; and soon after Amalric became king of Jerusalem in 1162, the opposition of the magnates forced him to put away his wife. The reign of this king is so full of contradictions that some historians have seen in it the attainment of the apogee of royal power, while others have identified in these years the final decisive tilt in favour of the baronage. The difficulty of reaching a verdict is well exemplified by the reign's most famous piece of legislation, the Assize on Liege Homage.

This arose from a situation in which Gerard of Sidon, one of the leading barons of the kingdom, arbitrarily ejected one of his vassals from his fief. The vassal complained that he had been punished without the judgement of his peers in Gerard's feudal court. The king took up his cause and, after a brief episode of civil war, compelled Gerard to reinstate him. There followed the Assize to which reference has just been made. All sub-vassals were given protection against arbitrary dis-possession in future, because the Assize introduced an innovation: in addition to the oath of homage they customarily took to their immediate lord, sub-vassals were now to take an oath of homage to the king which was to be liege-homage, more binding than any other. This new, direct link with the king also made them, in certain circumstances, members of his feudal court, that is, of the High Court of the kingdom, of which hitherto only the king's tenants-in-chief had been members.

It all looked like a notable advance in royal power. A magnate had been humbled, and means had been created whereby in future the king might ally with the sub-tenants against his own tenants-in-chief, and so subject the magnates to a kind of war on two fronts which had been waged to the profit of the monarchy in other parts of feudal Europe. But in Jerusalem such exciting possibilities were not to be realised in practice. There seems to have been too great a gulf between the magnates and their vassals, unbridged by any effective middle group. Although there were some individual exceptions, the sub-vassals as a whole never effectively became members of the High Court, which remained very much in the hands of the leading barons as an assembly in which they could co-ordinate their own resistance to the Crown. And there was one element in the Assize which they came to use against their suzerain: that no lord, be he even the king, could dispossess his vassal without judgement.

The political role of the magnates became increasingly evident in the kingdom during the troubled reign of Baldwin IV. A group of them resolutely opposed Guy of Lusignan both before and after Hattin. When Henry of Champagne became head of the government in 1192, and tried by his own arbitrary decision to send Aimery of Lusignan into exile, the magnates, assembled in the High Court, were ready to support

Aimery. In 1197 Aimery himself became king of Jerusalem and attempted in his turn to impose a similar sentence on Ralph of Tiberias. Once again the accused was backed up by his fellow magnates; on this occasion the Assize on Liege Homage was read at a session of the High Court and, in accordance with its provisions, the barons withdrew their service. Only Ralph's voluntary departure from the kingdom prevented a worse crisis.

The most serious collision was delayed until 1228, the year in which the western emperor, Frederick II, came to the East as a crusader. He bore the title of King of Jerusalem although, in the opinion of many in the East, he was only regent acting for the legitimate hereditary ruler, his newly-born son, Conrad. Frederick seems to have taken the view, which was not without foundation, that the kingdom needed strong govern-ment, but he attempted to impose it in a way certain to incite baronial opposition. In particular he tried to coerce the most powerful and respected of the barons, John of Ibelin, by depriving him without judgement of his fief of Beirut; and he followed this up by similarly ejecting from their fiefs some of John's principal supporters. Once again the Assize was invoked and the dispossessed were reinstated by force. But the attack on John of Ibelin continued. In 1231, after he had returned to Europe, Frederick sent to Syria a small but well-equipped military contingent under an imperial marshal, Richard Filangieri. The first main task it undertook was to besiege Beirut. The resistance that developed against Filangieri was led by John of Ibelin and other baronial figures, but it also drew in the burgesses, of whom something must now be said.

Reference has been made to the part played by burgesses in the ad-ministration of the law, by their work both in their own courts and in some of the market courts, and there had been occasions when the king of Jerusalem had associated some of the greatest of them in the solemn process of law-making. In the more agitated conditions of the thirteenth century some of them played a more active part in politics. This emerged earliest and most clearly in the principality of Antioch in times of military crisis. On two occasions during the twelfth century, in 1119 and 1149, when the army was annihilated and the prince killed in battle, the city of Antioch itself seemed to be in danger. On both occasions the Latin Patriarch took charge of the situation and organized the Frankish burgesses to defend the city if need be. In 1193 similar measures were given more durable and institutional form. Bohemond III had been kidnapped by Leo of Armenia, who sent a force to take over Antioch. Once again the Patriarch placed himself at the head of Frankish resistance, and those who rallied to him included knights and burgesses. On this occasion they formed a commune, that is, they bound themselves by a common oath to resist the Armenian occupation and to preserve the Norman line of princes. There is evidence that this sworn association remained in being for at least twentyfive years.

In Syria the commune was the child of political crisis, and political capitals were its birthplace. Such an organization had been formed during the last months of 1187 in Tyre, then the principal city of the kingdom still in Christian hands. In 1231 a commune came into existence in Acre, and in 1289 another in Tripoli. Except that they were sworn associations, they did not resemble the contemporary communes of western Europe. There the communal movement had been concerned with the government of towns and with the extent to which the leading citizens were to be concerned in that government. Often they were able to negotiate or purchase from the lord of the place the right to organize and control some part of the town's affairs. But if the lord refused to grant them any such facilities –and some lords, especially the ecclesiastical, were unwilling to contemplate change – then sometimes the citizens formed a sworn association, appointed officials, adopted a constitution, set up a treasury, assumed a seal and sought to achieve their aspirations by force and even bloody revolution.

There were no communes of this kind in Latin Syria, mainly because urban society was differently constituted. Towns were not, as in the West, communities of burgesses with the lord, like the feudatories generally, living outside it. Many of the feudal barons and knights, and in the thirteenth century most of them, were themselves town dwellers; important areas in the most important towns were immunities, conceded to the maritime republics of Italy and southern France. The Franks who were ranked as burgesses in the crusader states were not the sole inhabitants of the towns; they lived side by side with the indigenous population, both Christian and Moselm. This mixed society seems to have produced no craft gilds and no communal movements on the western model.

This does not mean that there were no gilds of other kinds. The society of medieval Christendom, wherever it existed, was characterized by a mass of voluntary organizations formed for religious and social purposes. It was such a fraternity that provided the framework for the commune in the Latin East of which most is known – that formed at Acre in 1232.

Something has been said of the arrival in Syria, in 1231, of Frederick's marshal, Richard Filangieri. It was Frederick's intention that Filangieri should represent him in the kingdom as his lieutenant, or *bailli*, and the marshal presented his credentials to an assembly at Acre which included not only magnates of the High Court, but knights and burgesses as well. Many were prepared to recognize him as *bailli*, but one obstacle to his general acceptance proved to be insurmountable. It was part of his mission to wrest Beirut by force from John of Ibelin. He had already taken the town, and the bulk of his forces were besieging the citadel. So flagrant a breach of the Assize on Liege Homage made him so many opponents that he was rejected as *bailli*.

This rejection was an act of resistance against the greatest temporal ruler in the Christian world. This crisis without precedent called for extraordinary measures, and action was quickly taken to mobilize all Franks who were prepared to defy imperial authority. How should they be organized? They did not think of themselves as revolutionaries, but as defenders of the law. So they shrank from revolutionary acts, but looked for some existing organization which they could use for their present purposes. They found it in a charitable gild, the Fraternity of Saint Andrew, which had officers, a seal, formal royal recognition and membership open to all. Within this prefabricated framework the barons, knights and burgesses opposed to Frederick set up in Acre a sworn association. They elected a mayor, who was John of Ibelin, and appointed a galaxy of subordinate officers.

The commune remained in existence for a long as Filangieri and his army were established in the country; after their expulsion in 1243 no more is heard of it. Historians differ as to whether it provided the government of Acre, and perhaps of other parts of the kingdom, during the 1230's, or whether it was no more than a means of organizing resistance to Frederick. In this second role it was certainly capable of rapid and decisive action. There was an occasion in 1233 when it seemed that Frederick might succeed after all in appointing one of the nominees as regent. But a young member of the Ibelin family gave the alarm, the tocsin was rung and members of the commune responded immediately to the alarm. There was an instant demonstration in the streets of Acre, with the crowd shouting 'Kill, kill!'

The movement against Frederick found recruits among the knights and burgesses, but it was mainly a victory for those barons who had inspired and organized it. After 1243, the main power in the government of the kingdom lay with the magnates assembled in the High Court. They were sometimes joined there by the heads of the Military Orders, the privileged merchant communities and the urban confraternities, an extension of the Court in which Professor Prawer sees the precocious beginnings of parliamentary development; but the nobility remained the leading element, and the absentee Hohenstaufen kings were unable to challenge them. Their absence, moreover, made necessary the appointment of regents, and on the numerous occasions when there were disputed claims to that office, the High Court established the right to adjudicate; and after 1268, when the Hohenstaufen line was extinguished, it was before this tribunal that the rival candidates for the crown argued their claims in due legal form.

The barons were men of action who won a military and political victory; they consolidated that victory, not only in legal forms, but in legal literature. Some were famous for their learning in the law and for their skill as practitioners in the courts, none more so than Bohemond IV of Antioch and Ralph of Tiberias. Others have won immortality as authors. Philip of Novara, client of the Ibelins and heroworshipper of the Old Lord of Beirut, was not only poet, historian and moralist, but compiled a major work on the laws of the kingdom. In this he was surpassed by the Old Lord's nephew, John of Jaffa, also a manysided figure. The books of Philip and John are the same kind of literature as that of the nearcontemporary Bracton in England, Beaumanoir in France and Eike von Repgow in Germany. The authors not only gave an account of the laws as they themselves understood them, but embodied their own views about the law, and gave those views a historical basis which, so far as Philip and John were concerned, was severely distorted. But the fame of their books led posterity to suppose that their baronial, highly partisan view of the constitution and its origins was the true one.

Historians have continued to believe that government in the Latin East was always characterized by weak rulers whose powers were from the beginning severely limited and, when necessary, successfully defied by their great vassals. Only during the last twenty years have historians, led by Professors Prawer and Richard, been able to reveal the very different state of affairs during that age of effective monarchic rule, the twelfth century. The barons of Jerusalem defeated the Hohenstaufen and for six hundred years misled posterity; such was the full extent of their victory. There have been uncountable references to them in discussions of medieval feudalism, yet until 1972 they were never studied in detail. This lacuna in the history of European society and institutions has now been admirably filled by Dr Riley-Smith's important book, *The feudal nobility and the kingdom of Jerusalem, 1174–1277.*

One baronial family has been mentioned frequently in these pages – the Ibelins. In their original homeland, now thought to be Italy, and even at first in the Latin kingdom, they were not magnates of the first rank. Subsequently they were favoured by what have always been the surest means to worldly fortune – a generous patron and prudent marriages. King Fulk first gave the head of the house the castle from which it later took its name. Even then the Ibelins were showing that irresistibility to heiresses and influential widows which carried them into the royal family and, in the thirteenth century, gave them an interest in every major fief in the kingdom. There is no space here to recount that history, but some of the salient points emerge from even a simplified

Table II   family tree.

Two other kinds of organization were at first subject to monarchic control, then eluded it – the Military Orders and the foreign merchants. The crusader states, and especially the Latin kingdom, annually drew pilgrims from all parts of the western world, and the needs of these pilgrims gave rise to new forms of the religious life. In the native land of Christ the Healer, men remembered particularly their duty to the poor and sick, and even before the First Crusade merchants from Amalfi had founded a monastery in Jerusalem, which in turn established a hospice for the care of pilgrims. This institution, under the same Master, continued in existence and was endowed both by Duke Godfrey and King Baldwin his brother. With the increased pilgrim traffic the work extended, especially its care of the sick, and its fame as a hospital spread. By 1113 it had received properties in western Europe, had set up hospices at western ports used by pilgrims, and had received its first major papal

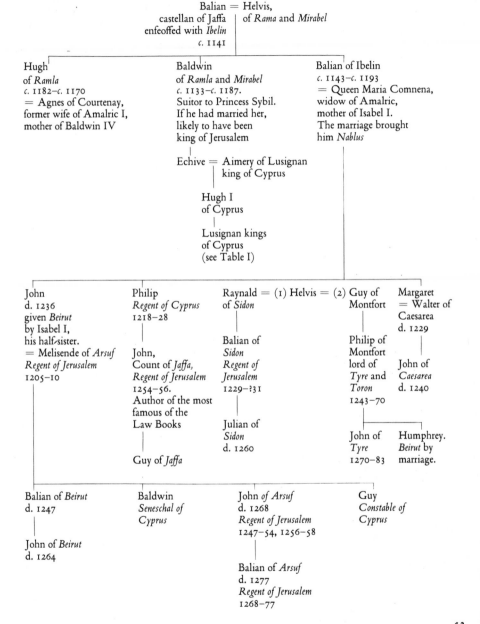

Balian = Helvis,
castellan of Jaffa | of *Rama* and *Mirabel*
enfeoffed with *Ibelin*
c. 1141

Hugh
of *Ramla*
c. 1182–*c.* 1170
= Agnes of Courtenay,
former wife of Amalric I,
mother of Baldwin IV

Baldwin
of *Ramla* and *Mirabel*
c. 1133–*c.* 1187.
Suitor to Princess Sybil.
If he had married her,
likely to have been
king of Jerusalem

Balian of Ibelin
c. 1143–*c.* 1193
= Queen Maria Comnena,
widow of Amalric,
mother of Isabel I.
The marriage brought
him *Nablus*

Echive = Aimery of Lusignan
king of Cyprus

Hugh I
of Cyprus

Lusignan kings
of Cyprus
(see Table I)

John
d. 1236
given *Beirut*
by Isabel I,
his half-sister.
= Melisende of *Arsuf*
Regent of Jerusalem
1205–10

Philip
Regent of Cyprus
1218–28

John,
Count of *Jaffa,*
Regent of Jerusalem
1254–56.
Author of the most
famous of the
Law Books

Guy of *Jaffa*

Raynald = (1) Helvis = (2) Guy of
of *Sidon*   Montfort

Balian of
Sidon
Regent of
Jerusalem
1229–?31

Julian of
Sidon
d. 1260

Philip of
Montfort
lord of
Tyre and
Toron
1243–70

John of
Tyre
1270–83

Margaret
= Walter of
Caesarea
d. 1229

John of
Caesarea
d. 1240

Humphrey.
Beirut by
marriage.

Balian of *Beirut*
d. 1247

John of Beirut
d. 1264

Baldwin
Seneschal of
Cyprus

John *of Arsuf*
d. 1268
Regent of Jerusalem
1247–54, 1256–58

Balian of *Arsuf*
d. 1277
Regent of Jerusalem
1268–77

Guy
Constable of
Cyprus

privilege, confirming the Master's control of its European possessions. During the first half of the twelfth century it acquired its first Rule, and a new international Order of the Church had come into existence. Its professed members, both priests and laymen, took monastic vows, but their work was in the world, serving the sick poor, and especially pilgrims. The Master and the principal House of the Order were to be found in Jerusalem.

Pilgrims needed not only medical care but physical protection. They might need this even in the Holy Land, especially when the Franks had not yet completely subdued it, and the Moslem garrisons of Tyre and Ascalon could still make the roads unsafe. In 1118 two knights pledged themselves to police the road between Jaffa and Jerusalem. Others joined them and the pious work gained them powerful friends. The first palace of the Latin kings of Jerusalem had been at the southern end of the Temple area, in buildings by the Aqsa Mosque, called 'Solomon's Temple' by many Franks. King Baldwin II moved his residence to an area (part of which is now being excavated in the Armenian Patriarch's garden) once occupied by Herod's palace, in the neighbourhood of the Tower of David. On moving house he gave the premises he was vacating to the new company of knights, who took their name from their new habitat, and became famous throughout the Christian and Moslem worlds as the Knights of the Temple, or Knights Templar. Their total dedication to a Christian cause attracted the enthusiasm of St Bernard, who eulogized them in a literary masterpiece, which spread their fame and brought them new recruits. Like the brethren of the Hospital, they too were quickly internationally organized and endowed, lived according to a Rule, were patronized by Popes, who confirmed them in their role and possessions.

Hospitallers and Templars developed in parallel during the earlier half of the twelfth century. The main difference between them lay in the military role possessed by the Templars from the beginning, and which at first the Hospital must have lacked. The Templars began as a body of knights, the Hospitallers did not. But just as in the thirteenth century the two main Orders of Friars, after different beginnings, came in the course of time more and more to resemble each other, so too the Templars and Hospitallers. As early as 1136 the Hospital accepted custody from King Fulk of his newly fortified castle at Beit Jibrin, and in 1144 they were granted a number of strong places by the count of Tripoli, including a castle that was to become known as the Krak des Chevaliers, which they would make the most splendid building of its kind in the world.

The acceptance of these responsibilities does not necessarily mean that the Hospital was already militarized in the sense that the Order included at this early date knights and serjeants. A brother knight is not mentioned in a Hospitaller document before 1148, while the first statutes in which the Order appears as an organization based on knights and serjeants belongs to the years 1204–06. It is possible that in the twelfth century, and especially in its earlier half, the military forces organized by the Order were composed, wholly or in part, of mercenaries. Whatever the form of their organization, there is no doubt that their military capabilities rapidly increased in the second half of the century. In 1157 they organized a column for the relief of Banyas; in 1168 they were able to promise King Amalric that they would provide 500 well-equipped knights and as many lighter-armed horsemen, known as Turcopoles, for an expedition into Egypt. Such a contingent would have been larger than the Latin kings often took on campaign.

The Hospitallers had military responsibilities, no matter how they discharged them, from the 1130's, and the earliest military activities of the Templars are recorded from the same period. They took charge of their first castle – Gaza – in 1145. During the Second Crusade they were prominent in the fighting march of the French across Asia Minor in 1147. They were equally prominent in the siege of Ascalon in 1153. From this time the armed contingents put into the field by the Military Orders became increasingly important to the military effort of which the Latin East was capable. Well before the end of the twelfth century, and throughout the thirteenth, their military contribution was indispensable.

This fact alone was enough to make the Masters of the Military Orders figures of major importance in the politics of the kingdom. The powers allowed the Master by the Rule, though not absolute, were considerable. He had behind him, and could throw into the political balance, the weight of a highly organized, immensely wealthy organization. The part played by one Master of the Temple, Gerard of Ridefort, in the last days of the first Latin kingdom, and by another, William of Beaujeu, in the last days of the second, are familiar episodes in crusading history. As time passed, the position of the Orders in all the Latin states became relatively stronger. The rulers became less effective, members of the baronage were often at odds with each other, some of them, though not the greatest, became poorer. Already in the twelfth century the Orders were buying in lands and castles from laymen too improverished to maintain and defend them. In the thirteenth not only some of the main castles, especially in Antioch and Tripoli, but some of the main towns as well, Tartus, Safad, Ascalon, came into the Orders' possession.

In these circumstances no other authority or group in Outremer could control them. Even in the twelfth century, when the Orders had not yet grown to their full stature, and when they existed within a system still effectively controlled by royal and princely power, they had striven for a measure of independent action: in both Antioch and Tripoli it was conceded to them that truces they made with their Moslem neighbours should be respected by the prince, though they need not observe truces negotiated by him. Such aspirations were not fully achieved in the days of the first kingdom. Amalric could hang twelve Templars whom he thought to be in dereliction of their duty in failing to defend a castle, and could give serious thought to a project for suppressing the Order. But in the thirteenth century, with absentee rulers in Jerusalem and Antioch, with regents whose authority was often under challenge, with an often divided baronage, none could discipline the Orders. The Hospitallers based on Marqab and Krak could make war and take tribute from their Moslem neighbours as if they were sovereign powers. The Templars could adhere to a treaty with the Ayyubid prince in Damascus, directed against Egypt, at a time when the leaders of a crusade, supported by the Hospitallers, could make a treaty with Egypt directed against Damascus. In this way they could contribute to the division, and so help to weaken, the Latin settlement. At the same time no other organizations were so dedicated to preserving it. This is a point to which we must return.

Other Military Orders were founded in the Holy Land; that of St Thomas of Canterbury was made up mainly of English knights, while St Lazarus was for knights stricken with leprosy. All but one were small organizations which did not compare with the Temple and Hospital in wealth and importance; the exception was the Teutonic Order. When the forces of the Third Crusade were besieging Acre, men from Lübeck and Bremen set up a hospital for the care of German pilgrims. This

enterprise outlasted the siege and became the nucleus of a larger organization which, in 1198, was formally constituted as a Military Order.
This action was taken when a German crusade, despatched by the
Emperor Henry VI, was in the Latin kingdom, and from the first the
new Order was, in a number of ways significantly different from the
rest. It was not international in character, but was for German knights;
it served to promote Hohenstaufen interest in the Levant, and it maintained close connections with that monarchy. It came to be well endowed
in Galilee, where the knights built and developed Montfort as their
principal castle and, later in the thirteenth century, in the kingdom of
Armenia; but from early in its existence it was looking for other areas in
which to settle and govern, briefly in Hungary and then, for the rest of
its existence, in Prussia.

The crusading movement was launched at the end of a century in
which western Europeans, so long under Moslem pressure, had themselves gone over to the attack, not only in Spain and Sicily, but on the
waters of the Mediterranean. This maritime offensive was part of a
commercial expansion led from Venice, Genoa and Pisa. At a time when
they were beginning to make new trading connections in all parts of the
Mediterranean – western European, Moslem, Byzantine – they saw fresh
opportunities in the crusade. They were there from the first. The crews
of a small Genoese squadron helped in the sieges of Antioch and
Jerusalem. In the autumn of 1099, little more than two months after
Jerusalem had been taken, a large Pisan fleet appeared in Syrian waters.
It was followed next year by that of the Venetians, and the year after that
by the Genoese, who were there again in 1104.

These fleets were essential to the extension of the Latin conquest.
Without them the seaports could not have been blockaded and reduced.
But why did the Italians sail eastwards in such force and in such quick
succession? In part because they were moved by the preaching of the
crusade, but in part because of the new opportunities it provided for
commercial enterprise. In the eastern Mediterranean there were markets
in which they could buy, for import into Europe, highly valued products
of the Far East. These came into western Asia by way of those arms
of the sea and major rivers along which they were drawn to the great
religious, political and commercial capitals. By way of the Persian Gulf
and the Red Sea, the Euphrates and the Nile they came to Baghdad,

Fig. 1

Cairo and Alexandria. Thence they were transported by river between Baghdad and Raqqa, or by trading caravan through the desert to Damascus, Aleppo and the cities on the Orontes, and ultimately to the Syrian ports.

Some light is thrown by a variety of documents from the crusader period on the commercial interests of European traders in these ports. Notarial records in Genoa include some particularly fine series of commercial contracts of the twelfth and thirteenth centuries; maritime legislation includes an informative Venetian sea statute of 1233; tariffs of duties payable in certain ports on commodities of the Syrian trade have survived; that for Acre, included in the 1240's in the *Livre des Assises des Bourgeois* gives the rate of duty on more than a hundred items. We know something, therefore, of the goods most in demand by European traders. Always high on the list were condiments to temper the rigours of the medieval European cuisine, especially sugar, loaf and granulated, some of which was grown and processed in the crusader states. Still more important was pepper. The Genoese historian who described the part played by his fellow citizens in the conquest of Caesarea in 1101 particularly recorded that, from the spoils of war, each of them received two pounds of pepper; and there was a time in the twelfth century when pepper in Genoa became almost an alternative currency, used for gifts, dowries, endowments, loans, payments of all kinds. Other culinary spices included ginger, nutmeg, cloves, cardamon, cinnamon. Closely allied to flavours were not only perfumes, like musk and the resin from aloes – some of them liturgical necessities, like frankincense and myrrh – but also natural products used in the preparation of drugs; galingale, indeed, might appear equally in the recipe book or in the pharmacopoeia. Other medicinal substances included camphor, ammoniac, senna, arsenic, borage and zedoary. The dyers were an important element in western cloth manufacture; for them were bought brazil-wood, sandal-wood, gum lac and alum. Other highly priced products included ivory and costly fabrics, damasks, camlets and silks.

In return for the naval help they gave the rulers of Latin Syria, the Italians charged a price which enabled them to extract the maximum trading profit from the conquests. The early history of the three maritime crusader states is punctuated by a series of treaties with the Italians. The documents differ in detail, but all embody the main advantages sought by the merchants. They wanted, in the first place, to be able to trade in favourable conditions. They wanted in particular to be able to keep their costs to a minimum, and so they bargained for as much exemption as they could get from the charges which governments have always laid on merchants – import and export duties, customs payments, harbour taxes. At a time when weights and measures varied in accuracy, they wanted to be able to use their own. In order to offset the disadvantages of trading in a strange land, they wanted to be able to do so not as individuals, but as a community. They sought the concession of a territorial area in which they could have their own quaysides, warehouses and communal services – church, bath-house, abattoir, public oven. They did all they could to acquire the right to police and administer the area so conceded. They needed protection against the hazards of litigation in a foreign land, where unfamiliarity with the language, law and procedure in the courts might put them at a serious disadvantage. They sought to negotiate, therefore, the privilege of pleading before their own tribunals in as many foreseeable circumstances as possible.

The territorial areas conceded them were often considerable. By the treaty which preceded the conquest of Tyre in 1124 they were given one-third both of the city and of the villages in the surrounding country-side. Even earlier, the Genoese had acquired the whole town and port of Jebail in the county of Tripoli. In all the coastal towns which mattered to them the foundation had been laid of communities largely immune from the operations of the government which had granted the immunity and the inhabitants of which were therefore less answerable to its authority than the bulk of the population. Once again, the consequences of this were more serious in the thirteenth century than in the twelfth. In the earlier period, the urban governments in Italy were unable to exercise effective direct control over their Syrian concessions; therefore they enfeoffed or leased them. Nor were connections between Italy and Syria continuous; the Genoese records show that trading voyages were irregular and were the concern of comparatively few investors. It has been said already that the Italian cities active in the crusader states were equally active in other parts of the Mediterranean. They successfully established themselves in Alexandria, for example, where they could buy the same Far Eastern luxuries as in Acre or Tyre, but in greater abundance and presumably at a lower price.

It is possible to argue that the grants made to them in the crusader states were of little use, since there were better markets open to them in Egypt and the Byzantine Empire; but the high value they placed on their privileged position in Latin Syria is shown by their constant efforts to extend it and by the major efforts they were ready to make to recover their losses to Saladin. The naval help they gave during the Third Crusade led to a fresh series of grants, and during the period of the second Latin kingdom they were more firmly established than ever in the coastal towns, and especially in Acre, the kingdom's commercial and political capital.

In the thirteenth century the character of the Italian commercial colonies was different from that in the twelfth, and so too was their role in the affairs of the Latin states. The connection between the colonies and their mother city was far closer. Gone were the leases and enfeoffments of the earlier period. The Italian communities in Syria were administered by consuls, appointed, controlled and frequently changed by the city government in Italy. Trading voyages were now annual; a far larger number of citizens invested in them. Many more went to Syria not only as traders, but as servants and craftsmen, with the intention of spending a number of years there, before returning to Italy.

Closer connection with and control from Italy meant that the colonies were more directly affected by the politics and diplomacy of the mother city. War between Genoa and Pisa usually meant war between those Genoese and Pisans who, afloat or ashore, were in Syria and its waters, with increasingly disruptive effects on the Latin states. As with the Military Orders, so with the privileged merchant communities. In the twelfth century they existed within the framework established by the secular rulers and especially by the Latin kings. Since their connections with Italy were tenuous, they lacked the power, as well as the wish, to disregard or defy constituted authority in Latin Syria. But in the thirteenth century, when that authority was much reduced, when the privileged communities were more populous and powerfully organized, when they felt themselves part of and subject to Italian city states which were themselves Mediterranean powers, the needs of the Latin states took second place to the ambitions of the commercial empires of which they were part.

Such were the principal European groups in the crusader states – the secular government, the major and minor feudatories, the established

Latin Church, the Frankish laity who were neither feudatories nor serfs, the Military Orders, the exempt merchant communities. All these were always a minority of the population; what were their relations with the majority?

These indigenous communities had been established in that country too long for their customs and institutions to be easily changed, and the Franks were too small a group to bring such changes about. To do so by force was certainly beyond them, the more so because all the force they could muster was too often needed against the external enemy. There is no evidence, except perhaps in the very earliest years, that they ever contemplated such a solution. They showed the normal medieval respect for what was customary and established. An example of that conservatism has been given earlier in this chapter, during the discussion of a matter fundamental to all government, and especially to medieval government – the application of the law to matters of everyday life. In the villages this was left in the hands of rays and elders; and if the new Frankish landlords loomed large in village life, then so for centuries past had their Turkish, Arab and Byzantine predecessors. There is no more attractive feature of the crusader regime than their respect, so evident in the law books, for local communities and their customs, and their concern that they should participate in the all-important business of making the law work. It cannot be too strongly emphasized, however, that, with rare exceptions, their participation was limited to the lower echelons of that society. The highest powers in legal and public affairs never passed outside the wealthiest and best organized groups of the European minority – the secular rulers and their households, the baronage, the episcopate, the Military Orders and the privileged merchants.

The law books say, 'In the *Cour de la Fonde* these people shall take the oath thus: the Jew, on the Torah; the Moslem, on the Koran; the Armenian, the Syrian and the Greek on the Cross and on the gospels written in their script; the Samaritan, on the Pentateuch; those of other religions, on the holy books of that religion.' When the authors of the law books mentioned the whole society in the crusader states to which the laws applied, they commonly did so in terms of a list which constantly recurs – *Suriens, Judes, Sarasins, Samaritans, Nestorins, Grifons, Jacopins, Ermines*. In other words, the Franks thought of their subjects in terms of religious communities, Christians, Moslems, Jews and Samaritans. The first-named were not of one Church, but of many. Centuries before the crusades the Christians of Asia and North Africa had fallen apart on a number of theological and metaphysical problems of great complexity, and especially on that of the relation between the human and divine elements in Christ's nature. Religious and political unity were so closely associated that the East Roman emperors had a particular interest in averting doctrinal schism. From the fourth century into the eighth a series of General Councils of the Church were held so that orthodoxy might be declared and preserved (it will be seen that during the crusader period these were recorded in mosaic at Bethlehem); but these efforts were not enough to keep Christians within one fold. Among the individuals who were unreconcilable dissidents from official policy, some attracted followers who formed a Church; such were Nestorius and Jacob Baradaeus. Sometimes regional or ethnic groups rejected the authority of Council and emperor and went their own way, again as a separate Church – Armenians, Copts, Georgians, the Maronites in the Lebanon.

Down to the seventh century, when Syria and the Holy Land were still Byzantine provinces, all the inhabitants were Christian and were members either of one of the dissident Churches, or still maintained their religious allegiance to Constantinople and to the supreme ecclesiastical authority of its emperor and patriarch. During the centuries following the Arab conquests there were two gradual developments: large-scale conversion to Islam and the spread of Arabic as the prevailing colloquial language. There remained, and remain, a multiplicity of liturgical languages: just as Europeans, whatever their vernacular language, then heard Latin in church, so Arabic-speaking Syrian Christians heard Syriac or Greek.

Although the leaders of the First Crusade initially regarded all eastern Christians as heretics, the western settlers never attempted persecution or coercion. The Church over which they probably exercised the greatest degree of control was the Greek. Many Latins regarded the Greeks as Christians who ought rightfully to be in communion with, and therefore subject to, the Roman Church. Certainly many Greek hierarchs were replaced by Latin; the patriarchs of Antioch and Jerusalem provide the principal examples, and in many places and at many times Greek clergy and laity must have been subordinated to the Latin hierarchy. The picture is far from clear, however, because Greek bishops are sometimes mentioned in the records of the crusader states; we hear, for example, of the Greek bishops of Gaza, Sidon and Acre. Was there an unbroken succession of such prelates, or could they establish themselves only when the crusaders' relations with Byzantium were particularly friendly, as in the time of Amalric I, or when Byzantine pressure on the crusader states was particularly severe, as it was on Antioch in 1138 and 1158? We need to know more in detail about the status of the Greek clergy and their congregations in the crusader states, and their relationship with the Latin rulers. We know in general that, though there were difficulties, the relationship worked well enough. In crusader Antioch, the large Greek community played a constructive part in the city's affairs, especially in the thirteenth century. It will be seen in a later chapter how closely Latins and Greeks cooperated to transform the interior of the Church of the Nativity in Bethlehem.

As for the other eastern Churches, their members were subject to Frankish government, and therefore their clergy were in a sense subordinate to the Latin; at the same time the crusaders recognized that they were separate and autonomous, and soon came to accept them as facts in their new life. Armenians, Jacobites and the rest were fellow Christians among whom the western settlers lived and with whom they freely intermarried for nearly two hundred years. Hereditary succession in the royal house of Jerusalem was first secured by an Armenian, and later continued by a Greek, marriage. It is no surprise to find in the records, therefore, many examples of harmonious relations between Latin and eastern Christians. Michael the Syrian, historian and Jacobite Patriarch, was cordially received in Jerusalem by Latin king and clergy; Meletos the Syrian, described in a charter as 'Archbishop of the Syrians and Greeks' in the region of Gaza and Beit Jibrin, and who is associated with the Hospitallers as a confrater, received a gift from the Master of that Order; on the intervention of Queen Melisende, judgement in a property dispute was made in favour of the Jacobite Metropolitan. Greek monasteries continued to flourish on Mount Carmel, Mount Tabor and in the Judean desert. Masons and sculptors were busy in twelfth-century Jerusalem not only at the Church of the Holy Sepulchre but at the Armenian Cathedral of St James the Great.

Friendly co-existence was no mere superficiality. It could raise hopes of reunion which in the 1180's were shown to be more than a Utopian dream when the Maronites, some 40,000 in number, entered into communion with Rome, and so remain. In 1198 the Armenian Church followed the same course although, as a calculated move in an unstable international political situation, it did not last. The Jacobites considered the possibility, and in the 1230's their patriarch made a profession of obedience to the Pope; but he could not carry his fellow hierarchs with him, much less his Church as a whole.

In the sphere of secular activity, some eastern Christians gave important military assistance in establishing and maintaining the crusader states. The fame of the Maronites as archers may well have played its part in drawing them closer to the Franks and Rome. The first Baldwin's creation of the county of Edessa at the head of so small a Frankish retinue is to be explained only by the strong Armenian support he received, and the same is true, though to a lesser extent, of the principality of Antioch. And throughout the crusader occupation there were no doubt many Syrian Christians who served the Franks among the infantry or the Turcopoles. It is known that many of these were Syrians, or were born of one Syrian and one Frankish parent.

Between eastern and western Christians in the crusader states there came to be bonds of many kinds. But there could also be serious friction. This was particularly the case in the early days when the eastern Churches were deprived of buildings and sources of income by their new masters; it was circumstances such as these that caused relationships to become strained and the native Syrians to think of the Franks as aliens, heretics and oppressors. There were also westerners, especially newcomers (a few exist still) who were antipathetic to Levantine men and manners, to whom the eastern Mediterranean peoples were supple, untrustworthy opportunists, effeminate, unprincipled, militarily useless. Such sentiments might well reflect the exasperation of Europeans outwitted in the market place, or unable to understand why foreigners whom they ruled should be less than enthusiastic in fighting their battles; but they were repeatedly expressed, and not only by excitable writers with a taste for invective like James of Vitry; they are not entirely absent from the pages of so sober an observer as William of Tyre, who was himself a native of Latin Syria.

When community relations deteriorated, the consequences for the Franks could be serious because all eastern Christians had centres of loyalty outside the crusader states. In the Taurus ranges Armenian leaders established principalities beyond crusader control. By the end of the twelfth century these had become a kingdom, whose history in the thirteenth was much involved with that of crusader Antioch, but which was independent of it. Armenians under Frankish rule could look to an Armenian king, just as Greek Christians could look to a Byzantine emperor in Constantinople or Nicæa. The communities of Nestorians, Jacobites and Copts outside the crusader states were more numerous and important than those inside. Their primates and patriarchs usually lived in lands under Moslem rule, and were more experienced in dealing with Moslem governments and in securing concessions from them than with any other.

This is a point of major importance which connects with another. Not only had Syrian Christians lived under tolerant Moslem rule for centuries, they had lived among Moslems as well. Though a common Christianity might link them with the Franks, they were at one with their non-Christian neighbours of long standing in everything else – habits, customs, common memories, language. Throughout the Christian era, and for centuries before that, they had lived under a succession of imperial masters, of whom the most recent had been Moslems, and they could contemplate with equanimity the prospect of doing so again. They lived peaceably enough under crusader rule, and many of them assisted it; but they were not as a whole fully committed to it, and would certainly not risk everything in its defence.

Much of this could also be said of the Franks' Moslem subjects. Like their Christian neighbours, many of them were peasants, accustomed to a succession of rulers and landlords. They found the Franks to be no worse than their predecessors in either capacity, and we have it from Ibn Jubair, a Moslem pilgrim who crossed crusader territory on his way from Damascus to Acre in 1184, that in Galilee men of his own religion regarded their Frankish landlords as milder and more benevolent than the Moslem. The comment provides only hearsay evidence relating to a small area at a particular time, but it does not go entirely unsupported. Usamah ibn Munqidh, who was closely acquainted with the Franks over a long period, tells us that Franks long settled in the country, in contrast with those newly-arrived, could treat Moslems with courtesy and understanding, even to the extent of showing consideration for their religious needs. But his examples of friendship between Moslems and Christians are nearly all drawn from the ruling social groups, from the world of seigneurs, amirs and their knightly retinues, with their common interest in bloodstock and the most skilled pursuits of the well-mounted gentleman – combat and the chase. Of the Moslem population as a whole it has to be said, as of the Christian, that in normal times they submitted to Frankish rule. But when that rule was threatened, they did not stake everything in its defence. They either remained passive or gave their support to the Moslem conqueror.

Amalric I, the fifth Latin king and the second to be born in the East, appointed as his personal doctor a Moslem recommended to him by the caliph of Egypt. He chose that doctor's son to be riding-master to his own heir, Prince Baldwin, whose academic education was directed by William of Tyre. There is no reason to suppose that these Moslem court officials, one of them in a position of the highest trust, gave the royal family anything else than their skilled and devoted service; but while they were doing so they remained in contact with Saladin and his circle, and when Saladin reconquered Jerusalem, they continued to live there under his patronage. No case history could illustrate more sharply the equivocal position of those Syrians subject to crusader rule.

Town and Country

Many crusaders came from regions of Europe far from the Mediterranean and where, at the end of the eleventh century, town life scarcely existed; in Palestine and Syria it had been unbroken for millennia. The life of the Europeans who settled there was much more centred on towns than it would have been in the West and this urbanization was assisted by two other developments – first, the trading activities of the Italian merchants, who made some of the Syrian ports, and especially Acre, commercial centres of international importance; second, the territorial losses to the Zengids, to Saladin and the Mamluks which deprived the Franks of rural territories, made their hold on the countryside increasingly pre-carious, and drove an increasing proportion of them behind town walls.

The visitor to the Near East can still form some idea of what those towns were like. Some medieval sites are not yet swallowed up in modern conurbations. From west of the Orontes it is still possible to see the immense circuit, from the river to the summit of Mount Silpius, on which the Byzantine walls of Antioch once stood, and on which they survived, in large part, until the nineteenth century. The modern town, which covers only a fraction of the ancient site enclosed by the wall, is probably rather smaller than its crusader predecessor. Tyre, standing on the former island which, since Alexander's siege, has been joined to the mainland, has also shrunk since it was the seat of Archbishop William, in days when one-third of it was held by the Venetians; but it is not difficult to see the size and sort of place it was in the twelfth and thirteenth centuries, nor to form an idea, helped by medieval descriptions, of its physical appearance. And the same is true of Acre.

The process can be further assisted by material remains. At Tartus and Jebail, to mention two of many possible examples, stretches of the crusader town walls still stand a few courses above ground. We can still see the trace of the rectangular towers which projected from them, and of the gateways by which they were entered. At both towns the crusader cathedral has survived, and something remains of the citadel, more at Jebail than at Tartus. In addition there is at Jebail the small harbour

Plate 7

67

which the Genoese must at one time have hoped to develop, and at Tartus fragmentary remains of the superb conventual buildings of the Templars.

Fig. 4

At both towns these features stand among modern buildings; at Caesarea they can be seen on a now deserted site. There the crusader town stands within the limits of the city built by Herod the Great in honour of his friend Augustus, of which the aqueducts and the amphitheatre still survive. The site has for centuries been littered with so great a profusion of marble columns that they have since been re-used at many other points on the neighbouring coast, and especially in Acre. At Caesarea the crusaders used them in quantity as the foundations of a mole in their harbour, and nearly a hundred of them are still visible on the sea-bed.

The crusader town occupied only a small part of the area once covered by Herod's splendid city. Much of it has been buried for centuries beneath the sand dunes and a major clearance which began in 1960 has more fully uncovered some of its civil and military features.

Plate 1

Within the town parts of two streets have been cleared, and the ground plan of some of the small shops and houses exposed. One of these streets ran beneath a succession of stone arches, between which awnings could be stretched to provide shade from the full glare of the sun. To this evidence of daily life in crusader Caesarea can be added the ground plan of its archiepiscopal cathedral, with its triple eastern apses still standing to a height of some four metres, and the rocky outcrop on the water's edge which was the site of the citadel.

Most of the recent work has been done on the defences. The fosse immediately outside the town walls has been cleared down to the paving stones which mark its thirteenth-century depth, so that those walls can

Plate 2

now be seen to their full surviving height. They now lack rampart walk and crenellation, but everything that remains is part of the reconstruction begun on the orders of St Louis in May, 1251; examination of the masonry shows, however, that the line on which they stand is older. The north and south walls run inland nearly 300 metres from the sea-shore; the eastern wall, parallel to the coast, is twice as long; to the west the town was protected by the sea. The line of the curtain wall was strengthened by projecting, broad-faced towers of rectangular plan. There were plenty of them: one at the northeast and another at the southeast angle,

Fig. 4 Caesarea. Plan of the crusader town's visible remains. (After M. Benvenisti)

and on the intervening 550 metres of the eastern wall another eight. Of these, the largest was also a gatehouse, containing the main entrance to the town. Approached by a bridge over the fosse, the outer gateway was in the northern flank of the tower. This gave access to a handsome entrance, divided into three rib-vaulted bays; entry into the town was made through an inner portal at right angles to the outer. A gatehouse in the north wall likewise imposed a sharp right turn on those entering the town. The task of an attacker was also made more severe by the pronounced batter of the lowest courses of curtain wall and towers to a height of some twelve feet above the floor of the ditch.

Visible urban links with the medieval past are strongest in Jerusalem. The present walls are mostly of the sixteenth century and were built at the order of Suleiman the Magnificent; but, with small exceptions, they

Plate 3

69

70

Fig. 5   Jerusalem. Plan of the Old City. A Church of the Holy Sepulchre;
B Hospitallers' convent; C Citadel and Tower of David; D Dome of the
Rock (Templum Domini); E Aqsa Mosque (Templum Solomonis), Temp-
lars' convent; F Abbey of Mount Zion. (After M. Benvenisti)

stand on the line, and perhaps on the foundations, of much older walls, and must present much the same aspect as those of the twelfth century. The area of the medieval citadel, which occupied much of the site of Herod's palace, is still preserved, and so is that citadel's donjon, the Tower of David, raised on the lower courses of one of Herod's towers. Within the city, then as now, the Dome of the Rock dominated the Temple area. Then as now, pilgrims from all over the Christian world flocked to Christ's tomb, housed in buildings which are discussed in a later chapter. Then as now, the main streets through the Old City, from the Jaffa Gate towards the Golden Gate, and from the Damascus Gate to Mount Zion, were those of the Roman military colony, established by the Emperor Hadrian early in the second century A D. Among the histories of the Latin East written in French in the thirteenth century, and used as continuations of the French translation of William of Tyre's great work, there are some which contain a description of Jerusalem before its loss to Saladin. It is easy to follow the medieval writer from street to street as they existed in his time and as they still exist in ours. It is possible to fix the location of the specialized markets for corn, fish, poultry, herbs and fruits, and of the streets where pilgrims could be washed and shaved, and buy a cooked meal – in Malquisinat, the Street of Bad Cookery. There were also shop-keepers and craftsmen in more lucrative lines of business: there were streets in which money could be changed, textiles sold, and where goldsmiths exercised their art.

Fig. 5

It must have been from among those Franks who rose to affluence by providing for the pilgrims and for wealthy patrons who, in the twelfth century, were concentrated in Jerusalem as nowhere else in Latin Syria, that those burgesses were drawn who feasted the king on his coronation day and who from time to time played a part in great matters of state. Until 1187 Jerusalem was a capital. Medieval kings and their households were constantly on the move, but the kings of Jerusalem seem to have spent more time in their palace in the Holy City than at any other place in the realm. It was the focal point for some of the most powerful organizations in the kingdom – the Latin Patriarch, the canons of the Holy Sepulchre, the Hospitallers and Templars. These latter were established at the southern end of the Temple area itself. The conventual building of the Hospitallers which, except for St John's church, have not survived, lay immediately south of the Church of the Holy Sepulchre.

In and around the city were other religious communities, internationally famous and internationally endowed.

Jerusalem was often the scene of great occasions in Church and State. Annually on Palm Sunday a solemn procession made its way from the Mount of Olives, down into the Kidron valley and up into the Temple area of the Old City by way of the Golden Gate, which in the course of each year was opened only on this occasion and again on Holy Cross Day. On Easter Saturday a crowd gathered in the Church of the Holy Sepulchre, as they do still, for the miracle of the Holy Fire, when the lamps in the Sepulchre are believed to be lit, not by human agency, but by a flame sent down from heaven. Some westerners suspected clerical sleight of hand even then, and in the thirteenth century Pope Gregory IX denounced it; but even if it be thought, to use a recent phrase, 'a piece of pyrotechnic nonsense', no one who has looked down on the scene from the upper galleries of the church can forget the mounting fervour and excitement as the moment is awaited when the sacred flame is brought from the Sepulchre, followed by the rapid spreading in the dimness of tiny points of light as the devout ignite their candles from it and from each other's. In the same church, from 1131 until 1186, the kings of Jerusalem and their consorts were anointed and crowned. After the solemn ritual they came from the church in a procession which passed through the narrow streets to the Dome of the Rock, regarded by most Franks as the Temple known to our Lord, where the king offered his crown at the altar and then, with a princely gift, redeemed it. Finally the procession crossed the paved courtyard of the Temple area to its southern end where, in buildings adjoining the Aqsa Mosque, which had been the royal palace but became the Templar convent, the coronation banquet was held, with the leading Frankish burgesses of the city waiting on the king.

Jerusalem was never an international trading centre, so that Italian merchants were not entrenched there as they were in the major seaports, but the city was unique in its magnetism for Christian pilgrims. Something is said in other chapters of the pilgrims' part in the life of the Latin East, of the burgesses who ministered to their needs and of the shrines which drew them to crusader Jerusalem.

After the conquests of Saladin, and the success of the Third Crusade in setting up an attenuated second Latin kingdom, some of the earlier functions of Jerusalem were transferred to Acre. But between these capitals there were two great differences – Jerusalem was something that Acre could never be, a Holy City and the scene not only of much of Christ's ministry, but of his last days on earth; while Acre was what Jerusalem had never been, an international market and port of such activity that, even before it became capital of the kingdom, an experienced Moslem traveller, Ibn Jubair, could compare it with Constantinople. In the thirteenth century, it grew still further in size, as it did in political and commercial importance.

The history of crusader Acre can be reconstructed from a wide variety of source material. Some of this comes from the twelfth and thirteenth centuries – descriptions by pilgrims, maps, hundreds of legal documents which record transactions in property. When details of the properties' boundaries are given, streets and public buildings are named and their relative position sometimes indicated. Travellers from every century since the thirteenth have left descriptions and drawings. This material has been intensively studied by scholars like Professor Prawer, Dr Riley-Smith and Mr Benvenisti, but even more work is needed, especially archaeological, before a map of the crusader town can be firmly and fully drawn.

Between August, 1189 and July, 1191 it was the scene of one of the greatest sieges of the Middle Ages; the length of the operation is sufficient evidence of the strength of its walls. Additional testimony is provided by maps like those of Marino Sanudo, where the double line of walls is shown, and the principal towers named. It also illustrates the growth of the town. While the Franks still held Jerusalem, Acre had been defended on the south and west by the sea, and on the north and east by a single line of walls. The citadel was at the mid-point on the northern wall. Even at that time settlement had begun outside the walls, especially to the north, which in the thirteenth century became the crowded suburb of Montmusart. While St Louis was in Syria the suburb, shaped like a shield, was fortified by a double line of land walls. Those parts of the old city wall not covered by Montmusart had been strengthened by the addition of an outer wall in the last years of the twelfth century.

Protection against sea-borne attack was also necessary, and defensive works were placed in the harbour which, as the map shows, lay south of the town. It was sheltered both from north and west by the site on

Plate 4

*Fig. 6   Acre. Key to Marino Sanudo Torsello's map. A Hospitallers' hospice;
B St Mary of the Knights; C St Laurence of the Knights; D St Anthony's
church. 1 Templars' sector; 2 Maupas gate; 3 Hospitallers' sector; 4 St
Anthony's gate; 5 Venetian sector; 6 English tower; 7 Accursed tower; 8 St
Nicholas' tower; 9 Pilgrims' tower; 10 Bridge tower; 11 Patriarch's tower;
12 Germans' tower; 13 Iron Gate; 14 St Lazarus gate. (After N. Makhouly
and C. N. Johns)*

which the town stands, and from the south and east by two long moles, both built before the crusaders' time. The western mole, by its extension northwards, enclosed an inner harbour, whose narrow entrance could be closed by tightening and raising a heavy chain. Each of these works was fortified at the seaward end by a strong tower. The Tower of Flies, on the eastern mole, played a notable part in the siege of the town by the forces of the Third Crusade.

The map also indicates some of the main subdivisions of thirteenth-century Acre. The communities of the Genoese, Venetians and Pisans each had their quarter, protected by a measure of administrative and judicial immunity, in which stood the shops and warehouses necessary for the organization of their business activities, as well as other buildings, both private and public, serving their spiritual and bodily needs, church, baths, bakehouse. The areas conceded to the Venetians and Pisans were, as we should expect, close to the harbours and the waterfront. The Genoese were nearer the middle of the town but a little further from the port, which is surprising in view of the fact that they helped King Baldwin I to take the town in 1104, and were therefore the first privileged Italians to be established there. The Templars were established in the southwest corner of the town on a site with a western waterfront to the open Mediterranean. The Hospitallers were further north and further inland. Their extensive property abutted on the north wall of the old town.

Fig. 6

The evidence for all this is mainly provided by medieval maps and legal documents, confirmed at a number of points by visible remains and which could be further tested by archaeological investigation. For example, in the former harbour area there are still two khans, quadrilateral courtyards bounded by ranges of two-storeyed buildings which look inwards towards the court. On the first floor was accommodation for merchants and at ground level storage for their merchandise. Neither khan is medieval in its present form, but both stand on older foundations, and both include re-used masonry of the Middle Ages. And there is strong support in the documents for the probability that Khan al-Afranj was the *fondaco*, the main warehouse and market accommodation, of the Venetians. It is also possible that the Khan al-'Umdan occupies the site of the main customs house and the seat of the Harbour Court. The best-known remains certainly of the crusader period were the work of the

Plate 34

Hospitallers. In recent years the Knights' refectory, often misnamed 'the crypt of St John' has been cleared to its original floor level. The trio of cylindrical piers and the rib-vaulted bays have long been visible but now, for the first time for centuries, it is possible to see them in their true dimensions and proportions. A narrow passage has also been cleared which links the refectory to another vaulted interior of a much plainer kind. There the groined vaults are carried on massive square piers; it looks designed for strictly utilitarian purposes, and may well have been for storage. Of the Templars' buildings nothing has survived, not even of that massive citadel which was the scene of the Christians' last stand before the final Mamluk victory in 1291.

The only crusader defensive work to have survived to its full height above ground is the Burj as-Sultan, which stood near the Arsenal. Below the present ground level there is much more to be recovered. Wherever there is excavation in the old town, or even just outside it, something is likely to be recovered from its medieval past. Meanwhile many smaller items, capitals, fragments of mouldings or carved figures, inscribed gravestones, pottery, are being collected and displayed in a museum of medieval antiquities housed in what were once the baths of Turkish days.

We know all too little of life as it was lived in the crusader towns, but we can probably make more contact with that of thirteenth-century Acre than with any other. The medieval maps show us not only town walls heavily fortified against the external enemy, but internal defences maintained by groups for protection against the invader who had broken in, and also against each other. Marino Sanudo's map shows, for example, Plate 4 the Tower of the Germans, presumably the Teutonic Knights; in the streets of Acre today we can still see part of the wall and a fortified gateway in the Genoese quarter; we know from contemporary historical accounts of other defences of the same kind. Such works were needed when the city was convulsed by episodes like the war of St Sabas.

Acre in the thirteenth century was crowded with a rich variety of people and institutions. Reference has been made to the areas of the town occupied by some of the major organizations, like the Military Orders and the communities of Italian and Provencal merchants. To these must be added the lay and ecclesiastical magnates of the kingdom itself – the large household, for example, of the king, or the regent, or the lieutenant who might represent either in their absence. Further than this, Acre became the home of an émigré Church and an émigré nobility. All the V.I.P.'s, individual or corporate, displaced by Moslem conquest, took refuge there – the Latin Patriarch of Jerusalem, the canons of Holy Sepulchre, the Archbishop of Nazareth, the Bishop of Bethlehem, the monks from Mount Tabor, the nuns of St Lazarus in Bethany, all concentrated in Acre; and this is to name but few examples among many. The Frankish population was swollen not only by those driven from the lost lands in the east, but by immigrants and visitors from western Europe also. Not only merchants, sailors and pilgrims, but soldiers of fortune, felons and ne'er-do-wells, some as penitents sent to expiate their crimes, some in search of fresh hunting grounds, some sent to the East to relieve harassed families. All the vices flourished, and especially prostitution. Many contemporaries were eloquent in their condemnation: they included James of Vitry, moralist and preacher, sometime Bishop of Acre, and a long succession of Popes.

Yet whatever wealth of colourful detail moralists might supply, Acre was more than a sink of iniquity. It served a variety of necessary social functions – as a political capital; as a market for its own industrial production and for the agrarian produce of the neighbouring coastal plain; as a focal point for international trade. With scarcely a break – and only the extremes of plague or warfare in the West could bring about such an interruption – fleets from Europe appeared twice a year in the spacious harbour. Some landed or took on board pilgrims, others discharged or loaded cargo. From Europe they brought mainly woollen textiles; from Acre they took back the Far-Eastern products discussed in the previous chapter. These commodities were handled in the harbour area and duty was levied by officials in the Chain Court, named after the obstacle commonly slung across the narrow entrance of many medieval ports, or at least their inner basins. When the chain was in its normal, lowered position, ships passed over it. When it was raised, the anchorage was effectively closed.

Away from the port was the Fonde, the large urban market in which local products were exchanged to meet local needs. We know from many sources what goods were sold there, especially from a list of more than a hundred articles on which duty was charged. The list is given, together with the rate of that duty, in the Law Book which sets out the customs of the burgess court at Acre. The market dealt largely in the rural produce which will be the subject of the second part of this chapter: goats and poultry, corn, vegetables, fruit, cheese, wine, oil from the sesame and olive. Most of this came from the city's Galilean hinterland, but some local merchants imported from further afield. Sugar came in by sea, as well as by pack-horse and camel; flax came from Damascus and Egypt, which also sent dried fish; from Antioch and Latakia came wine and textiles. In addition to its other social functions, the city was a centre of consumption and redistribution.

We are given a glimpse of the commercial life of the kingdom in general and of Acre in particular by Ibn Jubair. He was a Spanish Moslem who between 1183 and 1185 made the pilgrimage to Mecca and who kept a journal as he travelled. On 13 September, 1184, while on his homeward journey, he left Damascus with a caravan of merchants whose destination was Acre, where he hoped to book a passage for the West. On 6 October he boarded a Genoese ship which was also carrying Christian pilgrims whom he numbered at two thousand.

Ibn Jubair was so observant a traveller that we wish he could have stayed in the kingdom for a little longer. Every few lines he brings momentarily to life some fresh aspect of crusader society. What he has to say about its commercial life is full of interest. Trade was so important that it continued in war as in peace. The year 1184 was the third in succession in which Saladin had invaded the kingdom. This campaign had taken him to Kerak and Nablus. Ibn Jubair saw the first of the prisoners and spoils of war being brought into Damascus as he and his companions were leaving the city. The local Moslem merchants were taking their wares to Acre because, like Constantinople, it was a port of call for all ships, and its markets drew Moslem and Christian traders by land also. Two merchants of Damascus who did all their trading with places on the Frankish coast were among the wealthiest in that city, and they were influential in government circles both there and in the Latin kingdom.

The caravan's entry into crusader territory was a well regulated affair, doubtless born of long familiarity on both sides. The merchants, unlike some of the other travellers, paid no dues at Tibnin, the charge of four per cent on the value of their merchandise was collected at Acre. There they went to the market court, which was a khan of a kind already described. They did their business with the official clerks, all of them Christians who spoke and wrote Arabic. They sat on stone benches spread with carpets; their ink-stands were of ebony decorated with gold. In discharging their duties they were polite and manifestly fair, but at the same time they were thorough. They searched the luggage of those who, like Ibn Jubair, were not merchants, in case goods had been hidden there which were liable for duty. An organized customs system in an urban setting, smoothly operated with thoroughness, efficiency and courtesy, with written records kept in Arabic, these are scarcely characteristic of European administration as it then existed. It is tempting to see in the clerks of the customs and their sahib a piece of organization inherited by the crusaders from their Moslem predecessors.

So much has been said of Acre in this chapter because no other crusader town can match either the quantity of medieval evidence available for its study or its peculiar combination of functions. Three other capitals, Jerusalem, Antioch and Tripoli, ran it close, but the first and second of this trio were not seaports, and the second and third did not draw to themselves pilgrims and immigrants in the same number. Many places could reproduce this or that feature of Acre's life; even the brief references in earlier chapters show how many of them knew the shock of violent political crisis. But political assassination, and civil and communal strife, were exceptional. Crusader towns resembled each other as well in the more normal aspects of life. There were other busy harbours – the double port of Tyre; Beirut, developed by the efforts of the Old Lord, John of Ibelin; the old port of Tripoli, which became a suburb of the new crusader town inland; St Simeon, the port of Antioch, which also might well repay archaeological investigation by medievalists. In many towns on the coast and inland there were urban markets, with burgess courts and viscounts presiding over them, and the viscounts' staff policing the streets and markets. The greater towns were protected by elaborate defences and dignified by large buildings – churches, the convents of monks, friars and military orders, the palaces and strong towers of noble families. But there were in towns both small and great, narrow streets sheltered from the sun by vaults or awnings, with goods displayed in front of shopes which were like small, dark caves (such as may still be seen in the medieval streets surviving in Jerusalem), the flat-roofed houses presenting to the passer-by blank walls in which openings were few and small, in which life and the living rooms centred on the inner courtyard.

Professor Prawer considers that nearly all Syrian Franks were townees, without roots in the countryside and, as always, his arguments are well-grounded. Some of the charters which record transactions in rural property include the names of peasant cultivators; the overwhelming majority are the names of Syrians, either Christian or Moslem. There are a few examples of landlords who attempted to attract European settlers by offering them particularly favourable conditions of tenure and legal status. The canons of the Church of the Holy Sepulchre were successful in settling such colonies at al-Birah and al-Qubaibah, both a few miles outside Jerusalem; the Hospitallers established a community of European cultivators in the neighbourhood of their castle at Beit Jibrin; and so did the king himself on the coast at Achzib (Casal Imbert) between Acre and Tyre. But such instances are few in number, and form only a small proportion of the total agrarian evidence. The conclusion seems irresistible that Europeans were rare exceptions among a rural peasantry composed almost entirely of indigenous Syrians. This was certainly the impression of Ibn Jubair as he rode from Tibnin down to Acre. 'Our way lay through continuous farms and ordered settlements, whose inhabitants were all Moslems. . . . All the coastal cities occupied by the Franks are managed in this fashion, their rural districts, the villages and farms, belonging to the Moslems.'

When they first settled in the country the Franks found in its rural areas social arrangements and institutions which, if not identical with, at any rate strongly resembled some of those with which they were familiar in the West. For example, the land and its inhabitants were not all directly administered by officials in the service of the public authority. Everywhere there was the *iqta'*, land granted to a magnate in which he exercised authority and enjoyed the profits, on condition of rendering service, including military service, to the government in Damascus or Baghdad. Eastern *iqta'* was not in all respects the western fief; but there were some strong likenesses, and the Frankish knight could replace his Turkish predecessor without serious dislocation.

The peasantry, for their part, were not free, and most of them perhaps never had been, in the sense that they could, at their own choice, leave the village community to make their living elsewhere, or freely dispose of their land by sale, gift or bequest, or themselves enjoy the whole of its produce. They were instead tenants of a landlord, who not only took a proportion of their produce, but regarded them as in some sense his property. So here again the new European landlord found what he already knew in the West, a dependent peasantry. In the Latin of legal documents he could continue to use the same European vocabulary to describe them and their affairs, though there were also differences which that vocabulary sometimes obscured.

There was, in fact, a mixture of the familiar and the unfamiliar, but with the familiar predominating, especially for those settlers whose homeland had been in southern Italy or Provence. Syria and the Holy Land were lands not of scattered hamlets and homesteads, but of villages, not much more than a mile or two apart in the most thickly settled areas, which varied in size, but in which about twenty households was a common number. Such communities needed to take certain decisions in common, including those about the village agriculture. The agri-cultural year began in the autumn, with the final ploughing and the sowing of the main winter crops, wheat and barley. Thus far, all was familiar. The unfamiliar, certainly to the northerners, lay in the time of the grain harvest, some two months earlier than in the West; the pre-dominance of wheat over barley; the fact that the beginning of the agrarian year was marked by the coming of the rains. Familiar was the three-course rotation of local agrarian practice. One part of the village fields was sown with the grains just referred to; a second, with leguminous crops, mainly peas, beans and lentils; the third part was left fallow. Unfamiliar to north Europeans was the raising of a quick-growing summer crop on land which had been fallow during the winter – chick-peas, maize, millet.

Such were the main crops of the village arable, but there were others of major importance. In a land in which not only bread, but oil and, for some, wine also, were staple items of diet, the olive and the grape were widely grown. In most villages, besides the arable and the olive groves, there were patches of garden and orchard in individual possession. Cultivated too were specialist crops, in those areas where physical conditions suited them: citrus, figs and dates as well as sugar and cotton.

How did landlords derive their profits from these small village groups and the agriculture by which they lived? In large areas of western Europe at that time it was usual for village lands to be divided. A portion of them was occupied by the villagers as tenants of the lord, another portion kept by the lord in demesne, that is, as a home farm which he cultivated partly by paid farm workers, partly by the labour services owed by his tenants. These same tenants also owed a variety of payments, both in money and in kind. Landlords also maintained certain profitable monopolies: the villagers must grind their corn in his mill, they must bring their dough to his bakehouse, and they must pay for the service; furthermore the jurisdiction of his court, petty though it might be, provided a steady source of income.

Once again, conditions in East and West were both like and unlike. Profits of court, mill and oven were common to both regions. Arabic-speaking peasants, like English-speaking peasants at the other end of Christendom, paid hens to their French-speaking lord at Christmas and eggs at Easter. But there was one area of major difference. Landlords in crusader Syria did not cultivate demesne farms and therefore did not take labour services from their village tenants. No generalization about any aspect of medieval society can ever be absolute, and there were exceptions. There is evidence that a few landlords held some demesne arable; the lords' orchards and vegetable gardens were sometimes worked by villagers as a corvée; tenants sometimes provided and manned transport for the carriage of their lord's crops and other goods. But these were peripheral to a general situation in which the farming of the demesne arable by peasant labour service had no significant part.

As a general rule, all the village arable was farmed by the villagers themselves; the Frankish landlords, like their predecessors for centuries past and their successors down into modern times, took a share of their tenants' crop. This share might be as much as a half; it seems rarely, if ever, to have been less than a quarter. It applied to the produce of fields, orchards, olive groves and vineyards. Such transactions in kind were a common feature of the world we have lost. We have only to think of the lengthy, time-consuming arrangements by which many village parsons in England, less than two hundred years ago, were still going out into the fields to collect on the spot the tithes from their parishioners. In crusader Syria the division of the grain was carried out at the village threshing-floor in the presence of officials who ensured that the lord had his share.

These officials were essential to the working of the system. Medieval landlords did not normally live in a village among their tenants; the greatest of them, with rights in perhaps scores of villages, could not possibly do so. The lord of a single village might live in its manor house; but in Latin Syria many landlords, who as time went on perhaps became the overwhelming majority, lived in a town house, connected with the rural tenants only by rights and rents. Hence the importance of those officials who administered or collected them.

Nearly all landlords needed a man of business – in the West he was often called a steward – to deal with matters of estate management. In the East French-speaking landlords – those who learned Arabic were always a small minority – needed interpreters in their dealings with the native peasantry. The word by which these were known, dragoman, already existed in Greek and Arabic. A European steward could have worked through the medium of an interpreter, but it was to the advantage of all concerned if he could speak the languages of the rulers and the ruled, and so deal directly with both. The records make it clear that this often happened. The dragoman, who might be Frank or Syrian, was normally much more than a simple interpreter. Like John of Tibnin as early as 1151, or Geoffrey of Arsuf as late as 1261, he held his office in respect of a whole fief; a Hospitaller document shows us a dragoman on progress through the villages under his control. Like many administrative offices in that age, it was normally held as a serjeanty, that is, the holder performed not military service, like a knight, but the duties of his office in return for hereditary tenure and its profits which, as we know, could be considerable.

Akin to the dragoman was the scribe. There were several points of resemblance – both posts could be held as serjeanties and could therefore be hereditary; some scribes were Franks and some Syrians; they too were often men of substance enriched by perquisites in kind from the estates they helped to administer. Dragoman and scribe often resembled each other so closely that it has been asked whether both offices were not normally held by the same man. Close examination of the evidence by Dr Riley-Smith has shown that this was not usual. The work of the scribes was the more specialized. While the dragoman seems to have been in general charge of the administration of his lord's fief, the scribes were more particularly concerned with the collection of his dues.

These officers dealt with the dependent peasantry on their lord's behalf, but in each village their business was transacted not with the cultivators as individuals but through the hierarchy established in each community. At the head of the village elders stood the rays, of whom something has already been said as president of the village court. He also had the leading role in the economic and social life of his village. He was either chosen, or his appointment confirmed, by the lord and, to carry out his role effectively, he needed the confidence both of lord and villagers. He was spokesman for each to the other. He was best placed to convey and explain in detail to his fellow cultivators the lord's require/ments and instructions; if they for their part wished to present any petition or protest to the lord, they did so through their rays. The arrange/ments within the village for the sharing out of payments and services owed to the lord, arrangements about the village agriculture which required a decision taken in common; in such matters the rays took the main initiative and bore the main responsibility. He must have earned the larger allotment of land and the more commodious house he some/times enjoyed.

In western Europe an abundance of records sometimes makes possible a detailed reconstruction, in a limited area and within a limited time, of some aspects of a particular medieval village or lordship. The scanty documentation of the crusader states provides material for no more than a sketch of such matters, though Professor Prawer has provided an exception in his masterly study of the lordship of Tyre. But in the West, and particularly in this country, local historians have taught us how the study of the documents can be supplemented by a study of the land and landscape, and of the material remains which stand on or lie within it. Some indeed would put the land as the main source, to which documents are the ancillary. Can our knowledge of agrarian society in the crusader states be increased by these means?

Between the crusader period and the early twentieth century there were sufficient strands of continuity for the very recent to illuminate a more remote past. During that long period of time many features of the Syrian rural scene underwent little change or none. They included the social structure of the village, the rights and profits of landlords, methods of cultivation, techniques of milling grain or sugar or of extracting oil from the olive and juice from the grape. Broad facts of demography and settlement remained virtually the same. In his work on Tyre Professor Prawer has placed side by side statistics derived from Marsilio Giorgio's report to the government of Venice in 1243, and those published by the Turkish government not long before 1914. Just as observation of primitive peoples who still exist can enable anthropologists to fill in gaps in their knowledge of similar peoples who lived in the remote past, so can the fellahin of the twentieth century throw light on their predecessors in the thirteenth.

A landlord took his dues in kind. His share of the grain was collected from the village threshing floor, and the greater landlords sent their officials to make such a collection in a number of villages. What was then done with it? Surveys in the West often record that commodities due from tenants were taken to the lord's *curia*, to the manor house, with its yards and farm buildings, from which the demesne was administered and where the renders in kind could be stored. The European tenants settled by the canons of Holy Sepulchre at al-Birah, were required to take the canons' share of their produce 'to the *curia* of the Holy Sepulchre in Mahumeria, or to whatever place in the town the *dispensator* there (he was the canons' agent) might order.' Other tenants at Ramatha were to take the corn and vegetables due to the canons 'ad voltas nostras', to the vaulted grange in the village where the canons stored their rents in kind. Have any of the manorial buildings survived?

The most visited and most studied buildings of the crusader period are the castles and churches, but in the countryside there are more modest structures which were presumably neither, lacking as they do either defensive or religious features. Nearly a century ago such buildings were duly listed by Captain Conder and Lieutenant Kitchener (a subaltern in the Royal Engineers whose name was one day to become a household word) in the *Survey of Western Palestine*, but only in recent years has an attempt been made to explain their function. When he was collaborating with Professor Prawer in the preparation of the best and most recent map of crusader Palestine, Meron Benvenisti studied on the ground every crusader site, major, minor and minimal, in the territory of modern Israel. In his book *The Crusaders in the Holy Land* he convincingly demonstrates that a number of lesser buildings of the crusader period served purposes which were neither religious nor military, but which answered the needs of Frankish landlords.

There are two such sites a few miles north of Jerusalem, on the road leading to Nablus. Burj Bardawil has generally been discussed as if its primary role was defensive but, although its buildings include a small tower, there are no military features on the wall which encloses the site. It is easy to be persuaded by Mr Benvenisti that it was the headquarters of a rural estate. The vaulted buildings which backed against the inner face of the enclosure wall provided residential and administrative quarters, with accommodation for animals, implements and produce. The tower was simply a local refuge.

Such an identification is still more convincing if applied to the site at Jifna. It is distinguished from similar sites by the fact that it is still occupied, by the extent to which the medieval structures have survived, by the high quality of some of its masonry, especially that of its well-proportioned gateway, and by the unexpected loggia within, with its large, slightly pointed arches which once opened on to the courtyard. This stood on that courtyard's eastern side; to the south stood a building which, like the loggia, was of four groin-vaulted bays separated by transverse arches. Most complete of all is the barrel-vaulted room on the north side of the court, a single unbroken space some 28 metres in length and 8 metres in width, which may have been the main hall of the manorial buildings.

Aqua Bella is better known. It is within easy reach of Jerusalem to the west, and the public authority has recently shown imagination and initiative in improving the amenities of the site and in making it more accessible to visitors. Once again a courtyard, though a small one, lay at the heart of the place, into which buildings of two storeys looked from all sides. The best of them is a hall at first-floor level, with rib-vaulted bays and large windows looking towards the stream and the trees growing in the small green valley – *aqua bella* indeed, especially in the hills of Judea. These buildings have long been identified as a nunnery of the crusader period, but there is no shred of medieval evidence for such an attribution, and on the site there is no sign of a chapel. Mr Benvenisti is inclined to place it among the other unfortified manor houses and estate headquarters which he discusses in his book.

The difficulties of identifying the uses of such buildings are made more difficult by the degree to which they are encumbered with debris and overgrown with vegetation. Secure information can be gained only by clearing and excavation. There is a very wide difference between the generalizations made about the Templars' great castle at 'Atlit by the succession of itinerant students who examined the ruins without disturbing them, and the facts established as the result of excavation directed by Mr C. N. Johns. At Belvoir, too, tentative probings among the abundant cacti or in the dark undercrofts of occupied houses have been replaced by thorough archaeological investigation and with surprising results. The smaller buildings need the same treatment. No one who has edged through spiky undergrowth, shoulder high, to examine the storehouse at Manueth would disagree with that, and Manueth is one example among many.

Already excavation has uncovered the most extensive monument so far known of crusade rural life. In a document to which reference has already been made, al-Qubaibah was named by the patriarch as one of those villages which the canons of Holy Sepulchre were building for occupation by Latin Christians. In that village the eastern parts of the twelfth-century church survived, and its three semicircular apses have always been known. Opposite the western door of that church, on the other side of what may have been a small square, was a medieval building of undeterminate function. Closer examination has shown it to be the *curia* of the canons, with accommodation for storage and perhaps for the *dispensator* who represented the canons' interests in the village, and with a defensive tower sited at one of its corners. But the most striking recovery made by excavation has been the remains of some forty houses of the crusader village. These are not dwellings which, as in most rural communities, have come into existence over a long period of time, with the variety and unevenness which are a consequence of such haphazard development. The medieval houses in al-Qubaibah were neatly laid out on either side of the wide, paved thoroughfare which was the principal street in the village. They are similar in style, dimensions and equipment. From the archaeological evidence it is clear that they were all built as part of a single scheme of development. The documentary evidence of the canons' ambitious colonizing plans has been dramatically corroborated and extended by the archaeologist.

One last illustration of the interdependence between documentary and material evidence. Something has been said of the importance of presses and mills, of the need to press grapes and olives, and to grind not only corn but also sugar cane to extract the juice for subsequent boiling and crystallization. Legal documents mention both wind/ and watermills, and some of these can still be identified. In that contentious decade, the 1230's, there was a dispute between Templars and Hospitallers about water control on the Acre river, and Pope Gregory IX himself came to hear how the Templars' waterworks at their Doc (Da'uq) mill made difficulties for the Hospitallers in their mill upstream at Recordane (Kurdaneh). Such situations arose because of the need to build up a head of water by raising its level. It could then be released down a steeply inclined chute, so that a final jet of water could be shot with great force on to a horizontally laid mill/wheel. In this way a vertical shaft fixed to its centre could be rotated, to the other end of which, in a room above, the mill/wheel was attached. Fifty years ago the Hospitallers' mill at Recordane was still working, and its buildings survive today, with a protective tower, and with the chutes and channels which once fed four mill/wheels. It is not unique. The remains of crusader mills can still be traced on the Yarqon river, while at Tawahin as/Sukkar, near Jericho, are the considerable remains of a sugar mill. To provide water/power the crusaders repaired and re/used aqueducts first installed in the time of Herod the Great. The vaulted chamber in which the water struck and drove the lower mill/wheel still exists, though not the two wheels and their connecting shaft. But the stone basin in which the upper wheel ground the sugar cane is still in position, and in its centre is the hole through which the shaft passed.

Mr Benvenisti's book is the best guide to the material evidence of the crusaders' life in town and country. Much more certainly awaits dis/covery and identification, which will be achieved only by the kind of field/work he has undertaken – carried further, where necessary, by excavation.

The Castles

Of the visible crusader remains from southern Turkey to the borders of Egypt, none is more common than the castle. In some instances foundations and defensive ditches alone are preserved; at the other end of the spectrum is a major castle which, like the Krak des Chevaliers, is practically complete

The castles and walled towns have often been discussed as if they constituted a planned system of defence, with an outer screen, support line and innermost bases and strongholds. Such a view needs modifi-cation because it is anachronistic. It presupposes the existence of an authority with the power and resources to make and execute such a plan; that all crusader castles were founded by crusaders; that the main functions of castles lay in the public sphere and were to provide defence against the external enemy. None of these presuppositions can be justified. In Syria, a battle-ground for millennia, many strong-places had been built as a result of earlier political and military situations. The crusaders occupied them, and subsequently maintained and extended many of them, but not originally at the bidding of a superior authority. In the first age of crusader conquest, before kings and princes were firmly in the saddle, ambitious men played their own hand, and the most successful of them occupied fortified buildings because of the many uses to which these could be put. They could serve as the residence of a magnate and his household; they enabled a newcomer to dominate the surrounding area and its inhabitants; they were a centre from which he could administer his estates. When in 1183 the castle of Kerak was the scene of its young lord's wedding to a royal princess, and bride and groom passed their first night together in one of its towers, its role was that of a baronial palace. It has already been noted how any castle of the Military Orders was also a kind of monastery. The military function of castles was but one among many, and even this related not only to the external enemy, but to the need to control subject Moslem populations who might become hostile. Because of this multiplicity of functions, castles were valuable not only on a frontier, but wherever they stood.

Castles also played their part in the social and economic development of the crusader states. Their garrisons could bring security to the surrounding countryside, and settlers could be brought to areas which had previously been uncultivated because they were too exposed to enemy raiding. The castle founded by Raymond of St Gilles as the base for his long-term siege operations against the medieval seaport of Tripoli was to become the nucleus of the modern town. William of Tyre, writing in the 1170's, emphasized that colonization of the surrounding area followed the building of the castle of Tell as-Safi and at ash-Shaubak (Montreal). Of others built during his lifetime, we know that the Hospitallers attracted settlers to the vicinity of their castle at Beit Jibrin, and that centres of Frankish population grew around those at Gaza and Yabna (Ibelin).

Some eighty years later an account was written on the refoundation of the castle at Safad in Galilee after the restoration of the region to the Franks as a result of negotiations during 1239–41. The author had a good deal to say on the benefits gained by the Franks from both the offensive and defensive role of the castle. Offensively it provided a pad from which attacks could be launched on the lands of the sultan of Damascus. In defence the castle could not bar the way against a large invading force, but its garrison could check the raids by Moslems – the author particularly mentions those by Bedouin, Turkomans and Khorezmians – to which the whole area between Acre and the Jordan had previously been exposed. The greater security of the area thus achieved had two principal results. First, pilgrims were better able to visit the many biblical sites and shrines in Galilee. Second, men and transport could move more freely in the area, a busy and well-populated town came to flourish in the shadow of the castle and the 260 villages in the neighbouring region, which were worth nothing to their landlords before the castle was rebuilt, became once more an abundant source of profit.

Further reference will be made to the document from which this information is taken. Written in the early 1260's, but imperfectly transmitted to posterity, it is now available in an improved text edited by Professor Huygens. Among its many points of interest are its author's statements on the purposes and functions of an important castle. Too often modern writers must make their own deductions on such matters from the mute testimony of the surviving monuments; an authentic medieval discussion is as valuable as it is rare.

Crusader castles have also often been regarded as a kind of inter-mediary through which the advanced principles of the science of fortifi-cation, long developed and applied in the Byzantine and Moslem East, were transmitted to the more primitive European West. Certainly most western castles at the time of the First Crusade were of a rudimentary kind. The area occupied by the garrison was protected by ditch, earth bank and timber stockade. Within this bailey, or at its edge, a strong-point could be provided by digging a circular ditch and throwing the soil towards the centre. The summit of the mound, or motte, thus formed could be raised a considerable height above the bottom of the ditch, and could be defended by a stockade or even a wooden tower. Thousands of such mottes still survive in western Europe, and the defences they once carried are illustrated in the Bayeux Tapestry. That defence was passive rather than active; it lay in the inaccessibility provided by the height of the motte and the steepness of its sides. Even in the eleventh century a wealthy magnate might use stone rather than timber in building part of the castle; in the twelfth, stone construction became even more common. When the strong-point was built in stone, it usually

Fig. 7

Fig. 7   A motte and bailey castle. (After R. Allen Brown)

took the form of a rectangular tower and also embodied a passive defence. Because of its very thick walls in which the openings were few and small, with the principal entrance at first-floor rather than at ground level, it was difficult for the attacks to come to grips with the garrison, and vice versa. The besieged sat within their massive defences, and waited for the relatively ill-equipped besiegers to withdraw.

During the early part of the twelfth century moves toward a more active kind of defence were slow and sporadic, but they gradually assumed a more positive form, becoming in the course of the thirteenth century, fully developed. Not only were experiments made in the planning of keeps, so that they grew less vulnerable to stone-throwing artillery, but greater attention was given to the defence of the bailey. Timber stockades gave way to stone curtain walls, designed and equipped as fighting platforms from which it was possible to conduct a hard-hitting, active defence. Mural galleries, sometimes placed in successive storeys one above the other, with arrow slits to the field; above them all an open rampart walk protected by a crenellated parapet; projecting towers from which archers could shoot along the face of the wall and take attackers from both flanks; postern gates for the launching of a sudden sortie. As such fortifications became more elaborate a succession of obstacles was presented to the enemy: fosse, an outer wall, an inner wall higher than and overlooking the defences which preceded it. When these walls were set with many mural towers, the keep was no longer necessary. If a strong-point were needed, it might be in the form of a heavily fortified gatehouse. So-called 'concentric' castles built on these lines reached their apogee in England at the end of the thirteenth century, in those great and costly castles constructed by Edward I to secure his conquests in North Wales.

Similar fortification had been a feature of the late Roman world, and had been continued in its eastern part which we call Byzantine. Not only were such buildings constructed, but general principles were evolved and expounded in text-books. Special attention was given, for example, to the relative heights and distance apart of outer and inner walls so that the enemy could be engaged simultaneously from both levels. No fortification more fully embodied the precepts of the theorists than the land walls of Constantinople, built by the prefect Anthemius in the early years of the fifth century and which cross five miles of country

Fig. 8

Fig. 9

Plate 5

Fig. 8   The development of Dover castle. 1 Prehistoric earthwork, Roman
pharos, and Saxon church; 2 the castle c. 1190; 3 the castle in 1216; 4 the
castle at the end of the thirteenth century. (After R. Allen Brown)

between the Sea of Marmara and the Golden Horn. This marvellous double line, much of which still stands, was a familiar sight to many crusaders of the twelfth century and to the Italian sailors and merchants who went in increasing numbers to Constantinople during the same period. The founders of the crusader states attacked, conquered and took over many strong-places which embodied similar principles of fortification.

At the beginning of the twelfth century the difference between East and West in this branch of theoretical knowledge and of the necessary practical skills was very wide. It therefore seems an irresistible conclusion that, since the West made undoubted progress in this field in the twelfth and thirteenth centuries, it learned the necessary lessons in the East. These were first applied by the crusaders in the fortifications they constructed in Syria, and were thereafter transmitted to the West.

Western castles did indeed develop along lines which could have been learned in the eastern Mediterranean, but it is not a simple matter. Do buildings develop by the diffusion of forms from one region to another, or are such developments worked out locally, in response to changing needs, independent of what already exists elsewhere? And if there was diffusion, and models of the more sophisticated defences of an earlier age were necessary to bring about change, then did not such models already exist in the West, in the form of survivals from the Roman period? Even if it is allowed that there *must* have been transmission from East to West, with the crusaders as intermediaries, then three riders must be added. First, it is remarkably difficult to demonstrate such transmission in terms of reasonably well-dated buildings. Second, the design of castles in the West changed only very slowly during the twelfth and thirteenth centuries. The defences of Constantinople, seen by tens of thousands of crusaders as early as 1096, and many other fortified places in the Levant, produced no early or rapid changes in the West. Third, many crusaders who settled in the East were so little influenced by what they saw, conquered and occupied, that they continued to build the simpler kind of castle they already knew in the West. It is only fair to add, however, that they were rather earlier in developing the stone defences of the bailey than were their western contemporaries.

T. E. Lawrence, in that most famous of undergraduate dissertations, was first to give proper attention to the traditionalism of crusader castle

NORTH
GATE

NORTH-WEST
TOWER

RUSTYCOKER
TOWER

OUTER
WARD

NORTHERN
GATEHOUSE

OUTER
WARD

MOAT

INNER   WARD

MIDDLE
TOWER

CHAPEL
TOWER

SITE OF
MOAT

SOUTHERN
GATEHOUSE

SOUTH-WEST
TOWER

PILARDESBATHE
TOWER

BARBICAN

GATE NEXT
THE SEA

MILL

GUNNERS
WALK

DOCK

R O A D

Scale of feet

20 10 0   20   40   60   80   100   200   300   400

Fig. 9   Beaumaris. Plan of the castle. (Her Majesty's Stationery Office)

The Crusaders

Plate 6
Plate 15

Fig. 10

builders and to the many fine tower-keeps in Syria. Some, like Safita and Sahyun, still stand to their full medieval height, and they are to be found in more than one kind of defensive scheme. At Jerusalem, Tartus and Jebail they formed the citadel, the ultimate strong-point in the urban defences. At Sahyun and Beaufort they can still be seen as the largest and strongest towers in complex and sophisticated castles which were equipped with many towers. At Chastel Ruge (Qal'at Yahmur) the great tower dominates the rest of the defences. It appears to do so at Chastel Blanc (Safita) where the tall keep is the finest in Syria, but this is partly an illusion, since the tower has survived the rest of the once considerable defences. All these keeps were major pieces of fortification. There were also many small rural towers, the equivalent of peel towers in our border country, places of refuge in areas exposed to hit-and-run raid and counter raid.

Fig. 10   Tartus (Tortosa). Plan of crusader town. 1 Outer court of Templars' citadel; 2 Templars' great tower; 3 chapel; 4 Templars' hall; 5 town wall; 6 town gate; 7 cathedral. (After W. Müller-Wiener)

In many important respects the large tower‑keeps resembled their western counterparts. Though none enclosed as large an area as that at Colchester or the White Tower of London, they were comparable in length and breadth. Sahyun is 25 metres square, Beaufort 23 metres square, while Chastel Ruge measures 16 × 14 metres: English examples on a similar scale are Middleham 30 × 29.5 metres, Castle Rising 23 × 20 metres, with Scarborough 17 metres square. Both in East and West the keeps had the same plain exterior, with little or no buttressing or other projecting features. Their defensive strength lay in the sheer thickness of their walls in which openings were kept to a minimum. The wall of the keep at Sahyun which faced the most likely direction of attack is five metres thick. At ground floor level there were only two small openings through which it was possible to watch or shoot at the enemy on the far side of the ditch. Within such walls it was possible to build

Fig. 11

Fig. 11   Sahyun. The main crusader defences. The keep, vaulted in four bays, overlooks the fosse. (After E. G. Rey)

flights of stone steps to give access between the different floors and the roof. Additional strength was sometimes gained by re-using those huge blocks of masonry which had characterized monumental buildings in the Hellenistic age. Squared stones of this kind can be seen in the keep at Jebail, while the lowest courses of the Tower of David in Jerusalem had been laid in the time of Herod the Great.

Plate 8

There were also important differences between the great towers of western Europe and those of Latin Syria. The East, deficient in big timber, had always been a land of vaulted buildings. Crusader keeps were vaulted throughout, with a number of important consequences. They were better protected against damage by fire, no mean advantage against an enemy expert in the use of combustibles. Their height was rarely their greatest dimension (Safita was the principal exception); further, the flat roof of the building provided a better fighting platform than the pitched roofs and narrow rampart walks of the West.

Plate 14

In Europe the great tower might be the only stone feature of a castle otherwise built of timber; and because the timber defences have long since disappeared, the keep now stands in isolation. In Syria, where good building stone was plentiful and timber scarce, the subsidiary defences have often survived, and at Chastel Ruge, Jebail and Subaybah the keep is tightly enclosed in a ring wall. Against the inner face of that wall it was normal to construct a continuous range of vaulted buildings of such a height that the flat roof provided a spacious rampart walk, affording easy movement round the circuit of the wall and facilitating concentration of the defence in a threatened sector. At such places the ground floor of the great tower was entirely masked from the attacker; the garrison could defend from the roof both of the tower and of the ranges backing against the curtain wall. Such a close association of a tower-keep and a very small inner bailey seems to be distinctively Syrian.

Plate 7

Unless it is merely a temporary refuge, a castle must consist of more than a tower, however imposing. There needed to be one or more court-yards in which everyday life could be carried on, and these had to be provided with defences. Early European castles might consist of two main elements, the keep and the bailey or, in the language of contem-porary documents, *turris* and *castrum*. There is no doubt as to which element was the more necessary. Castles could be designed without keeps, but not without baileys.

It has been seen that the crusaders built many castles with keeps, but even in the earlier half of the twelfth century they were building castles without them. Sometimes they adopted a rectangular plan with towers at the angles and perhaps flanking the gateway. Such forts resembled the *castrum* so widely used by Roman and Byzantine military engineers, and of which so many examples survive in the Mediterranean lands.

Once more the question arises: were the crusaders learning a more advanced design already available in the East which they transmitted to western Europe, or did they, without regard to the past, work out for themselves a form of defence which suited their immediate needs? Both are possible. We know that the castrum-like forts built by the crusaders were sometimes constructed in haste, in open country and in the face of the enemy. The occasion was treated like a campaign. An army was taken to the site, ready to ward off any attack on the building operations, which proceeded in all haste. What was needed in these circumstances was a simple design, giving all-round defence, which could be quickly and easily executed; what better response to such a specification than a rectangular enclosure with towers at its corners?

Significantly enough, some of the best examples of crusader castles of this type are to be found in the coastal plain where there are no mountain spurs and slopes to offer natural protection, and where all-round, man-made defences were therefore needed. In the 1160's Amalric I wanted to strengthen his control over the southern extremity of the coastal plain, the last inhabited area before the desert divides it from Egypt. William of Tyre records that he built at Darum 'a fortress of moderate dimensions, covering scarcely more than a stone's throw of ground. It was square in form, and at each corner was a tower, one of which was more massive and better fortified than the rest.' It would be interesting to know the difference in size and strength between this tower and the others. It may have been slight, or so great that this tower was virtually a keep. But the plan of the whole castle was that of a *castrum*, a form used by the Franks elsewhere on the southern plain. Twenty years earlier Amalric's father, King Fulk, who as a former Count of Anjou was descended from a long line of castle builders, had established a number of strongholds in the neighbourhood of Ascalon, to check the forays of its garrison and to prepare the way for its future conquest. At Ibelin (Yabna), we are told, he built 'a fortress of very strong masonry with deep foundations and four towers'. Blanchegarde (Tell as-Safi) was 'a stronghold of hewn stone, resting on solid foundations . . . with four towers of suitable height'.

Good examples of this castle type are visible at Minat al-Qal'ah, al-Qulai'ah and Kaukab al-Hawa, or, as the crusaders knew them, Chastel Beroart, Coliat and Belvoir. All three stood in open country which saw much of the passage of armies. Each was a rectangular *castrum*, without a keep, but with a tower at each corner of the enclosure and at certain intermediate points.

The most interesting of the three is Belvoir. It was one of that small group of castles in the Latin kingdom which, after the disaster of Hattin, held out against Saladin for more than a year. From the heights above the Jordan it surveys the course of that river from Lake Tiberias to Beisan, overlooking one of the main routes into the kingdom used by invaders from Damascus. A force crossing the Jordan by the bridge at Sinn an-Nabrah, just to the south of Lake Tiberias, in order to strike towards the Plain of Esdraelon or of Acre, could be observed and challenged by a force based on Belvoir. Saladin crossed the Jordan by this route in 1182 and 1183, and on both occasions was challenged by the army of the kingdom in the neighbourhood of the castle. Until 1947 the walls and ditch of Belvoir were the boundaries of an Arab village. The plan of the large *castrum* was therefore clearly visible, with its boldly-projecting symmetrically-arranged rectangular towers, one at each corner of the enclosure and one at the intermediate point on the three sides protected by the ditch. The fourth, eastern side was made almost secure by the steepness of the slope down to the Jordan valley, though here too there was an additional defensive work – of which more in a moment. The size and quality of the visible masonry bore witness to the castle's former importance. Medieval masonry in the undercrofts of village houses in the interior proved the existence of substantial buildings in the crusader period, but expert opinion was divided as to whether or not a tower-keep had stood within the enclosure.

The site, no longer inhabited, has in recent years been cleared and excavated. There could be no more striking demonstration of the necessity of such work for the proper understanding of castle sites, however much masonry is visible above ground. The outer wall is now shown to have been well equipped for the conduct of an active defence

Plate 9

Fig. 12

and to have had a main gateway defended with particular care and ingenuity. Active defence was assisted not only by the flat roof of the vaulted ranges attached to all the inner faces of the curtain wall, but to the provision of no fewer than four posterns or sally-ports. The main gateway in the southeast corner of the enclosure was preceded by a narrow outer entrance; between the two was a hairpin-shaped approach, every inch of which was exposed to attack from members of the garrison posted on the walls which overlooked it. Any assault on the entrance was impeded by a large barbican which, as the plan shows, was thrust well forward down the eastern slope.

Fig. 12 Belvoir. Plan of the castle. 1 Outer gate, whence entry leads by way of barbican (2) and hairpin bend to inner gate (3); 4 vaulted accommodation backing on to inner face of wall; 5 postern; 6 main gate to inner court; 7 refectory; 8 inner court; 9 kitchen; 10 outer court; 11 bath-house; 12 cistern; 13 west gate; 14 bridge. (After M. Benvenisti). 1 : 400

Within the castle excavation revealed not a keep, but an inner *castrum*, some 40 metres square and with five towers, one at each angle and the fifth, a gatehouse, set in the western face. All project well beyond the face of the curtain. This inner entrance was set well away from the outer, so that an enemy who had forced the first gate might still find difficulties in reaching the second. Both gateways embodied the defensive device of compelling the user to turn through a right angle before entering either courtyard. The inner court also had ranges of vaulted accommodation on all four of its sides. The discovery of three ovens indicates the kitchen or bakehouse, and it is reasonable to place the refectory in the adjoining section. Sculptured fragments in an upper room of the inner gatehouse tower suggest that this was the chapel. A bath-house and a cistern can be identified among the buildings of the outer court.

In 1168 the lord of the castle sold it to the Hospitallers, presumably because he could no longer afford to maintain it. The recent study has shown its buildings to be of a single period of construction. The unusual size of the place, the high quality of its masonry and scheme of defence, its provision of amenities for a numerous garrison, all suggest that period to have been during the twenty years of Hospitaller occupation. Israeli archaeologists have established a new landmark in the history of the European castle: a strong-place, fairly securely dated, in which there was no great tower; in which all the defences, carefully designed to provide both for defence and counter attack, were concentrated on a symmetrically-disposed, double-line of curtain wall. All these features would one day become common in the strongholds of western Europe, but not until the following century. Belvoir was therefore ahead of western practice, but it was also ahead of what the crusaders had built thus far in Syria.

Belvoir, Coliat and Chastel Beroart were symmetrically-planned enclosures to ensure all-round defence. But as much of the country ruled by the Franks was hill and mountain, man-made fortifications were usually far from symmetrical, since they were necessary in inverse proportion to the natural defence available. Where a rock face or a very steep slope afforded adequate protection, this needed to be reinforced only by a simple curtain wall, with or without occasional mural towers. But where level ground offered the enemy an easy approach, then artificial defences needed to be heightened, thickened and multiplied. Some sites were completely isolated from their immediate surroundings. Millennia of continuous habitation, not uncommon in so anciently settled and civilized an area, can raise the level of a town or village high above the surrounding plain. The top of the tell so formed can be treated as if it were a very large motte, and its flat top can be encircled by a ring wall. Such was the defensive strength of Harim and Qal'at al-Mudiq, both, in the early twelfth century, centres of Frankish power in that part of the principality of Antioch which lay east of the Orontes.

Plate 10

Nature can also isolate. There are two known sites, Tyron in southern Lebanon and al-Habis in the Yarmuk valley, at which garrisons were installed in a cluster of mountain caves. These could be approached only by vertiginous paths or by rope ladders down the cliff face and, if they were attacked, the besiegers had literally to dig out the besieged by sinking a shaft into the natural fort. The best example of a strong-place above ground isolated by nature is perhaps Musailiha, though Shaizar, the home of Usamah ibn Munqidh and his family, occupying a narrow steep-sided ridge overlooking the Orontes, is also worthy of mention.

Plates 32, 33

Strong natural protection was available on the site chosen for one of the most famous of crusader castles, one that nowadays is little visited. During the twelfth century, before Saladin's reconquests, the Franks controlled the country east of the Ghor, the Dead Sea and the Wadi 'Arabah. This *terre oultre le Jourdan* was one of the major fiefs of the Latin kingdom; its lords' profits were drawn not only from the peasants and the Bedouin, but also from the Dead Sea minerals and from control of the Darb al-Hajj, the trading and pilgrim route between Damascus on the one hand, and Egypt and the holy cities of Arabia on the other. This control was secured by the knights and serjeants based on a line of castles of which the most important were Kerak and Montreal, so called in memory of its foundation by King Baldwin I. In barren country Montreal occupies the whole summit of a bare rocky hill high above the village of Shaubak. The irregular shape of its ground plan and the slight projection of its towers are imposed by the natural edge of the defended area, that is, the line beyond which the emplacement of the castle is delimited by the steep downward slope.

Plate 24

The strength of some castles lay wholly in their man-made defences, that of others in the natural features of the site. Most, however, owed something to both art and nature. In the remainder of this chapter it is possible to mention only a few. Three in particular have been chosen for discussion – Sahyun, because it belongs wholly to the twelfth century, and is an example of a major baronial castle and shows the attitude of the Franks to earlier Byzantine work; Krak des Chevaliers, because we can learn from it how a castle grew through time, and because its size and completeness, to say nothing of its sheer beauty, make it the finest building of its kind in the world; Pilgrims' Castle at 'Atlit, because it is that comparatively rare phenomenon, a castle founded, rather than occupied and developed, by the crusaders, and because it belongs wholly to the thirteenth century. Both Krak and 'Atlit became the property of a Military Order, and our knowledge of both has been advanced by excavations of major importance.

Nearly all of the coastal plain of Syria and Palestine is overlooked by hill and mountain ranges. The country therefore abounds in spur sites, isolated on all sides but one by precipitous slopes, with the principal man-made defences concentrated on that one side where the spur is joined to neighbouring high ground. At Sahyun, where the protecting ravines are particularly deep, the isolation of the site is completed by a

Plate 12

Fig. 13 Sahyun. The castle. A, B Gateways to upper castle. 1–6 Crusader towers. Arrows indicate most likely direction of attack. (After R. C. Smail)

rock-cut ditch, which is overlooked by the castle's most powerful *Fig. 13,* Plate 11
defences. The ditch is a truly stupendous work, 128 metres in length,
18 metres wide and some 26 metres in depth. Because it was too wide
to carry a bridge in a single span, a tall needle of rock was left and capped Plate 13
with masonry to serve as a pier. A second ditch within the castle divides
it into a main, upper bailey to the east, and a lower to the west.

The natural strength of the site is so great that, on most of its perimeter,
it is sufficiently defended by a simple curtain wall which follows the
edge of the slope, equipped with no more than an occasional small
tower. Elaborate fortifications were thought necessary only on the east,
and at the eastern section of the south wall.

In the upper castle there are two kinds of masonry and two defence
schemes. The ground is not level, but rises gently to an eminence on
which stands a small rectangular enclosure. Between this and the main
ditch are a number of walls in the same masonry, which at first glance
seem to be a single defensive scheme, with a series of obstacles culmi-
nating in a citadel. It is preceded, however, by a different and more Plates 14, 15
massive scheme of formidable walls and towers, constructed in larger
blocks of drafted masonry on the eastern and southeastern edge of the
site. It is inconceivable that anyone should have wished to build,
behind the great barrier, the slighter citadel and the walls which precede
it. The only meaningful hypothesis is that the builders of the outer
defences found the citadel and its associated curtain walls already in
existence, decided to ignore them and to replace them with massive
defences of their own design.

Who were these successive occupants? It is known that the site was
occupied by the Byzantines during the late tenth century when they broke
out of Asia Minor, where they had long stood on the defensive, and
re-established the duchy of Antioch in northern Syria. The defences
that culminate in the citadel are Byzantine not only in their general
lay-out, but also in some of their details. In some wall sections, for
example, small blocks are laid diamond-wise and there is a polygonal
tower, a design never adopted by the Franks. The subsequent occupiers
who rejected these defences and provided their own were the crusaders.
The drafted masonry is typical of twelfth-century Frankish work, and
the masons' marks found on it include not only letters of the Roman
alphabet but kite-shaped shields of a kind carried by western knights of

the period. Most typical of all is the largest of the towers. Its form and arrangement, already described, make it 'like any keep in Normandy'.

In designing castles, did the crusaders learn from, or even imitate, their Byzantine predecessors? This problem has often been discussed, and it is one to which Sahyun contributes some interesting information. The evidence provided by a single castle does not permit far-reaching generalization, but it has to be said that at Sahyun the Franks fortified the site in their own way. They virtually ignored the earlier Byzantine defences or, if Deschamps is right in supposing that they maintained them in good order, they relegated them to a minor position.

The great rock-cut fosse is generally credited to the crusaders, but such an obstacle must already have existed before their arrival. The nature of the site demanded it, and it was a Byzantine habit to strengthen their fortresses in this way; they had done so at Urfa and Gargar. The crusaders, however, may have widened or deepened it. The distance from the edge of the ditch to the nearest surviving Byzantine wall is about 18 metres. The distance cannot have been less in the Byzantine period and, if the Franks did widen the ditch, it may have been greater. It is inconceivable that so great a distance would have been left; immediately overlooking the ditch there must have been a Byzantine wall which the Franks destroyed and replaced with their own differently designed and more powerfully constructed defences.

Sahyun is a warning against simple generalizations. On the site the Franks did not use their Byzantine inheritance as a model, but neither did they reject it in every detail. For example, the mural towers are cut off from the rampart walk of the curtain wall; except in the gatehouse tower access to each section of the ramparts was possible only by exterior staircases leading up from the courtyard. In the three rectangular towers there is no direct access from the ground floor room to that on the first floor. This interruption of communication, desperately inconvenient as it must have been in many ways, was presumably a defensive device. An enemy who had gained a foothold in a tower or in a section of the wall could be more easily isolated there. It is described and recommended in the works of theorists known to the Byzantines, and is embodied in some of their buildings. The design of some of the casemates and apertures provided for archers, and of the combination of lintel and shallow relieving arch over certain doorways, could also be found in

Fig. 14 Sahyun. A Main gatehouse to upper castle; B gatehouses to lower castle. Attackers are vulnerable from above as they approach and are compelled to make sharp turns. (After P. Deschamps)

Byzantine buildings. But the most characteristic adaptation by the crusaders concerns the design of entrances. The southern gate of the upper castle, like the southern and northern gates of the lower castle, was carefully placed in the flank of a tower. If the enemy wished to rush the entrance, his line of approach was exposed to lateral shooting from the curtain wall above. At two of the entrances he found that if he did

Fig. 14

succeed in forcing the first gate, then he must change the direction of his attack, since access to the second gate leading from gatehouse to bailey was at right angles to that of the door by which he had just entered.

Plate 16

Krak des Chevaliers also stands on a spur, the steep sides of which give protection from all directions but the south. From this quarter an attacking force was able to approach on fairly even ground at the same level as the castle; as it did so it was faced by the castle's most powerful defences.

Although Krak stands out as the finest castle in Syria or anywhere else, its history has features in common with other crusader strongholds. It was not originally founded by the Franks; it was already there to be attacked by a contingent of the First Crusade as the main expedition passed through the region. Further, the count of Tripoli found at a fairly early date that he could no longer maintain it, and as early as 1144 he made it over, together with many other places in his county, to the Hospitallers, who already had the resources not only to repair it, but later to extend it. The castle in its present state represents the extent to which the Hospitallers had developed it by 1271, the years in which they surrendered it to the Mamluks.

Fig. 15

The scheme of defence established by the knights was a double line of walls which enclosed in two concentric rings the area occupied and defended by the garrison. This had not been the plan of the castle when they first acquired it. Throughout the hundred and twenty-seven years of their occupation there was much rebuilding and new building. During the major archaeological work which he directed at the castle from 1927 to 1929, Paul Deschamps made a close study of the different types of masonry in the castle, of the masons' stone-dressing techniques, of architectural ornament and inscriptions, and thereby was able to identify the main stages of construction. Some of the evidence is clear enough. The vaulting and severe decoration of the chapel are as in-

Plates 17, 19

contestably of the twelfth century as the tracery in the cloister outside the chapter house belongs to the thirteenth.

Plate 47

The chapel stands in the innermost courtyard of the castle, and its eastern end, or chevet, is part of the inner defences. This chevet, like the curtain wall of which it is part and beyond which it projects, is in rusticated masonry – stones squared so that they can be laid in regular courses but with the central portion of each block's face left rougher than

Fig. 15 Krak des Chevaliers. Plan of the castle. 1 North gate; 2 Tower P; 3 chapel; 4 chapter house and cloister; 5 vaults added at southern end of courtyard; 6 substructure of main southern towers; 7 main entrance; 8 hairpin bend on entry ramp; 9–10 gateways into inner court. (After W. Müller-Wiener)

Fig. 16 Krak des Chevaliers. 1 Posterns; 2 aqueduct; 3 open cistern; 4 terrace above vaulted accommodation at southern end of courtyard; 5 inner courtyard; 6 chapter house and cloister; 7 Tower P; 8 chapel; 9 gateways; 10 main entrance; 11 terrace above entry ramp; 12 hairpin bend on entry ramp. (After P. Deschamps)

and standing in slight relief above the smoother margins. Both are integral parts of the chapel's original structure, which can be securely assigned to the twelfth century.

This masonry exists not only along the northern section of the inner wall, where it is exposed to view, but also along the western, where it is not. It was subsequently encased in the works which are now visible from outside the castle, that is, a wall set with rounded towers and strengthened by a sloping glacis, the whole laid out in regular courses of smooth-faced masonry. How do we know that it is later than the rusticated masonry? In the first place, the northern extremity of the glacis can be seen cutting across a window in the southwestern face of Tower P, showing that it was a later addition. Second, against the inner face of the inner western wall there is a long vaulted compartment, called by Deschamps 'la salle de cent-vingt mètres', from which it is possible to gain access to a narrow passage in the thickness of the wall. As one walks southward along this passage, the left-hand wall is of rusticated masonry. In places it is blocked or made narrower by a similar wall. It is in fact the old outer wall of the twelfth-century castle literally encased in additions of the thirteenth. It is therefore possible to establish the earlier plan of the castle, perhaps as it was when the Hospitallers first acquired it – the present inner court enclosed by a rusticated curtain wall, strengthened by towers of rectangular plan and shallow projection.

Fig. 16

To the original nucleus the knights made many additions. These included not only the encasing of the original curtain on its southern and western sides in a thirteenth-century shell, as already described, but the provision of a new, outer circuit of walls and towers, thus extending the castle by giving it a new first-line of defence, and the additional area enclosed between the inner and outer curtains. At a late stage in their occupation of the castle the Hospitallers took the precaution of adding, on the eastern side, a ramped and elaborately defended entrance between the inner and outer walls.

All these were major additions to the defensive strength of the castle. The rounded towers and the thickness of their walls gave maximum protection against stone-throwing artillery, just as the glacis kept the enemy well away from the foot of the walls and increased his vulnerability to attack from above. Even more impressive than their military advantages, these constructions have also remained proof against earthquake over the centuries, and help to account for the remarkable near-completeness of the castle's preservation. The great height of the defences gave them maximum command over the area likely to be occupied by a besieger. The machinery which could be mounted on the flat roofs of the towers or of the vaulted buildings had a decided advantage over those of the besieger, which could operate only from ground-level. The archers of the garrison could also engage the enemy at many levels below that of the rampart walk. The great height and successive storeys of the place were well brought out by François Anus, architect to the mission led by Deschamps. In preparing complete plans of the castle he had to make drawings at six different levels.

Plate 20

The new outer line of walls, built in the earliest years of the thirteenth century, was lower and slighter than that of the inner court, and was placed not far from it. By such an arrangement the enemy could be engaged from both walls at once and, if he seized the outer, his tenure of it could be made dangerously uncomfortable from the inner wall. But to take over the lower outer wall was no easy matter. It was not just an obstacle, but was abundantly equipped with means for the conduct of a vigorous defence. Archers at ground-level could man a series of casemates while others could be stationed on a mural gallery above and, above that again, on a rampart walk.

The entrance to Krak presents features of great interest. The main gateway of the original castle stood on its eastern side and still gives admission to the inner court. But the principal entrance to the castle as it had developed by 1271 had to be in its outer wall. This doorway was also on the eastern face, and was joined to the original inner gateway by an ingeniously defended approach.

Those who planned castles were always faced with the necessity of reconciling the needs of defence, which became paramount only at rare intervals, and the peacetime uses of the castle, which were an everyday affair. The buildings could be sited and planned so as to set major problems to an attacker. They would be put in remote and unapproachable situations, for example, or could be given no entrances at ground-level, all of which made them almost useless for daily living. At a place like Krak, an important provincial headquarters of an international Order, a balance needed to be struck between the needs of a siege and of daily routine.

Plate 18

Such a balance is admirably exemplified by the entrance. It rises gently from the outer gate to the inner in a series of broad, shallow steps, carefully designed for the easy use both of men and horses. At the same time, difficulties were multiplied for an attacker, although these were not obstacles at other times. An enemy fighting his way in was hampered by sharp changes of direction – a left turn through a right-angle as he entered, followed, after a short ascent, by a sharp hairpin bend. Doorways set in the walls exposed him to surprise attacks from the flank. His task was made no easier by sudden changes of light, from dusk to bright sunlight, and when his approach came into the open, he was exposed to missiles from overhead.

It is only fitting that Krak des Chevaliers should have been the subject of thorough archaeological investigation. The director of the investigation, Paul Deschamps, from whose book all subsequent discussions of the castle, including this one, are derived, demonstrates how narrow is the view that would regard such a place simply as a fortification. It was a barracks in which troops were quartered – hence the spacious accommodation, on many levels, for men, horses and stores; the thoroughgoing measures for the storage of water in quantity; the serried rank of latrines.

When Wilbrand of Oldenburg saw it in 1212, the Hospitallers assured him that even in peacetime the garrison numbered 2000 men. It is interesting to compare this figure with that given for the Templars' great stronghold at Safad by that anonymous thirteenth-century writer to whom reference has already been made: the daily ration strength was 1700 in peacetime, 2200 in war. The military force housed in Krak was based on the brethren of the Hospital, knights and serjeants, who lived under vows of poverty, celibacy and obedience, and so it was also a monastery – hence the principal buildings which open from the inner courtyard, the chapel and the chapter house with its small cloister. It was also a provincial headquarters of a wealthy, international corporation, a centre of decision-making and executive action, both in respect of its own government and of the vigorous external policy it pursued towards its Moslem neighbours, especially the ruler of Homs. The visual beauty of the place, surpassed by only a minority of the world's great buildings, is the result not only of its physical setting, but of the austere splendour of its southern and western faces. Design and execution go beyond the requirements of defence. They reflect the wider needs, the wealth and the standing in Christian society of the great Order.

Farther to the north the Hospitallers held another castle of comparable size and importance. Until 1186 Marqab had been the fortified seat of the Mansoer, a leading baronial family in the principality of Antioch. In that year they decided that they could no longer maintain it, for reasons which, in the legal document by which the place was conveyed to the Hospitallers, they succinctly stated – the cost was too great and the infidels too near.

During the ninety-nine years of their occupation the Hospitallers developed Marqab in a way which gave it many likenesses to Krak.

Plate 29

There is the same double line of defence, with the same low fore-wall even closer to the loftier works behind; the same massive round towers placed opposite the only sector in which an attacker could set up siege works; the same large chapel opening into the inner courtyard, the same vaulted ranges, set in storeys one above the other, to serve as barracks, store-rooms and stables. It resembles Kerak in Moab in that the spur on which it was placed could accommodate not only a castle but a small town. The Bishop of Banyas from the coastal plain was glad to take up residence in Marqab in the dangerous days of the thirteenth century. The great castle, set in a twisted, improbable black and white landscape of chalk and volcanic deposit, is not nearly as well known as Krak. Certainly its masonry is inferior. Instead of the Krak's finely-jointed courses of carefully squared limestone blocks, Marqab is of black basalt set in a thick mortar. It has never been cleared, so that much of it remains ruinous and overgrown. Let us hope that this castle too will one day be investigated as thoroughly as Krak.

Plate 27

Plate 28

Fig. 17

'Atlit, a few miles south of Mount Carmel, was that rarity among crusader castles – an original foundation by the crusaders. The preaching of a new crusade had brought many westerners to the Holy Land in 1217, and while they were waiting for the main action to begin (they were subsequently launched against Damietta in the Nile Delta) they not only re-fortified Caesarea, but dug the foundations and raised the first walls of a new fortress. The Templars took a leading part in this work; and since the site was on their land, and they had long garrisoned a tower a short distance to the east, the new stronghold was handed over to them. The part played by the western crusaders was commemorated in the name, *Castrum Peregrinorum*, Pilgrims' Castle.

There are likenesses between Templar Tartus and Pilgrims' Castle, just as there are between Hospitaller Krak and Marqab; and because there are differences between these respective pairs, some writers have distinguished between Templar and Hospitaller 'schools' of castle building. Such a distinction cannot be pressed too far, since both Orders acquired many castles whose form and style were determined before they took them over. Any differentiation should be confined to the four places under discussion, and the differences even here are not so much in the schemes of defence and the principles of fortification they embody, as in the physical appearance of the buildings. In the two Hospitaller castles

Fig. 17 'Atlit. Plan of Pilgrims' castle. (After C. N. Johns)

the face of the thirteenth-century masonry presents an even surface, and
at Marqab the blocks are rather small. 'Atlit and Tartus are of rusticated
masonry, and at 'Atlit some of the blocks are particularly large; they
came in part from the walls of ancient buildings uncovered during the
digging of the foundations. Finally, the major towers at Krak and
Marqab were round, while those at 'Atlit and Tartus were rectangular
in plan.

The site selected for Pilgrims' Castle was a small peninsula, and the
natural advantages of the site shaped the scheme of defence. The main
fortifications were built at the junction of the peninsula with the mainland, as this was the only direction from which a land-based attack was
possible. Since the central area of the little headland was a few feet higher
than the rest, it was available for development as an inner ward. It is also
important that, as the outer edge of the defended area was at sea-level,
besiegers were denied the most deadly and devastating means of attack

Fig. 18

Fig. 18 'Atlit. Castle and town. (After C. N. Johns)

Tower

North Harbour

North sea tower

Bath house

South Harbour

50 0 100 m

Crusader Church

South sea tower

Crusader stables

at their disposal, namely, the mining gallery driven into the foundations of a wall or tower.

The castle, and the small town which developed outside it, were excavated in the early 1930's by the Palestine Department of Antiquities. The work was under the direction of Mr C. N. Johns, and its importance gives him a secure place among the very small group of scholars – mainly French, more recently Israeli, with his as the only British name among them – who have made significant contributions to our knowledge about the military architecture of the crusaders. Unfortunately for the general reader the results of his investigations can be studied only in excavation reports published in a learned journal, and in his guide-book to 'Atlit, a small work of outstanding quality, which has been unobtainable since existing stocks were destroyed in military action in 1947. A larger book based on the investigations at 'Atlit, supplemented by his work at 'Ajlun and the Tower of David, would have the same importance in the historiography of the subject as those of Rey and Deschamps.

Of the many aspects of the castle which might be discussed, three are of particular interest. The first concerns the strength of the eastern defences, a masterpiece of scientific design. Ditch, outer and inner wall were a trio of obstacles planned to operate in combination both in barring the besiegers' path and in enabling the garrison to strike back.

Plate 21

The size and weight of the masonry and the sheer thickness of the walls made them proof against sap and bombardment. Their height gave defending archers maximum command of ground over which an enemy could advance. Archers in the mural gallery built in the outer wall were 3 metres above attackers on the far side of the fosse, those on the rampart walk were 5.5 metres, while the summit of the two main towers

Plate 22

of the inner wall was no less than 34 metres above ground-level. The enemy beyond the ditch could be engaged from all these levels simul-taneously. The difficulty of forcing an entrance was increased by placing successive doorways out of alignment with each other, so forcing attackers to change direction, often through a right-angle. Every step into the castle was vulnerable to attack from above. A double line of walls, less formidable than those of the eastern defences, was continued around the whole perimeter of the peninsula. They could be attacked only by water-

Plate 23

borne troops, a situation which the Templars had little reason to fear. These waters were dominated by the Italians, and the harbour they used most was only a few miles away at Acre. Irresistible naval help was always at hand.

To turn to the second aspect, these walls had another function besides that of defence; they also served as the outer walls of long ranges of buildings set up along the inner face. It has been seen how the courtyards of crusader castles became built-up areas, and at 'Atlit this development was unusually intense. As at Krak, the scale and style of such buildings remind us that the castle was also the home of a community devoted to religious as well as to military ends. The dominant group in that community were knights, who expected accommodation of a high standard; the Order had the resources to provide it and the incentive to display its own international importance. The north tower of the main eastern wall housed in its topmost and loftiest storey a vaulted hall which may well have been the main public room in the castle. Some evidence of its former splendour is provided by the stone brackets carved with male heads, still in position on the one surviving wall, and by fragments of the moulded vaulting-ribs which these brackets supported. The south tower must also have been a tall and commodious building, while the south-western corner of the inner courtyard was filled by the large polygonal church, probably modelled on the Dome of the Rock from which, being known to the crusaders as the Lord's Temple, the Knights Templar took their name. The undercrofts of buildings which bounded the western side of the court have survived with ribbed vaults and cross-arches still complete, while there are traces of similar structures both on the northern and southern sides. In the greatest days of the castle, when a royal household took up its quarters there for the lying-in of a queen of France, with the Master of the Temple standing as godfather to the newly-born prince, this inner courtyard was the busy centre of buildings

Fig. 17

which had become, for the time being, a palace. As the plan shows, those parts of the castle outside the raised inner ward were even more fully built up with long ranges in three, two, or a single aisle of cross-vaulted bays. Although only small traces of these buildings remain, they are enough to make possible a reconstruction of their scale and appearance. Visitors to castles in the more northerly parts of Europe think of life in their stone buildings as a grim ordeal made comfortless by gloom, damp and penetrating cold. But for much of the year in the eastern Mediterranean one of the main amenities is protection from the sun's heat and glare in the middle part of the day. In 'Atlit we can still sense how effectively these stone walls provided it, especially those at the western end of the peninsula, set as they were almost at the water's edge, and exposed to the sea-breezes.

Finally, the castle still stands, as few others do, in its full territorial setting. Too often the castle which survives as an ancient monument is only a fragment of the whole complex of buildings and defences of which it was once part, but from the walls of 'Atlit something can still be seen of the castle's wider context. Immediately outside it is the site of a small town. On the north and west its boundary is the sea-shore, on south and east a wall and ditch. The eastern wall, some 600 metres in length, lies 230 metres east of the shore and the main castle defences. Its mural towers are few and small, standing at the angle where the east wall joins the south, another at the extremity where each wall met the sea. These walls were useful as a boundary and were sufficient protection against raiders and others who disturbed public order; the three gates which took wheeled traffic and the fourth for pedestrians could be closed and manned at nightfall. Though it was only a slight obstacle to a well-equipped invading army, nevertheless, the little town in the shadow of the great castle throve to a modest importance and had its own burgess court. Whatever remains of most of its buildings lies buried beneath the sand-dunes though some, a church, a bath-house, a range of byres and stables, were cleared and investigated by Mr Johns.

Beyond the town, but still visible from the castle, is a larger supply area, bounded on the east by a low ridge, and equipped with means which enabled the garrison to protect and control it. The Templars quarried there much of the stone for the castle, just as ancient settlers on the site had done two thousand years earlier, and as the British were to do in the twentieth century for the new harbour works at Haifa. Roads converged on the town gates through these rock cuttings in the ridge which in the past had been the resort of highwaymen, and the Templars, who had been founded to keep the roads safe for pilgrims, had in their early days manned a small castle on the ridge. There is evidence that the cuttings were treated as entrances to an extended castle area, and were equipped with gates, and that a bank was raised at right-angles to the ridge to cross the coastal plain between it and the sea. Castle, town and banlieu were thus all controlled by an international religious order.

Fig. 18

The anonymous writer on Safad may be given the last word, for he paints a verbal picture of the castle in comparable terms. He refers to the surrounding district as the source of its supplies, of fish, corn, legumes, honey and fruit, especially that of the olive and the vine, with wide pastures and ample resources of water for the needs of animals and the irrigation of crops. The castle had a bakehouse and was well equipped with mills, some driven by wind, some by animal power. Outside the castle were twelve water-mills. All these were reckoned among the excellences of a castle built, as the writer put it, to weaken and drive back the heathen, to comfort and increase the faithful, to honour Christ and to exalt God's holy Church.

Why should garrisons protected by fortifications like those at Safad or Sahyun ever have needed to surrender? The siegecraft of the age was, after all, for the most part extremely simple. We read in the sources of scaling ladders, of a battering-ram swung by a crew sheltered by a timber penthouse, of wooden towers, perhaps made barely mobile by a wheeled undercarriage, such as those by which the crusaders of 1099 gained a foothold on the walls of Jerusalem. What could such primitive apparatus achieve against the towering defences of Krak, especially those sections thickened at the base by the great talus?

There is no single answer to such questions. In the first place, it has always been possible to reduce strong-places without ever putting the defences to the test; a fortress can be blockaded and starved into sub-mission. The employment of such means was not always practicable, since it needed ample time and the absence of a relieving force bent on raising the siege – conditions which were rarely satisfied. But it was by such means that some of the major castles beyond the Jordan were reduced after Saladin's victory at Hattin.

Events in that same period proved yet again the ancient truth that 'men, not walls, make the city'. Fortifications are means for the use of the garrison, not *vice versa*. If the morale of the garrison can be destroyed then walls and towers will not be effectively defended. The more determined the besieging army and the more protracted the siege, the more severely that morale will be tested. It was affected too by the prospects of relief by a friendly force which would challenge the besiegers and bring in supplies. If such help could be expected, then morale could be maintained in the face of heavy odds; if not, then the garrison's will to resist could break. The defeat of the Christian army at Hattin in 1187 was so complete that, in the weeks which followed, the garrisons of many strong-places in the kingdom judged it useless to prolong resistance because there was no early prospect that a relieving force could take the field. Sahyun, for all the strength of its defences, natural and artificial, surrendered to Saladin in three days. The strongly fortified city of Acre yielded in a single day; but from 1189 its garrison was able to hold the same defences for nearly two years against the forces of the Third Crusade, partly because throughout that period Saladin had an army in the field cooperating with the garrison.

That other great destroyer of crusader rule, the Mamluk Sultan Baybars, not only deployed massive force against the castles, but used his ingenuity to break the will and cohesion of the garrisons. While he was attacking Krak, the Hospitaller in command of the defence received, by the sultan's contrivance, a skilfully forged order, which appeared to come from his superior in Tripoli, to surrender the castle. At Safad Baybars broke the unity of the defenders by promising quarter to those who were not Franks.

There were of course many occasions when castles were reduced because their garrisons, though in good heart, were beaten by skilfully directed military attack. The sources show that, in the twelfth century, the technique of siegecraft developed both in western Europe and among the crusaders in the East. Rams, ladders, siege-towers and surface sapping continued in use, but we also hear more of effective stone-throwing artillery and of mining. The range and weight of great stones hurled against or over defensive walls may have been increased by the introduction of the trebuchet. The propellent force of this timber machine was provided by a massive weight at one end of a pivoted beam. When the weighted end fell, the other, to which a sling was attached, flew sharply upwards, so that a stone or other missile – there were occasions when it was a corpse, a carcase or a severed head – was thrown through a high trajectory. In 1191 parts of the defences of Acre were seriously weakened by prolonged bombardment.

But the deadliest weapon of all was the mine. Unless it was made impossible by water defences, hard rock, or physical inaccessibility, there was no effective defence against the mining gallery which enabled besiegers to destroy the foundations of a tower or a stretch of wall. It became increasingly normal for medieval armies to take the field with a corps of specialists recruited from mining areas. Saladin took them from the region of Aleppo, just as in England Edward I was to look to the Forest of Dean. However massive their construction and ingenious their design, crusader castles and their garrisons could be subjected to both material and moral pressures; and of these, the moral were the more destructive.

The Churches

The first crusaders came to the Holy Land in response to preaching begun and inspired by the Pope, and those who settled brought with them the ecclesiastical institutions of the western Church which looked to the Pope as its head. They consecrated bishops, at Albara and Ramla for example, while the First Crusade was still on the march. After the conquest of Antioch and Jerusalem, no time was lost in appointing a Latin Patriarch in either city, and thereafter the establishment of secular and ecclesiastical government proceeded together. The Christian conquest extended the Roman hierarchy, and over this extension the Pope, from the first, exercised undisputed authority. A normal two-way traffic was soon in evidence and continued as a common fact of life throughout the existence of the crusader states – papal legates were despatched from Rome to the East, while parties to difficult ecclesiastical cases in Syria took their pleas and appeals to Rome. Meanwhile Syria and the Holy Land were organized into provinces and dioceses; convents of monks and nuns concentrated around Jerusalem and Antioch, but more rarely elsewhere; though after Saladin's conquests displaced religious communities crowded into Acre. Most of our knowledge of the Latin Church in the crusader states is at diocesan level and above; and, as usual, we have a clearer picture of such matters in the kingdom of Jerusalem than in the other Latin states.

This new hierarchy provided itself with churches partly by using those which already existed. The first view of the Old City of Jerusalem is made unforgettable by one of the great buildings of the world, the Dome of the Rock, erected in the Temple area in the last decade of the seventh century. To the pious Moslem this centrally-planned mosque is less holy only than the shrine at Mecca. During the crusader occupation, for a brief span of eighty-eight years in its long history, its gilded dome was surmounted by a cross and it became a Christian church served by a community of Augustinian canons. Another building, even more ancient, is the Church of the Nativity at Bethlehem, which stands over the rock-cut grotto, venerated since very early Christian times as Christ's

Plate 3

birthplace. The first church built on the site was commissioned by Constantine in the early fourth century. This was replaced on the orders of Justinian in the mid-sixth century, and it is his basilica which has managed to withstand the perils of fire, earthquake and invasion and survive to this day. The crusaders made Bethlehem, for the first time in its history, the seat of a bishop, removing that dignity from Ascalon. The additions they made to the work of Justinian's architects were very small, but in the 1160's they undertook a thorough-going interior re-decoration of which more will be said in a later chapter.

In these places, as in many others, the crusaders made use of the inheritance from the past; but they also established new foundations. This was both necessary and natural. Necessary, because although the Holy Land has been richly endowed with churches in the Byzantine period, they had suffered from natural disasters and the first Moslem invasions. Natural, because in Europe the twelfth century was one of the great ages of church building, and it was to be expected that the westerners would apply that same creative energy in lands they now controlled, especially as these were the lands of the Bible.

Inheritance and development, the Roman past and the romanesque present, both were and still are combined in the holiest place in Christendom, the Church of the Holy Sepulchre; to this must be added a force which lay behind much medieval church building in the Holy Land – the devotion of pilgrims.

The crusading movement in the twelfth and thirteenth centuries always functioned on two levels. On the one there was papal organization, the composition and despatch of encyclicals, the planned preaching tours by Pope and legates, the negotiation of truces to enable princes at war to join hands in a crusade. With all this there was secular leadership, sometimes in the hands of emperors and kings, who made formal diplomatic preparations, negotiated major shipping contracts with Genoese or Venetians, attempted to concentrate supplies and organize markets along their likely line of march. All these were affairs of the great world of government, diplomacy and finance. Such transactions leave formal records in their wake, some of which are still accessible to us, and it is therefore these aspects of the crusading movement that we comprehend best. The other level, equally powerful in its day, is one which we do not easily understand; this is to some extent because, living as we do in a secularized age, we find the message contained in its records less readily accessible.

There was no medieval word for crusade. Among the words used to describe such an expedition, two of the most common were *iter*, a journey, or *peregrinatio*, a pilgrimage. And though those who took part might be called, from the cross stitched to their clothing, *crucesignati*, a more common term was *peregrini*, pilgrims. They were pilgrims of a special sort, carrying not staff and scrip, but weapons with which to fight their way to the shrines which were their objective; and the motives which drove them forward, and sustained them through extremes of hardship, included that religious zeal which sent men and women on normal peaceful pilgrimages.

Crusades were partly expeditions organized by heads of governments, partly manifestations of popular religion. There are modern writers who seriously underestimate the second element. Yet any major crusade depended for its existence on mass enthusiasm. Failure to arouse it may be the key to an understanding of those frequent occasions on which the Pope preached a crusade but none was launched. A major crisis during the First Crusade had been its near-collapse after the conquest of Antioch, when its principal leaders had competed for lands and towns in northern Syria. Only the forcible insistence of the pilgrim rank and file compelled the princes, or some of them, to lead the expedition to Jerusalem.

Once the settlement was established, pilgrims became a constant fact of life in the Latin kingdom. Each spring brought an annual influx, intent on celebrating Easter at the Holy Places and spending the summer in the Holy Land. Their needs and numbers affected the growth of Italian shipping and the design of their ships; the dues they paid and the money they spent were elements in the king's finances and the kingdom's economy; their presence might significantly reinforce the royal army during a difficult campaign. Two of the kingdom's most powerful institutions came into being in direct response to the needs of pilgrims, the Hospitallers to tend the sick and the Templars to police the roads.

The pilgrims came to the lands of the Bible to see with their own eyes the physical setting of those episodes in history they best knew and which were part of their deepest beliefs. In earlier centuries, when Christianity was still an advancing wave, irresistible even to the Roman imperial government, popular faith had gone to extremes in localizing scriptural scenes and characters. On the Mount of Olives, for example, the pilgrims could pray not only in the Garden of Gethsemane, but on the very spot where Christ had stood when he wept over the city of Jerusalem, or from which he had finally ascended into heaven, or in the place where he had first taught his disciples the Lord's prayer. At each of these places there was a church – Dominus Flevit, Ascension, Paternoster – just as there was a church south of the city in the place were St Peter heard the cock crow. Nearby pilgrims were shown the field bought by Judas with his thirty pieces of silver. Not only had the place of crucifixion been identi⁄ fied, but the villages in which the silver pieces had been minted, the nails of the crucifixion forged, the tree grown which had provided the timber for the Cross. Such a list could be continued for many pages, in terms of the Old Testament as well as of the New; but of the many hundreds of sites with such associations, none could compare with those few square yards of ground where Jesus had been crucified and buried and from which he rose again. When men vowed to make the pilgrimage to the Holy Places, or to liberate the Holy Places from the Moslems, they thought first of the scene of those events and mysteries central to the

Christian religion. This too had its church, Holy Sepulchre, the most sought and longed-for of Christian objectives. Here there were all the elements so far discussed in this chapter – inheritance from an ancient past; the building zeal of twelfth-century Europeans; continuous pilgrim devotion.

Calvary and Christ's rock-cut tomb had been revealed by the Christian community in Jerusalem to St Helena, Christian mother of Constantine, the first Christian Roman Emperor. Jerusalem had been destroyed by Titus in AD 70 and refounded by Hadrian as a Roman military colony some fifty years later. For nearly two centuries the holy sites lay under the paving stones of the streets and building at the edge of the forum – St Helena had them uncovered and nearby, in an underground chamber originally cut in the rock for water storage, she found parts of a cross which she and posterity accepted and venerated as that on which Christ had died. On her son's orders the sacred place was glorified by the most splendid means at his disposal. The site was levelled for building. The sepulchre became the central point of a round church under a conical roof; the grotto in which the Cross had been found became the crypt of a second, basilican church with western apse and

Fig. 19

Fig. 19 Jerusalem. Holy Sepulchre. The churches in the fourth century. (After L. A. Vincent and F. M. Abel)

double aisles. Between rotunda and basilica stood Calvary, reduced to a formal cube of rock, in a paved and colonnaded courtyard.

All this was done seven hundred and fifty years before the First Crusade. During those centuries the site was exposed to the dangers of fire and earthquake, to foreign invasion, like that of the Persians in 614 and that of the Arabs twenty years later and, at the end of the tenth century, to the malice of the only caliph who ever persecuted Christians, the mentally unstable Fatimid, al-Hakim. When the crusaders became

Fig. 20 Jerusalem. Church of the Holy Sepulchre in the twelfth century. 1 Christ's sepulchre; 2 crusader choir; 3, 4 cloisters of the canons; 5 Holy Trinity chapel (with belfry above); 6 St John's baptistery; 7 St James' chapel; 8 Calvary chapel; 9 Calvary porch; 10 refectory; 11 kitchen. (After C. Enlart)

masters of the city in 1099, the basilica had gone but the rotunda still stood. It had recently been heavily restored by the generosity of a Byzantine emperor, but it stood on Constantine's foundations and some of his masonry was, and is, still in the fabric. The church immediately became the cathedral of the Latin Patriarch and was served by a body of canons who, in 1114, were brought under Augustinian rule. A decision had already been taken by the new rulers that they would make their own distinctive contribution to the site. They joined to the rotunda, on its

Fig. 20

129

eastern side, transepts and a choir. For the first time in its already lengthy history Constantine's round church ceased to be a free-standing building. The additions were in the western romanesque style, though not without elements that were to become part of the gothic. It was sufficiently complete to be consecrated in the presence of the papal legate on 15 July, 1149, the fiftieth anniversary of the crusader conquest of the city. The only major addition between that date and Saladin's conquest was the bell-tower.

The late Roman rotunda and the romanesque additions still stand today. Much of course has been lost in eight hundred years. Only slight traces of the conventual buildings east of the church remain; the upper parts of the belfry, in the interests of safety, were taken down in 1719, and have never been rebuilt; the cupola over the crossing of transepts and choir fell as the result of the earthquake of 1927, but has since been restored. The state of the building at that time was so precarious that the western façade was shored up with scaffolding which also effectively concealed it. It has recently been taken down, having served its purpose for nearly forty years. The church had also been in danger of collapse after it had been swept by a disastrous fire in 1808. In normal circumstances the western Catholic powers would have come to the rescue but, since they were preoccupied with Napoleon, the Greek Orthodox were left to deal with it on their own. In the circumstances, which seemed desperate, immediacy of action was made the only consideration. Masons, un-instructed by architects, were called in to do their best; the building was saved, but at a price. The graceful colonnade of Constantine's church gave way to the succession of gross cement piers in which the columns were encased; the uninterrupted space between colonnade and outer wall was divided by a series of party walls; what had been a spacious processional way became a row of dark, cluttered store-rooms. In the crusader church the twin columns in the choir were similarly hidden, and the division of choir from ambulatory by party walls destroyed the medieval design as effectively as sectarian malice destroyed the inscribed tombs of the Latin kings at the foot of Calvary. Because of these ob-structions, and the excess of hanging lamps and ikons, the interior of the church is not easy to see and appreciate as a whole. Until the work of renovation now in progress was recently begun, its overcrowded appearance has been in sad contrast to the clarity and spaciousness of the

Plate 26

Aqsa Mosque or the Dome of the Rock. But the removal of the scaffolding in 1970 has once more revealed one major feature which is discussed
in the next chapter – the southern façade.

Plate 25

The additions made by the crusaders, both in general and in most of
their details, are recognizably European. The central compartment is a
choir of two bays of which the western, surmounted by the cupola,
marks the crossing of choir and transepts. At the eastern end of the other,
rib-vaulted bay stands the High Altar, set in an apse marked by four
pairs of columns, victims of the repairs of 1808. It will be seen from the
plan that the two transepts are linked not only by the crossing, but by an
ambulatory, a curving processional way which passes behind the High
Altar, between the paired columns on the one hand and the main eastern
wall of the church on the other, a wall which itself encloses an apse, and
from which radiate three apsidal chapels. Such arrangements were then
typical of a major pilgrim church, and could be found, for example, at
Cluny and in St Sernin at Toulouse, both consecrated by Pope Urban II
within a year of his beginning to preach the First Crusade. From the
central apsidal chapel a staircase led down into the crypt of St Helena,
which lay directly beneath the canons' cloister. This cloister gave covered
access to the normal conventual buildings – chapter house, frater,
refectory.

The literature of the crusaders is vast and still increases, but it does not
include a book for readers whose only language is English and which
does full justice to the architecture and history of this misused, much
visited and most moving building. It ought to be written because it is in
that small space, internationally venerated for more than sixteen hundred
years as the site of the crucifixion, deposition, entombment and resurrection of Jesus, as well as yielding relics of the Cross itself, that the key
to understanding the crusading movement is to be found. Small wonder
that, during the twelfth century, Holy Sepulchre became one of the
wealthiest churches in Christendom, with landed endowments not only
in every crusader state, but in every part of western Europe.

Churches were needed as soon as the crusader settlement was firmly
established. Most building was therefore undertaken, as at Holy
Sepulchre, in the early and middle years of the twelfth century and is in
the romanesque style of that period. The crusader occupation continued
into the age of the gothic, but less building was then undertaken and

comparatively little has survived in that later style. Its beginnings are visible in the slightly pointed arches and vaults of the twelfth century, and more emphatically in the rib-vaults of Holy Sepulchre, the exis-tence of which can be inferred also at Sabastiyah and the Church of Jacob's Well. It will be seen that at Tartus gothic details were first applied to a romanesque fabric, until the new style took over completely on the western façade. Mainly gothic, too, is the Cenacle on Mount Zion, a room visited by pilgrims as the scene of the Last Supper; much of the construction must belong to the second crusader occupation of Jerusalem negotiated by Frederick II. There were notable thirteenth-century buildings in Acre, but virtually all have been destroyed. We

Plate 34

can still admire the tremendous cylindrical piers and rib-vaults of the Hospitallers' refectory, and a seventeenth-century illustration has preserved the general appearance and much of the detail of the Church of St Andrew. All that survives of this building above ground, however, is the handsome gothic doorway carried off to Cairo and re-erected there as a trophy of the final Moslem conquest. There are other glimpses of gothic splendour in the carved brackets and moulded ribbing of the

Fig. 21

Templars' great halls at Tartus and 'Atlit and, at the latter, the fragments of their centrally-planned church. And it is in another castle that a small but exquisite early gothic display has been preserved, in the arches,

Plate 19

tracery and mouldings of the little cloister and chapter house at Krak des Chevaliers, and in the vaulting and decoration of the round room, set in one of the massive southern towers, that must have been reserved for the castellan, or even for the Master of the Order.

Most crusader churches in Syria and the Holy Land, however, belong to the twelfth century, and although no two buildings are ever exactly alike, the larger of them have features in common which it may be useful to discuss before passing on to a consideration of particular buildings.

The interior of such churches was normally basilican in plan, that is, a central nave flanked on either side by a single aisle, with nave and aisle terminating in eastern apses. Only the Church of the Holy Sepulchre, for example, had an ambulatory and radiating chapels, and only the basilica at Bethlehem had double aisles on either side of the nave. There was no elaborate eastern arm of the church. There might be a small space between nave and apse, a kind of attenuated choir, but that was all. The

Fig. 21   Tortosa. Vaulting in Templars' hall. (After C. Enlart)

elaborate arrangement of some churches, with choir, retro choir and perhaps Lady Chapel all east of the crossing, were unknown in Latin Syria. Even transepts were rare. In the cathedral at Tyre they projected some six metres north and south of the line of the nave, and they may have been part of the Church of Jacob's Well. These were exceptions, and some have thought it strange that in the Holy Land the plan of so few churches should have been in the form of a cross. And it seems stranger still that, in a number of churches, the outer walls of the easternmost aisle bays are slightly thicker than the rest, as if in formal and distant recognition of the existence of a transept. There could, therefore, be no true crossing of transepts and nave, no space in which the four arms of the church met. At Holy Sepulchre and St Anne's, both in Jerusalem, the easternmost bay of the nave was given special treatment, with cupola and lantern raised above it, but no such feature has survived outside the Holy City.

Plates 41, 42

Nave and aisles were vaulted in stone. There has always been a timber roof on the Church of the Nativity at Bethlehem and the Cathedral of St Paul at Tarsus, but these again are exceptions. Elsewhere all aisles and some naves were divided into a succession of groin-vaulted bays, usually separated from each other by transverse arches. Other naves were covered by a continuous tunnel vault, slightly pointed, and these too might be divided into bays for transverse arches.

Nave was divided from aisles by an arcade sometimes of round-headed, but usually of wide, slightly pointed arches, which were carried on rectangular piers, or on pillars, or on a combination of the two. On the south side of the nave at Jebail, and again at Abu Ghosh, four-sided piers stand in their simplest form, but they were more often cruciform in plan. This was a logical arrangement inasmuch as the northern and southern arms of the cross received the transverse arches of nave and aisle, the eastern and western the arch of the nave arcade; but still more elaborate schemes were possible, with pilasters or half-columns attached to the face of the pier. On the face towards the nave supports were carried up the full height of the nave to meet the transverse arch at the springing of the vault. At Gaza this was achieved by two columns, one placed vertically above the other; but it was more usual to employ a single tall shaft, either a pilaster, as at Ramla, or a column, as at Hebron or Tartus. At Sabastiyah, pairs of engaged columns were used.

Plate 44

Windows in such buildings were few and small. They were opened either through the tunnel vault itself or, when the nave was groin-vaulted, in the wall above the nave arcade. All this, again, is a far cry from the complex, highly organized nave elevations of the late romanesque and gothic cathedrals of the West, with their ascending bands of arcade, tribune gallery, triforium and clerestory.

The decoration of most of the surviving churches is simple and severe, the most prevalent form was moulding, applied to the voussoirs of arches, to the bases of piers and columns, to their imposts and abaci. A horizontal accent was often provided by a continuous string course, also moulded, which joined the abaci of the nave wall shafts, and which was sometimes continued round the curve of the apse. The carving of capitals was commonly derived from the corinthian style, and the most wide-spread motifs were different forms of the acanthus and fat, smooth leaves with the points curving outwards. But there are notable exceptions to these common themes, especially in the field of figure sculpture, and none more so than the capitals of Nazareth, discussed in the next chapter.

Church interiors were often adorned with mosaic and mural paintings. Past travellers and pilgrims have left accounts of the pictures and inscriptions which once glowed from the walls and vaults of Holy Sepulchre, but this decoration, like the paintings in the cathedral at Beirut or in the church at Abu Ghosh, has disappeared almost without trace. Human figures can still be seen on the pillars of St Phocas of 'Amyun, with the patronal saint himself visible in the half-dome of the apse. And on the walls of the cave-chapel at Daddah, near the Abbey of Belmont, there appear not only the figures of saints, but a scene from the life of St Marina. Of the inscriptions which accompany the paintings, some are in Latin and some in Greek. The famous stone at Bethphage, on the eastern slopes of the Mount of Olives, is painted with scenes with which that place was closely connected – Christ's triumphal entry into Jerusalem and the raising of Lazarus from the dead. The inscriptions are in Latin. The most complete series of mural paintings to survive from the crusader period, those at Bethlehem, are discussed in the next chapter.

Many of the churches were as plain outside as they were within. Buttresses, where they existed, were rarely bold enough in projection or varied enough in profile to count as decorative features. At the east end the curve of the apses sometimes appears on the outer walls, as at Caesarea, and these were sometimes decorated with corbel table, engaged pillars or pilasters, and shafted window openings, as they are still at Beirut and Jebail, and as the main apse once was of the cathedral at Sabastiyah. The main doorway into the church was often made the principal feature of its western façade and was given special attention by the designers. It was set beneath an archway arranged in successive orders, with moulded voussoirs and jamb shafts with carved capitals. The western windows might be treated in the same way and set symmetrically in relation to the central doorway. As will be seen, such a scheme could achieve a certain magnificence; but generally speaking those which have survived cannot compare in splendour with the west fronts of many European churches.

Plate 39

Other external features might include a free-standing baptistery or campanile. It is generally believed that the small arcaded building just northwest of the Dome of the Rock, which to Moslems now commemorates the ascension of Mohammed, was originally constructed as a baptistery in the days when the crusaders had consecrated the great mosque as a Christian church. The open arches that once gave access to the baptismal font placed centrally beneath the cupola are now blocked, but mouldings, arches and capitals are all clearly crusader work. The most elegant baptistery to have survived from Latin Syria still stands, fortunately unaltered, at Jebail.

Plates 36, 37

Among the belfries, earthquakes have claimed many casualties. By 1719 the tower at Holy Sepulchre had become so unsafe that its cupola and two upper storeys were taken down. Its near neighbours, those of the Hospitallers and St Mary Latin, have entirely gone. The most impressive survival is at Tripoli, where the heavy, rectangular tower, with its twin- and triple-arches and shafted openings, still stands to its full height of four storeys. Like the other and more fragmentary remains of Tripoli's crusader cathedral, it has since been part of the town's principal mosque.

Plate 26

It is perhaps time to consider to what extent the general characteristics discussed in the preceding pages are displayed in particular buildings. The major churches of the crusaders and especially the cathedrals have survived better than the minor, not only because of their more solid construction, but because many of them have been maintained in continuous use. Jebail, like Holy Sepulchre, is still a Christian church. Tarsus, Beirut, Ramla, Hebron and Gaza are mosques. Our Lady of

Tortosa (Tartus), after many vicissitudes in which it had been barracks, warehouse, mosque and deserted ruin, is now a museum.

Since 1291 the principal building of the Great Mosque in Beirut has been the former cathedral church of St John the Baptist, built by the Latin bishops of that city during the twelfth century. The masons they employed found an abundance of ancient and Byzantine material ready to hand, and so provided themselves with enough marble columns and capitals for the nave, the western doorway and porch and the exterior

Fig. 22

Fig. 22 Beirut. Plan of the cathedral. (After C. Enlart)

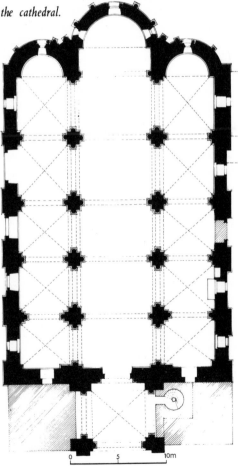

decoration of the main apse. During its centuries as a mosque it has undergone some alteration and its wall paintings have been obliterated. But for all that, it remains what Dr Boase has called it, 'as good a piece of romanesque architecture as any that survives in Syria', having many affinities with buildings which were its contemporaries in southern France.

Plate 31

Plate 30

It embodies many of the features already discussed. Its nave and aisles terminate in apses whose rounded shape is visible outside as well as inside the church. The nave walls are slightly thickened in the bay immediately west of the apses and choir as if in formal recognition of a transept. Nave and aisles are divided by cross arches into five bays. On either side of each bay a small window is pierced in the slightly pointed tunnel vault that covers the nave; each bay of the aisles has a groin-vault. The nave arcade is carried on square piers, on each face of which an engaged column supports either the transverse arch of nave or aisle or the inner arch of the arcade. Three stages of construction are visible. First, as was normal, the eastern apses; then the two eastern bays, between which and the apses there is a change in the level of the string course; finally, the three western bays, which are noticeably narrower than those to the east. The reinforcement of the westernmost nave piers probably shows that these were envisaged as the supports of western towers which may never have been built.

Externally the normal, plain exterior of a crusader cathedral, with its broad-faced buttresses of shallow projection, was relieved by two un-common features – a western porch with arched openings in three of its sides and a plain groin-vault within, and decoration of the eastern apses with corbel table, engaged columns and window opening with nook shafts and capitals.

Fig. 23

St John's cathedral at Jebail is like St John's cathedral at Beirut in its two unusual external features, but unlike in its lack of internal uniformity of design and decorative detail. The external features are, first, the three rounded apses decorated, as are those at Beirut, with round-headed windows, three in the main apse and one in that of each aisle, and with cornice and corbel table. The apses of Jebail, however, lack the engaged columns which are a feature of those at Beirut and Sabastiyah. The second external feature at Jebail, and perhaps its main glory, is the baptistery which backs on to the north wall of the church. This is a

Fig. 23 Jebail. Plan of the cathedral.
(After C. Enlart)

0   5   10m

domed canopy, rectangular in plan, supported by that north wall and
by two rectangular piers. It is open on three of its sides, and each opening
is covered by an arch of the usual kind, though each arch is differently   Plate 37
decorated. That on the north has gadroons, like the portals of Holy
Sepulchre; the eastern arch has an archivolt of three ranks of billets,
beneath which is a dentellated design formed by a series of uniform

Fig. 24   Jebail. The baptistery. Designs borrowed from Moslem art. (After C. Enlart)

Fig. 24

triangles, each decorated with a small flower or geometrical design; the western arch has more dentellation, but here the teeth are laid in a hori⁄zontal rather than a vertical plane. At the top of the wall above the arches is a cornice and corbel table, with decoration applied not only to each corbel, but to the metopes between them.

Plate 35

The most impressive part of the interior is the east end, with its uniform design of triple apse and small choir bay, its fine engaged columns which carry the chancel arch, and the handsome setting of the small apsidal windows. The rest of the building is less of a harmonious unity than Beirut or Tartus. In the first place it seems to have been noticed that the east end, presumably built first, was not correctly oriented, but faced a little south of east. The north wall and aisle were subsequently laid out on a truer east⁄west line, but were consequently out of alignment with the apses. In 1170 the cathedral in Jebail, like the castle, suffered heavy damage in the major earthquake of that year. The western half of the church was ruined for ever. Today there are only three aisle bays west of the chancel; before 1170 there were probably six. The south aisle needed to be entirely reconstructed and has many differences from that to the north. Its alignment is neither that of the apses nor of the north aisle, but is somewhere between. Its groin⁄vaulted bays are divided by transverse arches and its supports for the nave arcade are plain rectangular piers. In the north aisle there are no transverse arches (nor are there in the tunnel⁄vaulted nave), and in their east and west faces the piers have an

Fig. 25 Jebail. Section of the cathedral. (After C. Enlart)

engaged column to carry the arches of the nave arcade. All this does not
mean that the interior effect is displeasing. The worshipper who looks
towards the east end sees a finely ordered composition and, as with nearly
all crusader churches, its beauty is enhanced by the fine quality of its
masonry and its severe decoration.

Fig. 25

Perhaps the most interesting and impressive ecclesiastical building of
crusader construction outside Jerusalem is the cathedral at Tartus or, as
it was then more euphoniously called in the Latin documents of the day,
Tortosa. First occupied in 1099, conquered in 1102, evacuated in
1291, Tortosa was in Christian hands for longer than any other town in
Latin Syria, and building operations at its cathedral were more protracted
than elsewhere. More than once in its long history, the edifice suffered
damage through Moslem invasion. It has long been known that, in
1152, the army of Nur-ad-Din briefly occupied the town. Dr Riley-
Smith has recently published a newly-discovered charter which refers to
this episode, to its disastrous effect on the cathedral and to the arrangement by which the bishop called in the Templars to build a new citadel
for the town's better protection. Impressive remains of their castle and
other conventual buildings are still visible in Tortosa, and these alone

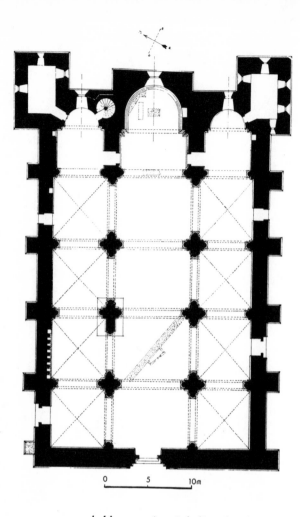

Fig. 26   Tortosa. Plan of the
cathedral. (After C. Enlart)

held out against Saladin when he occupied the town and damaged the
still unfinished cathedral in 1188.

Tortosa then remained in Christian hands, and resources were
available to make good the damage and to complete the construction.
From the earliest Christian centuries it had been credited with two
precious relics, an altar and an ikon of the Blessed Virgin, the one said
to have been dedicated by St Peter in her lifetime and the other to have
been painted by St Luke himself. Such links with Christ's mother and

disciples had made Tortosa the place of pilgrimage it still remained in the crusader period. At that time textiles manufactured in the town had achieved a local reputation and Joinville, when on crusade in St Louis' company, combined the two – he made his pilgrimage to Our Lady of Tortosa, and bought there, on the king's orders, a hundred pieces of camlet in different colours. Queen Margaret thought that he had been in search of relics – a more usual pursuit for pilgrims – and knelt reverently before the parcel he sent her. When it was opened, and the cloth revealed, the pious scene dissolved among the laughter of her ladies.

The first building operations in the twelfth century seem to have begun, as was normal, at the east end. Certainly the eastern bays of nave and aisles, and the apses which terminated them, show the normal roman-esque arrangement of the twelfth century: the nave arcade carried on cruciform piers, each with an engaged column on each of its four main faces; the arches in nave and aisles and the tunnel vault of the nave very slightly pointed; that vault strengthened by transverse arches, which are also provided between the groin-vaulted bays of the aisles. The western bays of nave and aisles embody all these features and are of the same

Fig. 26

Plate 38

Fig. 27

Fig. 27   Tortosa. Section of the cathedral. (After C. Enlart)

general design, but there are also a number of differences which show them to belong to a later period of construction. For example, in both bays of the western aisles the window was made longer by lowering the base and suppressing the string course which in the eastern bays had marked the base of the windows. More significantly, the starkness of the aisle vaults was relieved in the western bays by a carved boss at the intersection of the groins and, most important of all, the style of the capitals changed – from the formalized arrangement of thick, fleshy leaves with their points curled back, so typical of the twelfth-century crusader work, to the crockets of the thirteenth, terminating in small clusters of leaves and flowers, and more naturalistic details seen to best advantage on the capitals which survive in the window recesses of the west front. In the opinion of Deschamps this later carving compared favourably in quality with similar work at Chartres and Rheims.

    · It seems likely that, when Saladin's army occupied the town, the cathedral was still unfinished. When building was resumed the masons, in the interest of internal homogeneity, continued nave and aisles in the same style and dimensions as before, but added roof bosses and designed capitals in the style of their own day. When they came to the western façade they were no longer bound by earlier work, and its simple but harmonious composition is entirely of the thirteenth century. Above the centrally-placed main doorway there is a pair of large windows, and

Fig. 28

Plate 39

Fig. 28 Tortosa. Roof bosses in the cathedral. (After C. Enlart)

above and between these a third smaller window. All three, like the doorway, open into the nave, and the highest point of the uppermost window is level with the crown of the nave vault within. To the right and left of this central group are two more windows, each on the axis of either aisle. All five windows are tall, slender lancets and all, like the doorway, are set in recessed arches, with columns set in the jambs, four pairs in the doorway, two in each nave and one in each aisle window. Columns and arches were long ago wrenched from the door, and most of the columns from the windows, but their capitals and orders of moulded voussoirs remain.

After the main body of the church had been completed, a plan was made to crown the façade with angle towers. Had this been done, the cathedral would have looked even more like the fortress to which the Arab geographer, Idrisi, compared it. The east end was part of the town defences. By a close study of the masonry Camille Enlart, the great archaeologist and historian, was able to show that the original east end was strengthened externally by the addition of angle towers and the encasing of the main apse in a projecting bastion of masonry. These works overlooked the town wall and combined with it to present a formidable defence in that sector.

The characteristics of crusader romanesque architecture are best displayed in the cathedrals of the twelfth century, but they can be studied as well, and in an even more austere form, in some of the lesser churches. There are two, alike in size and scale, which are monuments not only of the crusader occupation, but also of French concern for such buildings and their outstanding skill in repairing them during the later half of the nineteenth century.

St Anne's stands just inside St Stephen's Gate in the Old City of Jerusalem. From the early Christian centuries pilgrim devotion had honoured the site as the home of Anne and Joachim, parents of Our Lady and therefore the scene of her childhood. The remains of a large Byzantine church are still visible. In the crusader period a new church was built as part of the Benedictine nunnery established there, which was sometimes graced by royal ladies, and this connection was revived by the sultan who in 1854 presented it to the Empress Eugénie in recognition of French help for Turkey during the Crimean War. As a result the nuns' church was superbly restored by Charles Mauss. It has recently

Fig. 29

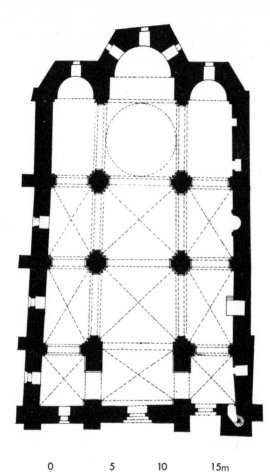

Fig. 30

Fig. 29   Jerusalem. Plan of the Church of St Anne. (After C. Enlart)

undergone extensive repairs as a result of damage sustained during the fighting in June, 1967.

Later on Mauss was also commissioned to restore the church at Abu Ghosh, another gift to the French from the Sublime Porte, this time in consolation for an erroneous judgement that had given to the Greeks the remains of the crusader cathedral at Lydda. The village at Abu Ghosh (its name preserves that of a local brigand well known to Chateaubriand and Lamartine) stands some seven miles west of Jerusalem on the road

*Fig. 30   Abu Ghosh. Plan
of the church. (After C.
Enlart)*

0   5   10   15m

to Jaffa; in the crusader period it was identified with the Emmaus of the
gospels. The site had been occupied by the Romans, and there is ancient
masonry in the walls and crypt of the crusader church, including an
inscription recording work carried out by a unit of the Tenth Legion,
who left their mark in so many parts of Palestine. It has been argued that
the unusually thick walls of the church are Roman work, but it is more
probable that Roman materials were re-used by the Hospitallers, to
whom the site was given in 1141.

Both St Anne's and Abu Ghosh have a nave and aisles with eastern apses and four bays divided by cross-arches. The plan of both is irregular; in neither church are north and south walls parallel, perhaps the result of using older foundations. Both interiors are simple to the point of severity. Everywhere are the plain, sharp edges of the groin-vaults which, except for the transepts and crossing of St Anne's, cover nave and aisles, and the hard, straight lines of piers and pilasters, unrelieved by the roundness of columns, except for one unpleasing instance at Abu Ghosh.

Besides the points of resemblance, each church has its own distinctive features. The internal organization of St Anne's can be read from the outside with unusual clarity. The transepts, while not apparent in the plan, stand out boldly in elevation, since they are raised above the aisles to the same height as the nave. This makes possible a true crossing of transepts and nave surmounted by a cupola on pendentives, a rare feature in crusader churches. As Deschamps has pointed out, the relative placing of the volumes of space enclosed by the cupola and the half-dome of the apse is a composition of particular felicity. The main decoration in the church, though even this is sparse by contemporary European standards, is applied to the western façade. A doorway with a plain tympanum is set beneath an arch of two orders, with moulded voussoirs but plain jambs. Its archivolt is decorated with small diamond shapes pierced at the centre. Immediately above is a horizontal band of billets with an upper border of ova; this feature also provides the base for a small, plain window, while above that is a larger window, with an outer arch of gadroons supported by corinthian capitals and a wide archivolt carved with acanthus.

At Abu Ghosh the thickness of the outer walls make buttresses unnecessary, except for that part of the nave wall that rises above the aisles. The east window is set in a deep recess; its arch of four orders has plain jambs and voussoirs and a minimum of moulding on archivolt and imposts. Inside the church the transverse arches of the nave are supported by columns with stiff-leaf capitals. The columns do not rest on the floor, but are in fact a kind of corbel turning at right-angles into the wall. This ugly device was much used by masons in Latin Syria: in the aisles of Abu Ghosh, as in the cloisters of Montjoie (Nebi Samwil) and Holy Sepulchre, such bent, truncated columns were used in pairs.

Plate 41

Plate 42

Plate 43

Plate 45

Plate 44

St Anne's and Abu Ghosh were each built by a well-endowed community, which no doubt helps to account for the excellence of their masonry and construction. There were other wealthy landlords who built substantial churches in the thickly-settled neighbourhood of Jerusalem. It was presumably the canons of Holy Sepulchre who provided substantial churches for their colonists at both Magna and Parva Mahomeria or, in more recent nomenclature, al-Birah and al-Qubaibah. At the first-named parts of the outer walls of a large church 43 × 17 metres, were still standing in 1917, but seem to have been obliterated during the final stages of the First World War. At Qubaibah the surviving lower courses of the medieval church, including those of the eastern apses, are built into the modern church of the Franciscan fathers. At Montjoie much of the Premonstratensian church still stands; a nave, a single apse, projecting transepts, of which only the southern arm survives, and a single northern aisle. To the south of the church are slight traces of the cloister. Down at 'Amwas, below the hill crowned by the castle of Latrun, are the lower parts of the walls and engaged piers of the twelfth-century church, built on and of the ruins of a large Christian basilica of the fourth century.

The only other area in which there is a comparable concentration of surviving crusader churches is between Jebail and Tripoli, then part of the crusader county of that name, now part of the state of Lebanon. These were smaller and no doubt poorer churches than those just discussed, perhaps more typical of those serving a normal parish. They may have survived because there has been and still is a substantial Christian population in the region. Two of the most complete are at Qubbah and Anafah, the crusader Nephin. Each is a single barrel-vaulted nave, without aisles or buttresses, and with an eastern apse. Qubbah has a western doorway that seems large in comparison with the size of the building (15 × 8 metres). The jambs are plain; voussoirs, imposts and archivolt have a simple moulding. Above the door is a small circular window. The same feature appears on the western façade at Nephin, which has a centrally-placed doorway in each of its four sides; here too arches and jambs are of the plainest kind. In masonry, mouldings and construction both churches are simple to the point of crudity. The oculus at Nephin, for example, is flanked by two lancet windows; but instead of achieving the symmetry normal in a western façade, the two windows are different in size and setting. The rustic effect is surprising in a town which was the capital of an important fief in the county of Tripoli, where in 1283 Burchard of Mount Zion counted twenty tall and strongly fortified towers and of which the town walls survived into the nineteenth century.

The church of St Phocas at 'Amyun is another small and simple building. Its single apse is embedded in a projecting rectangular chevet. Nave and aisles, unusually, are all barrel-vaulted, with the nave arcade carried on square piers as plain as those at Abu Ghosh. The simply moulded imposts of those piers and the string course in the apse are the only architectural decoration in the church. Of the paintings on apse and pillars something has already been said. In the opinion of Deschamps there are a number of signs that St Phocas was the work of indigenous masons and artists for the needs of indigenous Christians. He cites in particular its dedication to a Greek saint, the Greek inscriptions and eastern character of its mural paintings, and the stilted arch that frames its single, windowless apse.

Plate 46

Among the plainest and best constructed ecclesiastical buildings are castle chapels; the severity and functional character of the main fortress was extended into its place of worship. In the castles of the Military Orders the chapel was a building of major importance. The brethren, knights and serjeants alike, were not only a garrison but a religious community, bound by monastic vows, and the chapel was a focal point of their common life. It was also likely to be an element in the defences. At both Krak and Marqab, the two principal castles of the Hospitallers, the chevet of the chapel is part of the inner defences; at Marqab it is a section of the inner wall, at Krak it projects beyond. Within, both chapels have a simple nave without aisles, and an eastern apse. At Krak the nave has a tunnel vault of the normal twelfth-century kind, divided by cross-arches into three bays. The plain arches fall onto the plainest of pilasters, of which the imposts are joined in a continuous string course of the same moulding. The only other decoration is a blind arcading of double arches on the north and south walls.

Plate 47

At Marqab there is a little more decoration. The two groin-vaulted bays of the nave are divided by a transverse arch with engaged supported columns. These, and the pilasters to which they are attached, have carved capitals. There are also doorways in the north and west walls, set in recessed arches with moulded archivolts, and two jamb shafts on either side of each door with capitals of corinthian inspiration.

These two chapels are today bare monuments, visited only by tourists and occasional students; the chapel of the Templars at Safita is still a Christian church. It has an even more military character, since it lay at the heart of the defences, in the main storey of the tallest tower-keep in Syria. The openings from which it is lit are not church windows but military *archères*, set in deep embrasures. There is one in the eastern apse, and each of the north and south walls contains two. The entrance is through a simple doorway in the west wall, which is set some feet above the ground-level outside, and is approached by a tall flight of steps. Above the chapel, approached by a stairway in the thickness of the wall, is a handsome twelfth-century room which occupies the whole upper floor of the keep. Three equally-spaced free-standing piers on the central line of the hall divide it into two parallel naves, each of four bays covered in the groined vault. A window is placed in each outer wall of each bay. The room may have served as the Templars' chapter house. Above it the flat roof and its crenallated parapet still survive.

Plate 48

The prominence given to the chapel in the castles of the Military Orders emphasized the monastic element in their common life. In the crusader states there were also monasteries of a more ancient and normal kind, though not perhaps as many as might have been expected. Western Europeans were always more ready to visit the Holy Land as pilgrims or crusaders than to remain there as settlers, and this reluctance was as evident among monks and nuns as among laymen. When Saint Bernard was first offered that height on which Samuel was buried, and from which the pilgrim approaching from the west first saw Jerusalem (hence its crusader name of Montjoie), he declined it on behalf of Citeaux and suggested that the invitation be re-directed to the Premonstratensians. These duly established themselves on the site on which a small part of their conventual buildings still stand. Other houses of monks and nuns clustered in and around Jerusalem, most of which re-established themselves in Acre after 1191, and there was a similar concentration in Antioch and its neighbourhood. Elsewhere, although there were famous convents in holy places like Mount Tabor, they were in the country as a whole comparatively thin on the ground, and the exposure of the whole area to Moslem attack must have done much to account for this. For the same reason there are few visible remains of the monasteries and, once again, destruction has been most complete in Antioch and its region. Further south, even where the abbey church survives, as at St Anne's in Jerusalem, there is little trace of the other conventual buildings. There are fragments of the medieval cloister in Bethlehem, as there are in Jerusalem at Holy Sepulchre and St Mary Latin, but the most complete range of medieval monastic buildings is in the foothills of Lebanon, at a site which looks down on Tripoli and its coastal plain nearly seven hundred feet below. Its present name preserves the medieval; *Fig. 31* Dair Balamand is the Belmont of the crusader period. Despite St Bernard's earlier reluctance, it was Cistercian, a daughter house of Morimond, and founded in 1157, just four years after the saint's death. Its abbots and other dignitaries are attested in documents both of the twelfth and thirteenth centuries, and Cistercian buildings from both periods not only still stand but are in daily use, not always the use for which they were designed – the medieval chapter house, for example, is now a church – but they are still the home of a community of Greek Orthodox monks.

Approximately datable items like carved capitals and brackets show that the work of construction, begun in the twelfth century, was continued into the thirteenth, and the length of time over which the work was spread is best illustrated by the church. The interior, a barrel-vaulted nave with eastern apse, is stark even by early Cistercian standards. Unusually long in proportion to its width, it lacks transverse arches and therefore pillars or pilasters, and its bareness is relieved only by the horizontal line of a simple cornice at the springing of the vault. In the western façade there were two round-headed windows above the doorway, and above them a circular window set in a moulded stone frame. Thus far the chapel is of the twelfth century, but in the thirteenth *Plate 40* it was given a western porch and, at its eastern end, a small belfry which is one of the outstanding minor beauties of crusader architecture. It is almost complete, lacking only the colonnettes that once flanked the arched openings in each of its four sides. Above the arches it becomes, for a single topmost course, an octagon, and the whole is crowned with a small dome. The crocketed capitals, the string course joining their abaci and another between octagon and dome elegantly complete the whole harmonious design.

Fig. 31   Belmont. Plan of the monastery. (After C. Enlart)

153

The cloister has been reconstructed since the crusader period, but it must stand on the site of its Cistercian predecessor, since it is enclosed by and provides covered communication between the buildings erected by the western monks. Its northern gallery is bounded by the whole length of the church; the southern gives access to refectory and kitchen, which still retains its medieval hearth and chimney-piece; the chapter house, with two groin-vaulted bays separated by an arch lay between, opening from the eastern gallery. There are other Cistercian buildings of which the use is less clear. Next to the chapter house is a great hall, groin-vaulted within and strongly buttressed without, lit from its eastern end by a circular window above and between two lancets. A building at right-angles to the church may have been the infirmary; others in the western range may have been storehouses relating to the agrarian basis of the abbey's economy.

The plainness of these buildings has been emphasized, and it has been a recurring point in this discussion of crusader churches. At some places, however, there were more ambitious schemes of decoration, and these are discussed in the next chapter.

The Decoration of Churches

The beauty of the surviving crusader churches lies mainly in their masonry, their proportions, their clear and functional design. Ornament has generally been kept to a minimum, confined to the carving of capitals or to the mouldings of voussoirs, an impost, a string course or the base of a column. Their masons, however, were capable of more exuberant work and this is particularly evident, as Dr Boase has em-phasized, in the fragments of crusader sculpture re-used by the Moslems within and in the neighbourhood of the Temple area in Jerusalem. Some of these must have adorned the conventual buildings of the Templars and were likely to have been products of the yard in which the Order's masons and sculptors exercised their art. Nor is the richer work still visible confined to fragments. At some of the larger churches entire schemes of ambitious decoration have survived, and one of the best examples is provided, once again, at the Church of the Holy Sepulchre. Here the southern façade, by which pilgrims entered the church, was treated with special magnificence.

Plates 25, 49, 50

The twin portals are set in recessed arches of three orders, to each of which there are supporting columns. Each column has a capital, derived from the corinthian style and datable to the twelfth century. The outermost arch, supported by the pillars furthest from the doorway, is of flattish blocks with rounded corners and edges, called gadroons, a feature borrowed directly from Moslem architecture and which soon appeared in Europe. The pillars nearest the doorway carried the lintels, each decorated by a thin panel of carved marble, of which more in a moment.

This arrangement of twin archways and columns, the main element in the façade, is almost repeated, on the same scale, as a setting for two rather small windows, each of which is immediately above one of the entrance doorways. Each window is flanked by small columns, only half the height and less than half the diameter of those which carry the outer arches at this level. The setting of doorways below and windows above is unified not only by the similarity of scale and design, but also

155

because the gadroons of the portals are repeated as the outer arch of the windows, and also because the outline of both pairs of arches is em/ phasized by a richly carved archivolt. That below is in scrolls of spiky acanthus with a tiny flower at the centre of each, that above is a boldly carved arrangement of stalks and stylized leaves.

There is still another entrance on the same façade. Constantine's masons had reduced Calvary to a formal cube of rock. The chapels on its flat top are therefore several feet above the floor of the church, and the crusaders provided an entrance at the appropriate level from the outer courtyard. This doorway was approached by a flight of steps and was given its own domed porch. The arched openings in the sides of that porch are comparable in shape and width, and in their supporting columns and carved archivolt, with the other arches in the façade.

The various elements of the façade are bound together into a single composition by a number of strongly marked horizontal features. The division between the main doorways below and the windows above is emphasized by a boldly projecting, richly decorated cornice, on which stand the bases of the main columns framing the windows. There is another such cornice at the very top of the wall. Both features are con/ tinued across the whole breadth of the façade, and the lower is carried round the Calvary porch, thus tying it in with the other elements. In the same way the archivolt of the window arches is continued eastwards to include the arch of another window above the porch. The whole effect would be still more striking if the western part of the façade had not been obscured when the campanile was added in the years between 1149 and 1187.

Plate 50   The most ambitious work of the sculptors was applied to the lintels above the main doorways. These carved marble slabs have been removed into the safer keeping of the Rockefeller Museum, which stands just outside the northeast angle of the city walls. There are striking differences between the subject/matter on the two lintels. The one is carved with a number of scenes from the New Testament which include the raising of Plate 55   Lazarus from the dead, Christ's entry into Jerusalem and the Last Supper. Enlart judged this to be competent work, though not out/ standing, but Deschamps thought this verdict too severe. Certainly the scenes have some lively touches, with the boy climbing the palm tree to get a better view of the events of Palm Sunday and the friends of Lazarus holding their noses as they help him out of his grave clothes.

These scenes from Christ's life which took place in or near Jerusalem are entirely appropriate to the first of the city's churches, but the same can scarcely be said of the other lintel. Its sculptor covered the whole surface with a single vine-like plant, its leaves and fruit growing from a decorated stem arranged in a series of scrolls. Among the foliage a number of figures appear, a dragon, a centaur, a feathered bird with the head of a woman, but most prominent is a group of lively, naked boys. Such pagan scenes were sometimes used in the decoration of Christian churches, but it is perhaps surprising to find them at the entrance to one of the holiest places in Christendom. It is possible that at some time in the past the original lintel was destroyed, and that the present one is a substitute taken from a pre-Christian monument.

The design of appropriately splendid settings for the main doors of major churches inspired medieval sculptors in the West to some of their finest work. Examples in the Latin East are fewer, but Holy Sepulchre does not stand alone. The recessed arches which once framed the great doors of the Church of the Resurrection in Nablus were carried on four pairs of columns and the archivolt on pilasters. Each order of the arch was moulded with a double roll and the surface decorated with palmettes,

Fig. 32

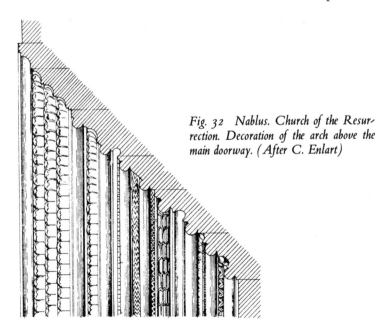

Fig. 32 Nablus. Church of the Resurrection. Decoration of the arch above the main doorway. (After C. Enlart)

diamond flowers, billets, zigzags. The archivolt carried three ranks of water-leaves. When Enlart studied and photographed the monument in 1922, it was much dilapidated. At some time in its long history it had, after the crusader occupation, been dismantled, moved and carelessly rebuilt. Tympanum, lintel and doorways had been lost. Even so, the effect of what remained was unusually rich for the Latin East, a reminder that it was the work of one of the wealthiest bodies of clergy in the western world, the canons of Holy Sepulchre. It was completely destroyed in the earthquake of 1927.

At Nablus the sculptors depicted no human or animal figures, save for a small scene on the side of an abacus, where the lamb is shown exposed to the raging of the lion on the one hand and the allurements of a siren on the other; but for Nazareth a display of figure sculpture was planned as fine as any then being executed in Europe. In that town the crusaders raised a large church over the cave venerated as the place in which the angel told the Blessed Virgin that she would become the mother of Jesus. Though the building of this Church of the Annunciation was already well advanced when Saladin's army threatened Nazareth in 1183, it seems to have been still incomplete when he took the town four years later. In the mid-thirteenth century the Franks once more held Nazareth, but in 1263 finally lost it to Baybars, who ordered the destruction of the church. His commands were executed so thoroughly that its ground plan has been recovered only by excavation carried out in the last century and this by Father Prosper Viaud, warden of the Franciscan convent of the Annunciation in Nazareth. In 1908 he extended his digging to an area beneath one of the main rooms of the convent. It yielded nothing, and he ordered the trenches to be filled in. An enthusiastic helper asked if he could continue down to the bed-rock. 'Je le lui permis par pure condescendance et je m'en allai, persuadé que c'était complètement inutile.' But the wholly unexpected result of Father Viaud's indulgence was the discovery in a rock cavity of five romanesque capitals of a quality far surpassing that of any other sculpture in crusader Palestine. All are carved with human figures and are bound as well by unity of theme and style. As to theme, all present scenes which concern the Apostles. The most familiar are doubting Thomas, being shown the wound in his Master's side, and the appearance of the risen Christ to his disciples on the Sea of Galilee where they had fished all night and caught nothing,

Plate 53

but who then received directions which enabled Peter to draw 'the net to land, full of great fishes, a hundred and fifty and three'. Other episodes are miracles wrought by the Apostles, taken either from the Acts or from the rich crop of apocryphal writings so well known among eastern Christians. A repeated theme is their power to bring the dead back to life – thus St Peter at Jaffa raises Tabitha, St Bartholomew in India the son of King Polymnius, St Matthew in Ethiopia the daughter of King Egisippus. These edifying scenes are enlivened by menacing beasts and devils, like the dragons who attend the Ethiopian magi vanquished by the saint or the demon from whom Bartholomew is rescuing the king's   Plate 52 daughter. One capital is rather larger than the rest, and its sculpture provides a general statement, as it were, of the subject-matter carved on the other four. A man, distinguished by a nimbus, is shown threatened by four fearsome devils, all armed, two of them archers. It is reminiscent of the tiny scene on the abacus at Nablus. But at Nazareth the man is led forward through the snares of the enemy, his wrist held by an upright and confident young woman, crowned and bearing a cross. He, surely,   Plate 51 is an apostle, she represents the strength of faith. Led by faith, the Apostles could accomplish the wonders shown on the other four capitals.

Unity is also provided not only by the artist's style, but by the setting in which his scenes are presented. On all the capitals the figures stand beneath round-headed arches decorated with spaced-out billets. On the arches stands continuous arcading with tall narrow openings, sur-mounted by roofs or decorated beams. At certain points there is a further storey of such arcading, giving the appearance of a small tower. This decoration gives a sure and valuable guide to its links with contemporary western European work. Sculpture having features in common with the Nazareth capitals can be found in many romanesque churches of central France, in Touraine, Berry, Nivernais and Burgundy. There are the same circular folds of drapery to render the projection of a shoulder, a knee or a breast; Christ and his Apostles are distinguished by the same large haloes; very small holes, sometimes arranged in groups of three, are used as surface decoration; some demons have the same shaggy bodies and bristling hair. In a capital in the nave arcade of the church at Plaimpied (Cher) there is a capital which comes very close to those at   Plate 54 Nazareth. It shows a seated Christ tempted by demons. This scene too is set beneath arches decorated with billets; at each corner of the capital, above the framing arches, is the same arcading with narrow openings, arranged in two storeys like a campanile. The figure of Christ has the same, large, cross-bearing halo, the features are similar and so is the arrangement of the hair, parted in the middle, leaving the ears exposed. The treatment of the draperies is the same and they are decorated with the same tiny holes pierced in groups of three. The devils of Plaimpied, both the smooth and the hairy, have their counterparts at Nazareth. The conclusion is irresistible that one of the great artists of the twelfth century, the Master of Plaimpied, came to the Holy Land not only as a pilgrim but to execute a commission at the new church in Nazareth. He was still at work and his capitals were not yet in position when Saladin won his victory at Hattin and threatened the whole kingdom. They were therefore hidden away against better days that never came, to remain undisturbed until their almost accidental discovery more than seven hundred years later.

It is possible that other church goods, buried for safe keeping when Moslem conquest seemed imminent, still await discovery. During building operations in 1869 at the present Franciscan convent in Bethlehem, silver and enamelled candlesticks were recovered together with an enamelled crozier and two bronze bowls engraved with scenes from the life of St Thomas. These can all be seen today in the museum in the Franciscan Convent of the Flagellation in Jerusalem and so can other objects also found at Bethlehem in 1906 – small bronze bells, some from a carillon, one from a clock and a set of bronze organ pipes.

It has been mentioned already that at Bethlehem the crusaders inherited a Byzantine church, founded by Constantine in the fourth century, rebuilt by Justinian in the sixth, spared by both Persian and Moslem conquerors in the seventh. The main fabric of Justinian's church has survived down to the present time. The only architectural features of the crusader period inside the building are the arches and flanking colonnettes of the two small doorways which, from the crossing, give access to the grotto of the Nativity. The interior decoration of the church, however, was a matter of major concern in the twelfth century, and survivals of the crusaders' contribution to this are still visible in patches of wall mosaic and in the faded paintings of the pillars of nave and aisles.

Plate 56

The major scheme was to cover with mosaic the eastern apse and the walls of nave and transepts. We know when this work was done because of one of those rarest of medieval aids to posterity – a dated inscription which includes the name of the artist. This inscription shows that mosaics and paintings were commissioned by Latin and Greeks working together, both as patrons and artists. We shall meet such collaboration again in discussing the illumination of manuscripts.

Only part of the inscription can now be read, but we know its complete text, as we do the whole scheme of the mosaics, from careful descriptions by earlier visitors, and especially from those published in 1626 by Franciscus Quaresimus, illustrated with engravings executed thirty years earlier by another Franciscan friar, Fra Bernardino Amico. The Greek portion reads: 'The present work was completed by the hand of Ephraim the Monk, painter and mosaic worker, in the reign of the Great Emperor Manuel Porphyrogenitus Comnenus and in the days of the great king of Jerusalem our Lord Amalric and of the right holy bishop of Holy Bethlehem our Lord Ralph in the year 6677, second of the indication.' Since the Byzantine era was reckoned from the year of the Creation, 5508 years before Christ's birth, this gives a date anno domini of 1169, which is repeated in the Latin text. At that time there had been for nearly twenty years a period of close collaboration between the rulers of Latin Jerusalem and the Byzantine empire. Both Baldwin III and Amalric had married princesses of the imperial family. In the year of the inscription the army of Jerusalem had undertaken a combined operation with the Byzantine fleet against Alexandria; further joint action was to be negotiated and attempted during the following decade.

Fig. 33

Fig. 33 Seal of Amalric I. Obverse: the king in coronation regalia; reverse: Jerusalem, showing the Dome of the Rock, the Tower of David, the Church of the Holy Sepulchre. (After G. Schlumberger)

Plate 56

The church at Bethlehem shows that collaboration went beyond diplomatic and military activity. The main feature of the parallel bands of decoration which ran the entire length of the nave walls was a record of the early Councils of the Church, the Oecumenical Councils on the south wall, the Provincial Councils on the north. Each assembly was symbolically represented, those on the south wall by a pair, those on the north by a trio of arches, supported by pillars of which capitals, columns and bases are richly decorated. On the north wall the arches are sur-mounted by a dome, roofs and turrets. In the lower part of the space between the pillars there are ornamented lecterns, some of them flanked by candles and censers. In the upper part there is a brief record, in Greek, of the place, year and size of the Council and of its principal achievement.

In all this the Greek language and events of earlier church history predominate. But the record of the second Council of Nicæa in A D 787 is in Latin characters; so are the names of the ancestors of Christ which form the lowest band of decoration, and so is the name of an artist who must be mentioned in the following chapter as well as in this.

Plates 57, 58

On each pillar of the nave arcade, and in some of those in the aisles, is painted the figure of a saint. Here the meeting of East and West is even more striking. Some of the saints depicted were Egyptian ascetics – Antony, Macarius, Onuphrius. Some were the founders of Greek monasteries in southern Palestine in the fifth century – Theodosius, Sabas. There are also St Euthymius the Armenian and St Marina from Antioch in Pisidia. But there are also many westerners – St Leonard from Gaul, St Catald the Irishman, St Vincent from Spain, St Fusca from Ravenna, to say anothing of Scandinavian heroes like King Olaf and King Canute. Of the thirty paintings, eighteen are inscribed with the name of their subject both in Latin and Greek, seven in Latin and one in Greek only, though four others have longer Greek inscriptions. Unlike the nave mosaics, these paintings do not seem to have been designed and executed as a single scheme of decoration. Certainly they do not belong as a whole to the period of Amalric and Manuel Comnenus, since a Virgin and Child on a pillar between the southern aisles bears the date 1130. It is possible that the paintings were com-missioned singly, from time to time, perhaps by pilgrims with the means to bear the cost of the work and the influence to secure the agreement of the bishop or chapter. This might well account for the variety of subjects and their treatment.

The mixture of languages, scripts and subject matter corroborates the evidence provided by the long bilingual inscription already quoted, that both Latin and Greek Christians were closely involved in the decoration of the Church of the Nativity. The name of one other artist appears there besides that of Ephraim the Monk, painter and mosaic-worker. Low down on the north wall of the nave, by the foot of one of the angels, there are the words Basilius Pictor. The name is Greek; the letters and language in which it is written are Latin. In the chapter that follows it will be necessary to discuss in another context the work of a painter named Basil. He might possibly have been the same Basil who worked at Bethlehem. But it will be seen that, for all that his name, style, models and the inscriptions on his paintings were all Greek, he was in fact a western European. The crusader states were a meeting place, not only of Islam and the West but also, to an extent that has still to be fully elucidated, of Byzantium and the West.

Books and their Illustration

Although few books were produced before the age of printing, they could not be dispensed with altogether. All churches needed service books. The greater the church, the greater the need, and no church can have been more famous or more visited, and few can have been wealthier, than the Church of the Holy Sepulchre in Jerusalem. Where were its books produced? Even if no other information were available on this point, we might guess that, like some of the great monastic houses, it produced its own. It certainly had the means and the organization. From the year 1114 the canons of the church lived a corporate life under the Augustinian rule. Presided over by their prior, they not only served the liturgical needs of the holiest places in Christendom, but they were a richly endowed property-owning corporation. It was highly likely that, somewhere in the conventual buildings to the east of the church, this great ecclesiastical organization maintained a scriptorium, a studio-workshop in which scribes copied texts and artists decorated them with miniature paintings and illuminated ornament.

Is anything more than guess-work possible? Have any books survived which could have been written in a scriptorium of Holy Sepulchre? In 1845 the trustees of the British Museum purchased from a M. Commarmont of Lyon, a richly bound and illustrated manuscript said to have been the property of the Grande Chartreuse before the French Revolution. This manuscript, a psalter, is still in the British Museum and so, kept as a separate item, are its medieval carved ivory covers. Besides the psalms it contains a calendar of church feasts, a litany and a number of prayers, and from these contents much has been done to identify the time, place and purpose of the book's production.

Medieval office books often commemorated events or saints associated with the locality in which the book was written. In the calendar of the British Museum psalter every day of the year is marked with the church feast or saint's name proper to the day; but against 15 July is written *Eodem die capta est Jerusalem*, that is, it commemorates the taking of Jerusalem by the forces of the First Crusade on 15 July, 1099. On that anniversary in 1149, exactly fifty years later, the romanesque additions to the Church of the Holy Sepulchre were consecrated. Some medieval calendars record this consecration; that of the British Museum psalter does not. So there are grounds for believing that it was written after 1099 but before 1149.

Such grounds are strengthened by two other entries in the calendar:

August 21 *Obiit rex Balduinus rex Ierosolimitanus secundus.*

October 1 *Obiit Emorfia Ierosolimitana regina.*

King Baldwin II and his queen are the only persons mentioned in the calendar who belonged to the age in which the psalter was written. Since they were husband and wife, it is likely that the book was made for one of their four daughters. For which? Alice and Hodierne were married respectively to the rulers of Antioch and Tripoli. They left the Latin kingdom when still young, but their two sisters spent their whole lives there, Melisende as Queen and Yvette, who never married, as a nun who became Abbess of the Convent of St Lazarus at Bethany. St Lazarus, however, is mentioned nowhere in the book, and it is therefore thought that its owner was Queen Melisende. Since the calendar commemorates the death of her father in 1131, but not that of her husband, King Fulk, in 1143, the book was probably written at some time during those twelve years. Its script and style are both consistent with such a dating.

The carved ivory covers may produce further corroborative evidence. They are decorated both on front and back with eight medallions within a border of leaves and branches. On the front cover each medallion is carved with a scene from the life of King David, and on the back with one of the eight acts of mercy recited by Our Lord: 'I was in prison and you visited me.' In the interstices between the medallions are carved birds and animals, and by a bird at the top of the cover is the name HERODIUS. The British Museum catalogue describes this as the name of the artist, but a century ago a French scholar noted that *herodius* was the word used in Latin bestiaries for the heron, for which a more common word was *fulica*. It is not far from Fulk, and closer still in sound to Foulques, as the king was known in the common speech of the day. Was the carved bird a rebus for the king? If so, what of Herodius? Possibly it was added at a later date by one who wished to label the heron, but who knew nothing of the connection intended by the original

Plate 62

artist with the husband of the royal lady for whom the book was written, illustrated and bound. It has in fact long been accepted as Queen Melisende's Psalter. It was certainly intended for a great lady. The prayers are for a woman's use – the sinner who offers them is not *peccator*, but *peccatrix* – and the outstanding opulence of the decorations testifies to her wealth and social standing.

Scattered through the libraries of Europe are other manuscript books with comparable signs of an origin in medieval Jerusalem. The Vatican Library has an office book of the Church of Holy Sepulchre. It was written in the early thirteenth century, but the contents provide good evidence that it is an exact copy of a book in use at the church before Jerusalem was lost to Saladin. Elsewhere in Rome is part of a richly illuminated sacramentary; the rest of it, the leaves on which the preface and the canon are written, is in the Fitzwilliam Museum at Cambridge. There is a missal in Paris, a psalter in Florence and another sacramentary which, like Queen Melisende's Psalter, is among the Egerton manuscripts in the British Museum. All three of these office books, and the Rome sacramentary just mentioned, commemorate in their calendars the conquest of Jerusalem on 15 July. The Florence psalter and the British Museum sacramentary also mark the day on which the romanesque Church of Holy Sepulchre was dedicated – *dedicatio ecclesie dominici Sepulchri*. All four note feasts particularly concerned with Jerusalem, those of six early bishops of the city, for example, and those of saints closely connected with the Holy Land – Cleophas, Sabas, Lazarus. Two of them mark all four feasts of St Augustine of Hippo, one marks three and the other two. All of these books seem to have been produced for use in a house of Augustinian canons in Jerusalem, in other words, for the canons of Holy Sepulchre, in whose scriptorium they were probably written.

This conclusion is corroborated by a study of the miniatures and the ornamented initials with which these books are decorated. Those in Queen Melisende's Psalter provide the best starting point. They fall into four groups: first, twenty-four miniatures, each a scene from the Old Testament; secondly twelve medallions, each a sign of the Zodiac, which adorn the calendar: thirdly, eight full-page initials; finally, at the end of the book, nine portraits of saints. Each of these groups is by a different artist.

The twenty-four Old Testament scenes have often been described as work of a Byzantine painter, and there are good reasons for this. The last of these miniatures is inscribed *Basilius me fecit*. Basil is a Greek name, and the names of some of the characters in the scenes he painted are in Greek letters. But detailed and expert examination by Dr Buchthal has shown that although the Greek models were carefully copied, even to the extent of using the Greek alphabet, the artist who copied them, whatever his name, was not Greek. He reproduced features from the originals without understanding them; he could not convey their life and action; he could copy, but not relate, the groups as the original artist intended, nor could he quite master the Byzantine skill of creating the illusion of space and depth. At the same time, his miniatures have characteristics which are entirely western. The colours are strong and often discordant; his figures do not stand convincingly on the ground; they sometimes overlap the frames in which they are set; the ornaments at the top and bottom of the frames differ from those at the sides. In Dr Buchthal's view the master who executed these miniatures had an initial training in the West, but had access to Byzantine models and was well taught in a Byzantine school, probably in Constantinople itself.

The portraits of the nine saints at the end of the psalter must also, it seems, be attributed to a western artist who copied from Byzantine originals, but his qualifications to do so were less than those of Basil. The human figures lack volume and their dress does not convincingly clothe them. The draperies are merely rhythmical patterns with little relation to the human forms they cover. The lively interplay of lines, which has close parallels in most western schools of the early twelfth century, is the dominating feature of the style. The byzantinism of these figures is more apparent than real; it is in fact little more than a surface decoration.

Yet though less skilled in copying Byzantine material than the painter of the New Testament miniatures, the artist who portrayed the saints has much in common with him. In some important respects their work is almost identical – in their duplication of loops of drapery, for example, and in the ornament which fills the frame of their pictures. In Dr Buchthal's view, they shared the practice of the same workshop. More than this, he sees them working side by side, with Basil as the master, the painter of the saints as the assistant, his western habits more in evidence

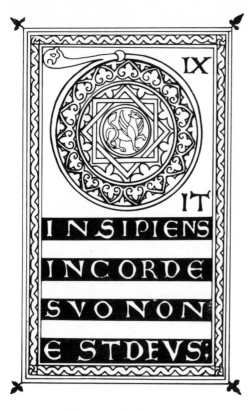

*Fig. 34 Scriptorium of Holy Sepul-
chre. Initial from Melisende Psalter.
London, British Museum, Egerton 1139*

because he had more recently arrived in the East, and because he had
not had the advantage of a training in Constantinople.

In turning to a third group of the psalter's decorations, the ornamented
initials, the erudition of the art historian again detects a wide range of
sources and influences. The richest effects were obtained by the use of
strong colours associated with pomp and power. There are full-page
initials in which the black pen-drawn letters stand on a background
entirely of gold, and on which the few lines of text are in letters of gold
on strips of purple. This technique was in use at the turn of the eleventh
and twelfth centuries in the scriptorium of St Benedict's own monastery,
Monte Cassino.

Mediterranean influence is likewise evident in the initial letters
themselves, but other regions also make their contribution, and especially

England. One example must suffice to show how the elements were combined. The artist, like many illustrators of psalters before and since, made a major effort in decorating the initial letter of the first psalm of all, the B of *Beatus vir* – 'Blessed is the man that hath not walked in the counsel of the ungodly.' He took the opportunity, and this too was common, of honouring the psalmist himself, and King David, seated at the harp, is shown in the lower part of the letter. But the ornament which surrounds him, and which fills the upper part, is of curving, intertwined stems of small leaves and flowers, and amid the foliage are little, living creatures – a bird, a beaked animal, a centaur with his bow. The upright shaft of the B is decorated at head and foot with interlaced ornament, and in its lower panel a dragon is climbing the shaft, its jaws open as if to seize a small flower.

Plate 61

All these features, the interlace, the leaf-scrolls and their inhabitants, the climbing dragon, are typical of English illumination in the early twelfth century, and they are repeated in other initial letters in the psalter – in the D's of *Dixi custodiam* (Psalm 39) and *Dixit dominus domino meo* (Psalm 110). But other initials in the same series by the same artist are decorated with other elements. The D's, for example, of *Dixit insipiens* – 'the fool hath said' – (Psalm 14) and *Dominus illuminatio mea* (Psalm 27) have as their centrepiece two squares, one laid diamond-wise upon the other; and the only animal in each letter is a winged griffin. For both elements there are Moslem sources, but they are even more common in southern Italy; and it is more probable that they came from the West than from the East.

Fig. 34

It has already been mentioned that the calendars and litanies of the Paris missal and of the sacramentary, part of which is in Rome and part in Cambridge, associate both books with the Holy Sepulchre scriptorium. Their illustrations show that they were produced in the same years as Queen Melisende's Psalter. In both books the intial of *Per omnia secula* is decorated with interlace at the top of the shaft and with leaf scrolls and a bird in the bowl of the P. In addition, that of the sacramentary has human figures climbing the shaft, as well as interlace at its foot; while the missal has in its foliage not only a bird, but two animals closely resembling those in Queen Melisende's Psalter. All these were characteristic of English illumination of the period, but once more, they do not stand alone. Half-way up the shaft of the initial in the sacramentary

Fig. 35

Fig. 35 Scriptorium of Holy Sepulchre. Initial from Sacramentary. Cambridge, Fitzwilliam Museum, McClean 49

are two squares placed at an angle to one another, which derives from southern Italy. The anatomy of the climbing figures is rendered with a skill beyond that of contemporary northern artists and seems to be due to Byzantine models and training. In the same letter in the missal there is a medallion at the mid-point of the shaft inspired by Monte Cassino, while the shaft itself is filled with geometrical ornament and the foot is decorated with a leaf of which the most likely source is central Italy, and most probably a manuscript illuminated in Rome.

The many other decorated initials in the two books cannot be considered here in detail. Interested readers are referred to Dr Buchthal's magisterial examination. But the same elements can be repeatedly demonstrated – English, central and southern Italian, Byzantine. He is able to show how closely the three books were connected, the respective artists of the missal and the sacramentary copied from a common prototype, which was in turn closely connected with Queen Melisende's Psalter. Further, the portraits of the saints in the psalter must have provided the model for certain medallions in the other two books. In other words, not only are the three works related, but the psalter was the earliest. Dr Buchthal assigns it to the late 1130's, the sacramentary to c. 1140 and the missal to the late 1140's. All were written and illustrated in the scriptorium of Holy Sepulchre in Jerusalem when the new romanesque church was nearing completion; and there are grounds for believing that its mosaics had features in common with the three service books.

The society of the Latin kingdom was so cosmopolitan that it is not surprising to find other regions influencing its art, particularly Italy, with which it was always in such close contact, and through which some of the Byzantine techniques and models might have been trans⁄ mitted. The strong English influence, however, is unexpected. English⁄ men had not played a leading part in the early crusades, nor in the foundation of the crusader states in the Levant. But there were English⁄ men who went south to the kingdom which their Norman kinsmen had founded in Sicily and southern Italy, and who made a career there: some in the church, like Richard Palmer, who was successively Bishop of Syracuse and Archbishop of Messina; some in government, like the Yorkshireman Robert of Selby, who was King Roger's chancellor, or Master Thomas Brown, who was a senior civil servant in the *duana* of the king of Sicily before returning home to serve in the exchequer of the king of England. Professor Francis Wormald has drawn our attention to William, surnamed the Englishman, who spent his working life in the Holy Land, became the first Latin Archbishop of Tyre in 1127, and of whom we learn something from the great historian who half⁄a⁄century later followed him in that see. Before his preferment, the earlier William had been Prior of the Holy Sepulchre. Holding this office so early in the kingdom's history, and so soon after the canons had been brought under the Augustinian rule, it is not impossible for him to have founded the scriptorium at Holy Sepulchre. The later William tells us also that his predecessor went to Rome to receive his pallium, and that the Pope gave him business to do on his return journey in the neighbourhood of Bari. England, Rome, southern Italy. William the Englishman, Prior and Archbishop, knew all three. Did he present to the scriptorium of the convent over which he had presided those exemplars which the artists of Outremer put to such creative use?

Among the service books already mentioned, which are shown by certain contents in their calendars to have originated in Jerusalem, is a psalter now in Florence and, among the Egerton manuscripts in the British Museum, a sacramentary. Their script can be dated by palaeo⁄ graphers to the second quarter of the thirteenth century; and since Professor Wormald proved that the same scribe wrote not only the Egerton sacramentary, but the so⁄called Pontifical of Apamea which was in Professor Wormald's possession, we have three works produced in the Jerusalem scriptorium during the period of the second Latin kingdom, that is, during the fifteen-year period of Frankish occupation of the Holy City made possible by Frederick II's successful negotiation with the Sultan al-Kamil in 1229. An attempt has been made to date the Florence psalter much more precisely. It has characteristics which distinguish it from most of the other service books written in Jerusalem, and it is possible that these differences provide significant clues. For example, the miniatures which illustrate the book depict scenes from the life of Christ. These are not grouped at the beginning of the book, but are distributed throughout its text. Each is placed at the beginning of a psalm, but has no connection, in content or otherwise, with that psalm. Such an arrangement of the illustrations was then common in books written in Germany. Once again, the prayers seem to show that the book was written for a woman, and the litany of saints has English and royal connections. It includes, for example, Edmund and Edward, each of them a king and martyr. High among the women saints stands St Elizabeth, mother of John the Baptist. In the 1230's, when the psalter was written in Jerusalem, the Latin kingdom was ruled by Frederick, Western Roman Emperor and King of Germany. In 1235 he married Isobel (another form of Elizabeth) sister of Henry III of England and daughter of another Isobel. Was the Florence psalter a wedding present for the English princess, commissioned in Jerusalem by her German husband?

Certainly the quality of its illustrations makes it a book fit for a queen. Once again the B of *Beatus vir* leads in magnificence. The bows of the letter are formed by two superb dragons. The compartments they partly encircle are filled with New Testament scenes, the Annunciation above and the Nativity below. Opposite each, in the upright shaft, is a prophet displaying an appropriate text. Between them, as ever, King David is seated at the harp. And since the whole letter is set in a rectangle, there is room for other figures, including that of the announcing angel.

Once again there is evidence of Byzantine inspiration and western execution. The texts displayed by the prophets, for example, are not from the Vulgate, but are literal Latin renderings of the Greek Septuagint. In the New Testament scenes 'the attitudes and groupings of the main figures as well as the secondary episodes correspond exactly to those in countless Byzantine versions'. But the hand of a western, and probably south Italian, artist shows itself in general and in detail: in general, in his rendering of the figures and their draperies. The tradition is Byzantine, but the versions closest to those of the Jerusalem master are to be found in miniatures painted in Sicily. And in detail, in the network of lines used to shade the figure of the angel.

Elements from the Greek East and the Latin West are present in the psalter of Queen Melisende as they are in the psalter of – dare we say it – Queen Isobel. But, in the judgment of Dr Buchthal they are differently related. 'The finest miniatures in Queen Melisende's Psalter and the two twelfth-century Gospels from Jerusalem were faithful copies of Byzantine works. . . . But here in the thirteenth century the Byzantine models are no longer painstakingly imitated; they serve merely as a source of inspiration. The Byzantine elements of iconography and style do no more than assist the finest qualities of the western tradition to come fully into their own.'

The scriptorium in Jerusalem which produced the Florence psalter can have been active only in the years 1229–44. Even then, Jerusalem was something of an outpost. Throughout the thirteenth century the chief city in the Latin kingdom was Acre. What evidence is there of book production in this second capital?

It scarcely exists outside those areas which are the monopoly of the art historian. But in the Chapter Library at Perugia there is a missal which commemorates in its calendar, on 12 July, *dedicatio ecclesie Acconensis*. It had been on 11 July, 1191 that Acre had at last fallen to the forces of the Third Crusade, and one of the earliest formal acts of its restoration as a Christian city would certainly have been the rededication of the Church of the Holy Cross after its four years in Moslem hands. The entry of this event in the calendar of the Perugia missal certainly shows that the book was closely associated with Acre, and probably that it was produced there. Once that fact is granted, it is possible for the art historian to demonstrate, by comparing its illustrations with those of other manuscripts, that these too must have been executed in the same workshop. A full-page miniature of the Crucifixion in the Perugia missal, for example, has its replica in a missal in the British Museum. But this kind of analysis goes far beyond such obvious comparisons. Close and minute examination has revealed a style which can be associated only with the Latin kingdom during the later part of the thirteenth century.

Plate 59

The identification of the Acre scriptorium and its products is made almost entirely on grounds of artistic style. Almost, but not quite. There is a manuscript of the *Histoire Universelle* in Brussels in which the scribe gives his name, Bernard Dacre, or d'Acre; and besides this possible connection with the thirteenth-century capital, it is known that the book was once owned by a Lusignan, a member of that royal house who were kings of Cyprus and, in the last years which preceded the fall of Acre, kings of Jerusalem.

The Acre style is nowhere better exhibited that in a manuscript Bible now in Paris at the Bibliothèque de l'Arsenal. It does not contain the scriptures in full, but twenty books of the Old Testament only, trans-lated into French. It is a selection which was superseded after the complete Bible had been rendered into French in the mid-thirteenth century, and very few manuscripts have survived. The one in the Arsenal has been confidently assigned to the Latin kingdom on account of the evidence provided by its illustrations.

Each of the twenty Old Testament books has a full-page frontispiece and an historiated initial. They are closely related in many ways to the Perugia missal mentioned. 'The common workshop tradition is obvious', writes Dr Buchthal, 'in the proportions of the figures, the identical repertory of types, groups and gestures, and the treatment of the nude bodies – the manner of joining arms and legs to the torso, and the undulating outlines which indicate the interplay of muscles of the arms. The black lines between eyes and ears, giving a spectacled look, appear prominently in most figures of the Arsenal Bible. The draperies, too, are treated very much like those in the initials of the [Perugia manuscript] – the folds of light-coloured garments are indicated by a system of black-line drawing, while most dark garments have white edges bulging out in bold curves, or forming rhythmical zig-zag patterns.'

In those illustrations both French and Byzantine elements are dis-cernible. Some frontispieces owe nothing to Byzantine art and are wholly western in character; but those from Exodus to Judges clearly derive in part from Byzantine work, though the eastern models are modified by scenes and motifs from contemporary French art. But the artist did much more than place eastern and western elements side by side. By combining the two into something neither western nor Byzantine he created a work of art with an original character, which takes its place among the greatest

Bible illustrations of the thirteenth century. And it was part of the artist's originality to be independent of pictorial models, and to draw on the resources both of his imagination and of his observations direct from life – from the life, that is, of the Levant in which he worked. Job's camels, and the attitude of the boy attending King Solomon, are details which he had himself seen.

Plate 66

The decoration of the manuscript has the kind of magnificence which makes it likely that it was intended for a royal patron, and this may account for the prominence given in the illustrations to the figure of the king. The frontispiece to each of the three books ascribed to Solomon – Proverbs, Ecclesiastes and the Song of Songs – is the portrait of a monarch, seated and attended. With whom in Outremer could this idealized figure of a king be associated? For forty years of the thirteenth century the Hohenstaufen kings were absentees, while the Lusignans who followed exercised authority only of a partial and disputed kind. But there was one shining interlude. After the failure of his crusade and his release from captivity St Louis spent four years in Acre. At that time he was the most powerful of European rulers, who seemed to fulfil in his person three contemporary ideals – as a saint, as a knight and as a king. Can the production in Acre of the Arsenal Bible be associated with his *de facto* rule in that capital? The western models to which the artist owed most were books associated with his court in France, just as the anointing of the first kings of Israel, Saul, David and Solomon, is portrayed in terms of the French rite. It has been suggested that the book was commissioned by St Louis himself.

Plate 64

The artists of the Acre scriptorium did not confine their talents to the decoration of religious books. The thirteenth century saw an increase of literature not only in Latin, but in the commonly spoken languages also, and in none more than French. Much of it, both in prose and verse, was on secular subjects, written by laymen for a lay audience. The literate, literary baronage of the Latin kingdom were not alone in their talents and interests.

The reading public, though so different in size and composition from that of today, shared with it a taste for history. Two works which were particularly popular were first, an *Histoire Universelle*, a history of mankind as known to western Europeans in the early thirteenth century, from the Creation to the time of Julius Caesar; and second, William of Tyre's history of the crusaders in Syria and the Holy Land, and the various continuations which came to be attached to it. William had written in Latin but his great history was so popular that, early in the thirteenth century, it was translated into French, which was also the language used by his first continuators. The work came to be generally known, from the name of the eastern Roman emperor mentioned in its first sentence, as the *Estoire d'Eracles*.

The *Histoire Universelle* survives in a large number of manuscripts, many of them illustrated. There are three which, by the style of their pictures, are linked not only to each other, but also to the Arsenal Bible, and therefore to the Perugia missal and other works executed in Acre. One of these books is now at Dijon, another at Brussels, a third in the British Museum. It is the Brussels manuscript of which the scribe was Bernard d'Acre, and which was once the property of a Lusignan of the royal house of Cyprus.

These three copies of the *Histoire Universelle* can be assigned to the Acre scriptorium because they share with other products of that work-shop the characteristics to which reference has already been made. 'There are the same short doll-like figures with round heads and sunken eyes, with the same black lines running from the eyes in the direction of the ears; a similar repertory of characters and gestures, and the same relation of figures to buildings and landscapes.' Further than this, there are signs of the same readiness to observe direct from nature, and the use of both western and Byzantine elements. The western influences are still those of thirteenth-century French work and those from Byzantium derive from what was then a very recent past. There are features in the Dijon miniatures which can be traced to Byzantine work which belongs to the years of Latin domination after 1204; while in the miniatures of the British Museum copy there are attempts to convey perspective, light and shade and the volume of the human figure that can be found in Byzantine painting of the period which followed, in 1261, the ending of Latin rule at Constantinople and the restoration of a Greek ruling dynasty, the Palaeologi.

Examples of the work of these artists from Acre are included among the plates at the end of this book. For the purpose of comparison the Plates 63, 65 illustrations of the opening chapters of Genesis are set side by side. Besides the resemblances already mentioned, there is a close similarity

Fig. 36 Acre scriptorium. Histoire Universelle. *Border of the Creation scene. London, British Museum, Add. MS. 15268*

in the designs which fill the spaces between the frames of the individual pictures in the Arsenal Bible and in the Dijon *Histoire*; and in the British Museum *Histoire* the same ornament is repeated in the interstices at the edge of the central panel. In all three sets of illustrations Adam, at the moment of Eve's creation, is portrayed from behind, and since this device is found in no known western version, it is a significant link between the three manuscripts. Byzantine influence is strongest in the British Museum version of God the Father and his human creations.

Although the artists of Latin Syria lived and worked in a cosmopolitan society in which Arabic-speaking Moslems were a large and important element, evidence of borrowing from the art of Islam is rare. When work of the Acre school reflected their eastern surroundings, it was the result of observation rather than of copying. But the border to the Creation pictures in the British Museum *Histoire* is an exception. In the strip at the top of the page an eastern potentate sits cross-legged as he is entertained by an ensemble of seven musicians, one of them a woman. They accompany the sinuous movement of a dancing girl, towards whom the eyes of the principal figure are appreciatively turned. On the other three sides of the page an array of figures, some human, some animal, some a mixture, are in lively action, in combat or pursuit, against a background of foliage. There is the same incongruity between the main contents of the page and its borders as there is between the two lintels above the twin doorways of the Church of the Holy Sepulchre.

Why was such a border used? It has been suggested that it has the force of a dedication. Similar scenes of conviviality, as well as of running animals, were painted by artists in Baghdad as the frontispieces of books commissioned by and dedicated to a sultan or amir. That the British Museum copy of the *Histoire* may have been intended for some great patron is corroborated by the quality of the manuscript and its illus-

Fig. 36, Plate 63

trations. The miniaturists who worked on it were more considerable artists than those of the Dijon and Brussels manuscripts. Not only are their pictures larger, but they are livelier, more detailed, more effectively descriptive of the scenes they portray. Once again, it is noticeable how high a proportion of the illustrations include the figures of kings and queens.

The British Museum *Histoire Universelle* belongs to the last years of the Latin kingdom; the late date of the Byzantine sources is sufficient evidence of that. To whom might it have been dedicated at such a time? It is natural to think of the festivities which accompanied the accession of the last Latin king of Jerusalem ever to be crowned in Syria. After his coronation at Tyre on 15 August, 1286, King Henry and his court moved to Acre, where they held high revel. There were memorable performances in the lists and on the stage, where the knights re∕enacted famous episodes from history. Some of the scenes, like those which featured the Queen of the Amazons, and for which young knights attired and made themselves up as women, were splendidly illustrated in that copy of the *Histoire* we are now discussing. Dr Buchthal has suggested that the book was produced for this very occasion; and he recalls that King Henry long survived the end of Latin rule in Syria. 'One wonders whether he turned over the pages of his splendid copy of the Histoire Universelle ever again, and what memories were evoked in his mind by the miniatures of what is now Ms. Add. 15268 in the British Museum.'

William of Tyre's great book on the crusades and the crusader states was written in the East by one who was a native of the Latin kingdom. He continued working on it almost to the end of his life, by which time it had become an account of contemporary politics in the kingdom, in which he himself played a leading part. It breaks off unfinished in discussing events which belonged to late 1183 or early 1184. It became widely popular in Europe; its traditional title, 'a history of deeds done beyond the sea' is that of a book thought of as being read in the West rather than the East. Early in the thirteenth century it was translated into French and, as surviving manuscripts show, existed as an independent book. But since it was unfinished, and since its author had not lived to see the tremendous climax of the events which he recorded in its final pages, attempts to continue or complete it were only to be expected.

Suitable material lay ready to hand. An author, or authors, writing in French, had taken as a theme the loss of the Holy Land to Saladin. The main subject matter was introduced with some episodes from the Latin kingdom's history in the earlier parts of the twelfth century, that is, the book was written independently of that of William of Tyre, and its independent existence is proved by manuscript survival. Such manu‑scripts commonly continue the history of the Latin East down to the period of Frederick II's intervention, 1229 or 1231, but no part of their contents is as detailed as their account of Saladin's final attacks on the Latin kingdom in the middle and late 1180's. It was therefore admirably suited to continue the history of William of Tyre. An editorial hand need only omit its earlier part, and the rest could be joined on to the French translation of the archbishop's work. A group of manuscripts show that this was done, and that a book was in circulation made up of William of Tyre's history translated into French, continued to 1231 by means of part of the independently written French history. Editorial work did not stop at this point. Subsequent additions were made, either written for the purpose, or by the adaptation of books originally written to stand alone, so that there were stages of continuation to 1247, to 1275, and to 1277.

Some of this history, in addition to that by the archbishop of Tyre, was written in the Latin East. The book used as the first stage of the continuation was by, or was based on a work by, Ernoul, a squire of Balian of Ibelin, who was in attendance on his master during the fateful summer of 1187. Another stage of the continuation, which deals with the period 1229–47, is by an author who knew Latin Syria at first hand. He is familiar with the terrain of which he writes and has a detailed knowledge of the Syrian baronage, of their family relationships and feudal service. Nor is he simply a well‑informed visitor – to him Europe is 'le pays de dela'.

If much of the material which made up the *Estoire d'Eracles* was originally written in the East, it would be surprising if some of the surviving illuminated manuscripts of the work were not produced there. There are, indeed, three with pictures in a style which not only displays the characteristics of the Acre scriptorium, but which connects them with the manuscripts of the *Histoire Universelle* already discussed. They are also by the same token connected with each other. To quote a small sample of the many pieces of available evidence, each of the three manuscripts of *Eracles*, two in Paris and one in Lyon, includes among its illustrations a painting of a siege, Nicæa (1097), Antioch (1097–98), Damietta (1249). In all three the defenders of the besieged town include Moslem bowmen, all alike in style and attitude. So are other members of the garrison who, in two of the pictures, lurk half-concealed behind the battlements. Each of the two artists concerned rendered this detail in the same way. In the picture of the siege of Antioch are two knights, one of them ascending a scaling ladder, who must have been copied from an illustration to the British Museum *Histoire Universelle*, which shows an attack on a strong place directed by the Queen of the Amazons. Again, in the *Eracles* there is a monotonous sequence of bedroom scenes in which successive kings of Jerusalem are shown about to expire. These seem to derive from the death of a patriarch which illustrates the *Histoire*. The only Latin king discussed by William of Tyre who did not die in his bed was Fulk, who was brought down at full gallop when in impromptu pursuit of a hare. Two of the illustrators of *Eracles* give a lively account of this episode and one of them includes not only Queen Melisende, but a small black hound which the artist seems to have taken from a painting of the finding of Oedipus which illustrates the Brussels manuscript of the *Histoire Universelle*. To sum up, all three manuscripts of the *Estoire* must be from the same atelier and, since they are connected with the *Histoire Universelle*, then the chain forged, link by link, by Dr Buchthal, leads to the conclusion that this workshop must have been the Acre scriptorium.

Plate 69

Plate 70

Plate 67

Plate 68

This conclusion is fortified by the evident first-hand acquaintance of the artists with life in Outremer. To return to the edifying death-bed scenes, among those shown in attendance are not only the Latin Patriarch of Jerusalem, but also an ecclesiastic in a white alb which shows him to have been an Augustinian canon, and who must be the Prior of the Holy Sepulchre. In the lower half of the same picture, the death of the old king is followed by the coronation of the new. In these miniatures the king is not enthroned as he would have been by a western artist, and as he is in the Arsenal Bible; he is shown kneeling before the patriarch. This is strictly in accordance with the account of the coronation proceedings given by John of Ibelin. It is hard to resist the conclusion that knowledge so detailed and so exact was the result, not of hearsay, but of observation.

Research even more recent than Buchthal's is building on the foundations he has laid. Among the granite mountains of the wilderness of Sinai stands the monastery of St Catherine, founded in the sixth century on the orders of Emperor Justinian. Its existence ever since has been unbroken, and it still has a number of features which date from its foundation, pre-eminent among them the great mosaic, depicting the Transfiguration, in the apse of its church. Its treasures include matchless collections not only of codices but of ikons, some two thousand of them, the oldest dating from the sixth century. In recent years they have been the subject of detailed examination by Professor Kurt Weitzmann, who has identified among them paintings linked with the miniatures, executed in crusader Jerusalem and Acre, which have been the subject of this chapter. The most striking example is a painting of the Crucifixion in which the only figures at the foot of the Cross are the Blessed Virgin and St John. If it is compared with that Crucifixion from the Perugia missal already mentioned, the likenesses between the two are unmistakeable. In both paintings the Virgin and St John are in the same attitude, each with a hand to the face, each with a thumb or a single finger extended. In both pictures the two angels above the Cross convey extremes of emotion; in both the type of Christ and details like the rendering of the folds of his loin cloth lead to Weitzmann's verdict that, when the two pictures are placed side by side, 'the three main figures coincide to an astonishing degree . . . These two paintings seem to us the products, if not perhaps of the same workshop, at least of the same artistic center.'

So many of the ikons display the now well-known characteristics of the miniatures from Jerusalem and Acre that a new area of crusader art is being revealed. Work is still in progress; but already Professor Weitzmann has begun to identify and distinguish between some of the ateliers in which these artists worked. And he reinforces the work of Dr Buchthal in emphasizing the importance of their achievement 'in absorbing the Byzantine style and transmitting it to the Latin West'. In painting, as in other fields, the significant contacts made by the crusaders were not with Islam, but with Byzantium.

Plate 60

Plate 59

Was there a Franco-Syrian Nation ?

Some historians have argued that the crusaders in Syria and the Holy Land built a new nation. In his monumental *Histoire des Croisades*, which appeared during the mid-1930's, René Grousset described crusader society as 'une nation franco-syrienne'. The same striking phrase had been used by Louis Madelin in a famous article twenty years earlier, while twenty years after Grousset Jean Richard wrote of the emerging nationhood of the kingdom of Jerusalem in the twelfth century and of its denationalization during the thirteenth.

Was there ever a Franco-Syrian nation? Certainly it is possible to observe the progress made in establishing conditions which in time might have given birth to such a unity. European settlers, and still more their children born in the country, were influenced by their new environment, and made many local customs their own. They lived in the same kind of houses as their Syrian neighbours and took advantage of the country's lighter textiles and its higher standards of medicine and cookery. Many Syrian Franks developed the eastern habit of taking frequent baths and some were even said to keep their wives in seclusion. Western newcomers and visitors noticed such differences and deplored them. Further than this, the settlers learned to live in peaceful tolerance among both Moslems and the Christians of other denominations. This was a long step forward from the state of mind inculcated by propaganda for the crusade, which encouraged Christians to hate and loathe Moslems as those who insulted God's Church and defiled its holy places. The Syrian Franks came to tolerate Moslems worshipping in their midst. Ibn Jubair found that in Acre he could make his devotions in part of the former Great Mosque, while in Tyre he entered a complete mosque still available for Moslems. In Jerusalem the Templars could make suitable arrangements for Usamah to say his prayers and could apologize for the angry newcomer from the West who was uncouth enough to interfere.

The peoples of Latin Syria not only came to understand each other better, but in some ways drew closer together and even began, though on a small and tentative scale, to merge. The importance of intermarriage and of religious reunion, like that of the Maronites with Rome, has already been mentioned. Native Syrians were thoroughly involved, even though in subordinate positions, in the machinery of Frankish govern ment. It has been seen that some of them served in offices like that of rays, dragoman or scribe, or in the customs service, or as light armed troops in the ranks of the Turcopoles. They could even secure a foothold in the all important group of feudal landholders; at least one Arab family in the Latin kingdom is known to have held its lands hereditarily and by knight service, and there may have been others.

The Franks could become more closely attached not only to the peoples, but also to the land of Syria. Fulcher of Chartres tells us that even in his day settlers who had come to the country as Franks or Romans were beginning to think of themselves as Palestinians or Galileans and that men formerly of Rheims or Chartres now considered themselves citizens of Antioch or Tyre. The settlers' children, born in the country, could regard it with the deep sentiment which is one of the ingredients of patriotism. William of Tyre's parents had made their home in the Holy City and he was born there. In both the prologues which appear in his history, the one which introduces the whole work, the other its last book, he writes with genuine emotion of his reluctance to record the disasters which had recently befallen his *patria*, his native land.

The developments discussed in the three preceding paragraphs have sometimes been regarded as evidence for the existence of a new nation. In fact they are no more than preconditions for the growth of such an entity, a growth which in the event was scarcely begun and never completed. The period of crusader rule was too short, and too many forces were pulling apart what might have become, in time, a fully integrated community. Something has been said of those centres of loyalty outside Latin Syria which prevented Armenians, Syrian Christians, and Moslems from giving to crusader governments their whole allegiance in all circumstances. The loyalties of many Syrian Franks were likewise divided. They always maintained strong ties with the West. They well understood the insecurity of their position, especially in the earliest years of the settlement, and again after the loss of Edessa to Zengi and of Egypt to Nur ad Din, the failure of the Second Crusade and the rise of Saladin. The long series of appeals for help addressed to western Europe reinforce the clear testimony of Fulcher of Chartres and William of Tyre that their contemporaries clearly understood the dangers of Moslem counter-attack. The same two historians, independent observers of events sixty or seventy years apart, both emphasize how public morale could be raised by the arrival of western pilgrims, especially if they included men of fame and substance. The Latins in the East knew themselves to be an outpost of a western world to which they increasingly turned.

The most constant and visible of all links with Europe were those maintained by the most powerfully organised groups in crusader society of which something was said in an earlier chapter. The Latin ecclesiastical hierarchy were part of the universal Roman Church, which was a unit of government as well as a unit of faith and over which the Pope presided as supreme judge and legislator. The transaction of ecclesiastical business at the highest level and the final settlement of disputes meant constant recourse to Rome, while from West to East came a succession of papal legates as well as European hierarchs who had been appointed to sees in the Latin East. Such traffic, like papal intervention in the affairs of the crusader states, became particularly heavy in the thirteenth century. The Military Orders made a large contribution to it. They were directly subject to the papacy, which was the source of their major privileges, and their exempt position involved them in constant disputes with the diocesan authorities. The Orders, too, were international in their scope and organization, and in the Holy Land they were constantly reinforced by newcomers from the West. As for the privileged commercial communities, enough has been said already of the extent to which they came to be controlled by the governments of their mother cities. Finally, the baronage of the crusader states received into their ranks from time to time members of European noble families.

By her third husband, Count Henry of Champagne, Queen Isabel I of Jerusalem bore two daughters. The elder of them, Alice, a princess of Jerusalem, was married when young to the king of Cyprus, and later to the heir of Antioch-Tripoli. She was regent both in Cyprus and Jerusalem, and in the latter kingdom laid claim to the throne itself. No one could have belonged more completely to the Latin East. Yet for more than twenty years her claims to the county of Champagne were a factor in French feudal politics and the concern of three successive Popes. Those claims were expensively bought out by the count of Champagne only in 1235, after Alice herself had spent two years in the West. She returned to Outremer. But her third and last marriage was with a baron from Champagne who accompanied the count on his crusade of 1239.

In the twelfth and thirteenth centuries forces were at work which were drawing the Europeans in the crusader states towards the land and peoples of Syria; but even stronger forces were drawing them westwards, keeping them part of Latin Christendom, preventing their integration with the peoples among whom they lived. William of Tyre had a foot in both worlds. He was a native of Latin Syria; through the impression-able years of infancy and early boyhood he knew no other land, and there is no doubt of his deep feeling for it; it was the scene of his main work for Church and State: he knew Arabic and, using Arabic sources, wrote a history of Islam. Yet in more important ways he was thoroughly western. When in his teens he was sent to Europe for his higher education which he continuously pursued, after the manner of the most serious students of his day, for nearly twenty years. Most of that time was spent in the two greatest European academies, Paris and Bologna, where he attended the lectures of the most renowned scholars of the age. Small wonder that his immortal history of the crusades and the crusader states give evidence of the width and depth of his reading in Latin literature, and that the book ranks high in the distinguished body of historical writing which was part of the western European renaissance of letters in the twelfth century.

When in his late thirties this highly educated clerk returned to the Latin kingdom, almost certainly in 1167, he quickly became Arch-deacon of Tyre and tutor to the heir apparent. Subsequently he became Archbishop and royal Chancellor and followed a distinguished public career in the kingdom. But his links with the West were regularly renewed. In 1169 he was in Rome on the business of the Church of Tyre. In 1178 he led the delegation from Jerusalem to the Third Lateran Council, held in the following year. Some five years later he was at the Papal Curia again, this time on his own affairs.

When in his prologues William discusses the people of the kingdom of Jerusalem in his own day, and their sad decline from the standards and achievements of their forefathers, it is not the whole population of Latin Syria that he has in mind. His heroes are the first crusaders and the men who founded and extended the crusader settlement; his concern is with the ruling group in the society of which he was part. Certainly William was influenced by the Arabic-speaking population among whom he lived from his earliest years; he knew their language and had written their history; he was bound by the deepest ties of sentiment to the country controlled by the Latin kings; it was his *patria*, the land of his birth and upbringing. But his culture and sympathies were those of western Christian society, in which he had spent the middle twenty years of his life, and to which he returned from time to time thereafter.

Essentially western, but influenced in some ways by his Levantine environment; was this not true of crusader society as a whole? The evidence provided by the monuments discussed in the second half of this book seems to point in the same direction. No one in the present century has yet studied the crusader churches as intensively as Camille Enlart. It was his considered verdict that 'if the churches of the Latin kingdom could be transported to the valleys of the Rhône, the Allier or the Garonne, not one of them would seem out of place.' And again, that 'the religious architecture of the crusaders is as French as any of the romanesque schools to be found in France itself', though it corresponded exactly with no one of them. There are of course exceptions to these generalizations. St Paul's at Tarsus is reminiscent of some of the churches of central Europe. Other elements seem to be of Italian inspiration: the bell-tower at Tripoli; the plain tympanum above the carved lintel in the main portals of Holy Sepulchre; the decoration of some of the corbels which support the cornices of the baptistery at Jebail or the Edicule of the Ascension on the Mount of Olives, some of the marbles and mosaics which once adorned certain churches in Jerusalem. But in plan, construction and in their main features, the crusader churches are closest to those built in the same era in central and southern France.

There was some borrowing from Moslem and Christian Syrian art. There were, for example, the gadroons of Holy Sepulchre, St Anne's and the baptistery of Jebail; Moslem motifs carved on parts of the corbel table of the apses of Jebail; the decoration of the string course which continues the archivolt above the main doorways of Holy Sepulchre. We expect transmission of this kind if only because indigenous masons and artists were sometimes employed on crusader buildings, as they had been, for example, on that elaborate scheme of interior decoration in

Fig. 24

John of Ibelin's castle at Beirut, which so impressed Wilbrand of Oldenburg. Yet in relation to the whole body of crusader church building and ornamentation, evidence of such borrowing is small. As for the illustration of manuscript books, the models and sources of inspiration were from artistic centres in western Europe and Byzantium. It is true that the artists of Jerusalem and Acre used these elements to develop their own characteristic local style, and that some of them drew parts of the Syrian scene from the life, but there is no good evidence that other Syrian communities contributed to these developments. In particular, there is only one well-authenticated instance of direct borrowing from the art of Islam.

Castle building scarcely helps to elucidate 'national' development, since there was an international style of fortification, inherited from the Roman Empire, developed in Byzantium, learned and adopted by the Moslem world. But here again, it has been seen that many crusader castles, especially those equipped with tower-keeps, were western in design, and that subsequent changes followed a similar course both in Latin Syria and western Europe.

The birth of a nation, however that elusive concept may be defined or described, seems an unlikely result of the crusader settlement, mainly because so complex an area had never then been, and has never since become, the home of a single nation. The intermingled peoples, ruled by a succession of foreign imperial powers, had too few of those common possessions which help to make a nation: language, literature, religion, history, true or false. It was highly unlikely that the thin, brief crusader occupation could succeed where other conquerors, more thoroughly in control of the country for a longer period, had failed. Too many of the best organized and most influential groups in crusader society, both European and Syrian, had interests and loyalties outside the country. There were, of course, those whose whole existence was bound up with the crusader states, and they must have included many of those born in the country of mixed Frankish and Syrian parentage, with kinsfolk on both sides of the line which divided Latin from eastern Christians and from Moslems. Here perhaps was the real nucleus of a new Franco-Syrian nation; but they seem never to have become sufficiently numerous or important to hold that society together in the face of mounting external pressure.

Bibliography

The best guides to the whole range of literature on the Crusades are:

ATIYA, A. S. *The Crusade: Historiography and Bibliography.* Indiana U.P., 1962.
MAYER, H. E. *Bibliographie zur Geschichte der Kreuzzüge.* Hanover, 1960. This work lists 5362 items.
— Literaturbericht über die Geschichte der Kreuzzüge, (1958–67). *Historische Zeitschrift,* Sonderheft 3, 1969.

CHAPTER I

Two works on the history of the crusades and the crusader settlements are outstanding. The first, by Mayer, is a single, short volume, the second, by Prawer, a more extended treatment.
GROUSSET, R. *Histoire des Croisades.* 3 vols. Paris, 1934–6.
— *L'Empire du Levant.* Paris, 1949.
MAYER, H. E. *The Crusades.* Oxford, 1972.
PRAWER, J. *Histoire du royaume latin de Jérusalem.* 2 vols. Paris, 1970.
RÖHRICHT, R. *Geschichte des Königreichs Jerusalem (1100–1291).* Innsbruck, 1898.
RUNCIMAN, S. *History of the Crusades.* 3 vols. Cambridge, 1951–4.
SETTON, K. (ed.) *A History of the Crusades.* 5 vols. Pennsylvania, 1955–. 2 volumes have appeared; vol. 3 is in the press.
1. *The First Hundred years.* 1955.
2. *The Later Crusades, 1189–1311.* 1962.

WAAS, A. *Geschichte der Kreuzzüge.* 2 vols. Freiburg, 1956.

CHAPTERS II AND III

The outstanding contributors to the subject matter of these chapters in recent years have been Professor Joshua Prawer, of Jerusalem, and Dr Jonathan Riley-Smith, formerly of St Andrews, now of Cambridge.
CAHEN, C. *La Syrie du nord à l'époque des croisades.* Paris, 1940.
— Le régime rural syrien au temps de la domination franque. *Bulletin de la faculté des Lettres de Strasbourg,* 29, 1950–51.
— Orient latin et commerce du Levant. *Ibid.*
HEYD, W. *Histoire du commerce du Levant au moyen âge.* 2 vols, augmented edition translated by F. Raynaud, reprinted Leipzig, 1936.
JOHNS, C. N. The attempt to colonise Palestine in the twelfth and thirteenth centuries. *Journal of the Royal Central Asian Society,* XXI, 1934.
LA MONTE, J. L. *Feudal monarchy in the Latin kingdom of Jerusalem, 1100–1291.* Cambridge, Mass., 1932.
— The communal movement in Syria in the 13th century. *Haskins Anniversary Essays.* New York, 1929.
MAYER, H. E. On the beginnings of the communal movement in the Holy Land:

the commune of Tyre. *Traditio*, 24, 1968.

PRAWER, J. *The world of the crusaders.* London and Jerusalem, 1972.

— *The Latin kingdom of Jerusalem. European colonialism in the middle ages.* London, 1973.

— Colonization activities in the Latin kingdom of Jerusalem. *Revue belge de philologie et d'histoire*, XXIX, 1951.

— L'établissement des coutumes du marché à St Jean d'Acre et la date de composition du Livre des Assises des Bourgeois. *Revue historique de droit français et étranger*, sér. IV, 29, 1951.

— The *Assise de Teneure* and the *Assise de Vente* – a study of landed property in the Latin kingdom. *Economic History Review*, IV, 1951.

— The settlement of the Latins in Jerusalem. *Speculum*, XXVII, 1952.

— Étude de quelques problèmes agraires et sociaux d'une seigneurie croisée au XIIIe siècle. *Byzantion*, 22, 1952, and 23, 1953.

— Les premiers temps de la féodalité dans le royaume latin de Jérusalem, *Tijdschrift voor rechtsgeschiedenis*, 22, 1954.

— La noblesse et le régime féodal du royaume latin de Jerusalem. *Le Moyen Age*, 65, 1959.

— Estates, communities and the constitution of the Latin kingdom. *Proceedings of the Israel Academy of Sciences and Humanities*, II, 1966.

PRUTZ, H. *Kulturgeschichte der Kreuzzüge.* Berlin, 1883.

REY, E. G. *Les colonies franques de Syrie au XIIème et XIIIème siècles.* Paris, 1883.

RICHARD, J. *Le comté de Tripoli sous la dynastie toulousaine, 1102–1187.* Paris, 1945.

— *Le royaume latin de Jérusalem.* Paris, 1953.

—Pairie d'orient latin. Les quatres baronnies des royaumes de Jérusalem et Chypre. *Revue historique de droit français et étranger*, sér. IV, 28, 1950.

— Colonies marchandes privilégées et marché seigneurial. La fonde d'Acre et ses 'droitures'. *Le Moyen Age*, 59, 1953.

RILEY-SMITH, J. S. C. *The Knights of St John in Jerusalem and Cyprus.* London, 1967.

— *The feudal nobility and the kingdom of Jerusalem, 1174–1277.* London, 1973.

— The Templars and the castle of Tortosa in Syria: an unknown document concerning the acquisition of the fortress. *English Historical Review*, LXXXIV, 1969.

— The *Assise sur la ligèce* and the commune of Acre. *Traditio*, 27, 1971.

— A note on confraternities in the Latin kingdom of Jerusalem. *Bulletin of the Institute of Historical Research*, 44, 1971.

— Some lesser officials in Latin Syria. *English Historical Review*, 87, 1972.

CHAPTERS IV, V, VI

BARASH, M. *Crusader figural sculpture in the Holy Land.* Jerusalem, 1971.

BENVENISTI, M. *The crusaders in the Holy Land.* Jerusalem, 1970.

BOASE, T. S. R. AND CLEAVE, R. L. W. *Castles and churches of the crusading kingdom.* Oxford, 1967.

BORG, A. Observations on the historical lintel of the Holy Sepulchre, Jerusalem. *Journal of the Warburg and Courtauld Institutes*, 32, 1962.

DEAN, B. The exploration of a crusader's fortress (Montfort) in Palestine. *Bulletin*

The Crusaders

of the Metropolitan Museum of Art, New York, 22, 1927.

DESCHAMPS, P. Terre sainte romane. Paris, 1964.

— Les châteaux des croisés en Terre Sainte. 2 vols and 2 albums. Paris, 1934–9.
1. Le Crac des Chevaliers.
2. La défense du royaume de Jérusalem.

— Le château de Saône dans la principauté d'Antioche. Gazette des beaux-arts, 30, 1930.

— Le château de Saône et ses premiers seigneurs. Syria, 16, 1935.

— Les entrées des châteaux des croisés et leurs défenses. Syria, 13, 1932.

— L'architecture militaire des croisés en Syrie. L'approvisionnement de l'eau. Revue de l'art ancien et moderne, 62, 1932.

— Deux positions stratégiques des croisés à l'est du Jourdain: Ahamant et el Habis. Revue historique, 72, 1933.

— Une grotte forteresse des croisés au delà du Jourdain: El Habis en terre de Suète. Journal Asiatique, 227, 1935.

— Une grotte forteresse des croisés dans le Liban. La cave de Tyron. Mélanges René Dussaud, I, Paris, 1939.

— La sculpture française en Palestine et en Syrie à l'époque des croisades. Mémoires et monuments de la fondation Piot, 31, 1930.

— Un chapiteau roman du Berry imité à Nazareth au XII siècle. Ibid, 32, 1932.

DUCKWORTH, H. T. F. The Church of the Holy Sepulchre. London, 1922.

ENLART, C. Les monuments des croisés dans le royaume de Jérusalem. Architecture religieuse et civile. 2 vols and album. Paris, 1925–8.

FEDDEN, R. AND THOMSON, J. Crusader Castles. London, 1957.

HAMILTON, R. W. The structural history of the Aksa Mosque. Jerusalem, 1940.

— Structural survey of the Church of the Nativity. London, 1935.

— The Church of the Nativity at Bethlehem. Jerusalem, 1947

— A guide to Bethlehem. Jerusalem, 1939.

HUYGENS, R. B. C. Un nouveau texte du traité 'De constructione castri Saphet'. Studi medievali, 3 ser., 6, 1965.

JOHNS, C. N. Excavations at Pilgrims' Castle ('Atlit). Quarterly of the Department of Antiquities in Palestine, 1–6, 1931–6.

— Medieval 'Ajlun. I. The Castle. Ibid, I, 1931.

—Excavations at the Citadel, Jerusalem. Ibid, 5, 1935.

— A guide to the citadel of Jerusalem. Jerusalem, 1944.

— A guide to 'Atlit. Jerusalem, 1947.

JOHNS, C. N. AND MAKHOŪLY, N. A guide to Acre. Jerusalem, 1946.

KING, D. J. C. The taking of Le Krak des Chevaliers in 1271. Antiquity, XXIII, 1949.

LAWRENCE, T. E. Crusader Castles. 2 vols. London, 1936.

MAUSS, C. L'église de St Jérémie à Abou Gôsch. Paris, 1892–4.

MÜLLER-WIENER, W. Castles of the Crusaders. London, 1966.

PILLET, M. Notre-Dame de Tortose. Syria, 10, 1929.

REY, E. G. Étude sur les monuments de l'architecture militaire des croisés en Syrie et dans l'île de Chypre. Paris, 1871.

RICHMOND, E. T. The Dome of the Rock in Jerusalem. Oxford, 1924.

SMAIL, R. C. Crusading Warfare, 1097–1193. Cambridge, 1956 (p'back, 1972).

VIAUD, P. *Nazareth et ses deux églises de l'Annonciation et de St Joseph.* Paris, 1910.

VINCENT, L. H. AND ABEL, F. M. *Jérusalem,* II. Paris, 1914–26.

— *Bethléem. Le sanctuaire de la nativité.* Paris, 1914.

— *Emmaus. Sa basilique et son histoire.* Paris, 1932.

VOGÜÉ, M. DE. *Les églises de la Terre Sainte.* Paris, 1860.

CHAPTER VII

This area of crusading studies was first discovered and charted by Dr Buchthal. The work of developing his original achievement is now being actively pursued.

BUCHTHAL, H. *Miniature painting in the Latin kingdom of Jerusalem* with liturgical and palaeographical chapters by F. WORMALD. Oxford, 1957.

WEITZMANN, K. Thirteenth century crusader icons on Mount Sinai. *The Art Bulletin,* 45, 1963.

— Icon painting in the crusader kingdom. *Dumbarton Oaks Papers,* 20, 1966.

Sources of Illustrations

The following persons and institutions kindly permitted use to be made of photographs taken or owned by them and their help is gratefully acknowledged.

Archives Photographiques 54; Institut Français d'Archéologie, Beirut 6, 10, 12, 29; Dr Meron Benvenisti 9; Trustees of the British Museum, London 61–63, 68, 69; J. Allen Cash 32; C. Enlart 30; Garrison Collection 59; Dr Martin Hürlimann 5; courtesy the Israel Department of Antiquities and Museums, Jerusalem 50; A. F. Kersting 1–3, 7, 11, 13–15, 17–20, 26, 27, 34, 35, 38, 39, 47, 48; Manoug, Beirut 36, 40; Bodleian Library, Oxford 4; Palestine Department of Antiquities 21–24, 56–58; Bibliothèque Nationale, Paris 64–67, 70; Professor E. K. Waterhouse 31; published by permission of the Michigan-Alexandria-Princeton expedition to Mount Sinai, photo courtesy Professor Kurt Weitzmann 60; Zodiaque 16, 28, 37, 41–49, 51–53, 55.

Mrs G. D. March redrew figures 6, 7, 11, 14, 16, 18, 21, 34–36. The original sources of these and the other line-drawings in the book are given in the captions. The maps (figs. 1–3) were drawn by H. A. Shelley.

3

4

5

6

9

13

14

15

16

17

18

19

20

21

22

23

24

26

30

31

32

33

39

40

45

46

47

51

52

53

4

55

58

59

60

61

62

D E faim & de mezaise come
nos auons dit ne veulet
oir paroles de laissier le
siege: Ains sembloit ale

prts entre ceaus dehors que la pie
ne eschaperoir. Cil qui orent eu
ces messages & ces letres se redou
toient mlt de nre gent. por quoil

Coment les dames de sare a leur
uengier los barons & los fiz & los

lune tourne requir. quant elles fu
rent uengies lautre uinst engie

Ntre elles auoit .y. ames.
wynes lune anomoit mer

Nsi par ceste achoison co
mensierent memiermet

Notes on the Plates

1   Caesarea. Part of a street in the crusader town.

2   Caesarea. The town walls. The fosse has been cleared to its thirteenth-century depth.

3   Jerusalem. The Old City from the Mount of Olives. The Dome of the Rock can be seen in the middle of the Temple area, with the Aqsa Mosque on the left.

4   Acre. Marino Sanudo Torsello's plan, made early in the fourteenth century. (A key to this plan is given in fig. 6.) Oxford, Bodleian Library, MS. Tanner, 190, fol. 207.

5   Constantinople. The double line of the land walls. Fifth century A.D.

6   Safita from the air. The tower-keep of the castle is the tallest in Syria. The arrangement of the houses has been shaped by the line of the castle's former outer defences.

7   Jebail. The tower-keep, tightly enclosed in a ring-wall with angle towers, a typical crusader design.

8   Jebail. Hellenistic masonry re-used in the crusader keep.

9   Belvoir. Air view of the castle, which was recently revealed by Israeli archaeologists.

10 Harim from the air. The castle was given all-round protection by the steep sides of an artificial tell.

11 Sahyun. The principal crusader defences.

12 Sahyun and the surrounding terrain seen from the air. This is the finest of the castles sited on a spur.

13 Sahyun. The rock-cut defences, showing the pillar of rock left to support a bridge.

14 Sahyun. The interior of the keep. Like all similar crusader buildings, it is vaulted throughout.

15 Sahyun. The keep, and other crusader work in similar masonry.

16 Krak des Chevaliers. The south and west fronts. Hospitaller work of the early thirteenth century.

17 Krak des Chevaliers. The inner court. On the left, the early gothic cloister.

18 Krak des Chevaliers. The first stages of the ramped main entry.

19 Krak des Chevaliers. The early gothic decoration of the chapter-house doorway, seen from the cloister.

20 Krak des Chevaliers. The western defences.

21 'Atlit. Left, the north tower of the inner wall; right, the outer wall.

22 'Atlit. North tower of the inner wall, preceded by the outer wall.

23 'Atlit. View inland, along the line of the southern defences.

24 Shaubak. The castle founded by King Baldwin I.

25 Jerusalem. Church of the Holy

225

Sepulchre. The southern façade, with the Calvary porch on the right.

26 Jerusalem. Church of the Holy Sepulchre. Left, the belfry of the late twelfth century; centre, the dome above the church originally built by Constantine; right, the cupola above the romanesque crossing. The scaffolding, having done service for forty years, was taken down in 1970.

27 Marqab. Distant view of the Hospitallers' castle on its volcanic ridge.

28 Marqab. The principal tower. Comparable with the main works at the Hospitallers' other major castle, Krak des Chevaliers, but with inferior masonry.

29 Marqab from the air. In the foreground the main defences which barred the enemy's most likely line of approach.

30 Beirut. Interior of the crusaders' romanesque cathedral, now the Great Mosque.

31 Beirut. The eastern apses of the cathedral. The doorway is a Moslem addition.

32 Musailiha. An extreme example of defensive strength achieved by physical isolation.

33 Shaizar. The home of Usamah ibn Munqidh (1095–1188). Town and castle are sited on an unusually narrow ridge overlooking the River Orontes.

34 Acre. The massive thirteenth-century refectory of the Hospitallers.

35 Jebail. The apsidal east end of the crusader cathedral.

36, 37 Jebail. The baptistery of the crusaders' Church of St John the

Baptist; detail of the carved decoration (37).

38 Tortosa. Cathedral of Our Lady, now a museum. A place of pilgrimage. The doorway is thought to have led to the original shrine, which was at first incorporated into the later building.

39 Tortosa. The gothic west front of the cathedral.

40 Belmont. The thirteenth-century belfry of the Cistercian church.

41–43 Jerusalem. Church of St Anne. The nave looking east (41); the cupola over the crossing, with the eastern apse below (42); view of the west front, in which the various architectural elements can be easily identified (43).

44 Abu Ghosh. The interior of the church. The severity of the decoration and the truncated column are both typical of crusader work.

45 Abu Ghosh. The church seen from the east, showing deeply recessed window and ancient masonry incorporated by the crusaders.

46 'Amyun. Church of St Phocas. Eastern apse with fragment of wall painting.

47 Krak des Chevaliers. The spacious twelfth-century chapel.

48 Safita. The Templars' chapter house on the upper floor of the keep.

49 Jerusalem. Church of the Holy Sepulchre. Detail of decoration on the south façade.

50 Jerusalem. Church of the Holy Sepulchre. A lintel, formerly above the main doorway, now in the Rockefeller Museum.

51–53　Nazareth. Twelfth-century capitals from the Church of the Annunciation: an Apostle led by faith (51); a miracle of St Bartholomew in India (52); Christ and doubting Thomas (53).

54　Plaimpied (Cher, France). Capital from the church, showing seated Christ. Stylistic resemblance to the Nazareth capitals is so close that the same Master must have worked in both places. Cast in Paris, Musée de Chaillot.

55　Jerusalem. Church of the Holy Sepulchre. The Raising of Lazarus, from a lintel above the main doorway.

56　Bethlehem. Church of the Nativity. An angel, part of the upper band of mosaic decoration, executed in the twelfth century.

57, 58　Bethlehem. Church of the Nativity. Twelfth-century paintings of St Stephen (57) and St John the Baptist (58) on the pillars.

59　Perugia. Crucifixion from a missal. Biblioteca Capitolare, 6, fol. 182v.

60　Sinai. Ikon from St Catherine's monastery. Compare the treatment of the subject with that of plate 59.

61　Beatus-initial from the Melisende Psalter. London, British Museum, Egerton, 1139, fol. 23v.

62　Twelfth-century ivory cover of the Melisende Psalter, showing the Christian acts of mercy. The bird marked 'herodius' is between the two upper medallions. London, British Museum.

63　The Creation from the *Histoire Universelle*. The borders of this biblical scene are a rare example of direct borrowing from the art of Islam. London, British Museum, Add. MS. 15268, fol. 1v.

64　Frontispiece to Ecclesiastes from the thirteenth-century Bible illustrated in the Acre scriptorium. Paris, Bibliothèque de l'Arsenal, 5211, fol. 337r.

65　Frontispiece to Genesis from the same Bible. Adam's posture at the moment of Eve's creation should be compared with that in plate 63. Paris, Bibliothèque de l'Arsenal, 5211, fol. 3v.

66　Frontispiece to Job. The camels can only be the result of the artist's own observation. Other figures clearly show the attributes of the 'Acre' style. Paris, Bibliothèque de l'Arsenal, 5211, fol. 269r.

67　King Fulk, when riding near Acre with Queen Melisende, is killed in a hunting accident. An illustration from the *Estoire d'Eracles*. The black hound appears in plate 68. Paris, Bibliothèque Nationale, MS. 2628, fol. 146v.

68　The finding of Oedipus, from the *Histoire Universelle*. London, British Museum, Add. MS. 15268, fol. 754.

69　Siege and capture of Antioch, 1098, from the *Estoire d'Eracles*. The attacker at the top of the scaling ladder, and another kneeling at the foot of the wall, should be compared with the similar figures in plate 70. Paris, Bibliothèque Nationale, MS. 9084, fol. 53r.

70　Scythian women on the attack, from the *Histoire Universelle*. The 'spectacles-like' rendering of the eyes, a hall-mark of the 'Acre' style, is particularly in evidence among the group of women. London, British Museum, Add. MS. 15268, fol. 101v.

Index

Entries with the Arabic definite article 'al-' will be found under the subsequent initial letter.